"*Execution of Justice* is exhilarating. It is theatre reasserting its claim on the country's moral conscience."

—David Richards, *Washington Post*

"*Annulla* is one bangup 90 minutes of theatre....I don't know when I've been stimulated as much by anything on the living stage."

—Jerry Talmer, *New York Post*

"The contradictions which Emily Mann has arranged and intercut to such terrifying effect are the contradictions of human beings....*Still Life* is *Heart of Darkness*, with apple pie and vanilla ice cream on the side."

—*Village Voice*

"*Greensboro* is a provocation, a potent exposé of the 'less-than-human thing' which fuels the politics of hate and injustice in America."

—*Forbes* newspapers

TESTIMONIES

TESTIMONIES

FOUR PLAYS

EMILY MANN

THEATRE COMMUNICATIONS GROUP

Testimonies: Four Plays copyright © 1997 by Emily Mann

Annulla, An Autobiography copyright © 1988, 1996 by Emily Mann
Still Life copyright © 1979, 1996 by Emily Mann
Execution of Justice copyright © 1983, 1985, 1996 by Emily Mann
Greensboro (A Requiem) copyright © 1996 by Emily Mann

Introduction copyright © 1997 by Athol Fugard

Testimonies: Four Plays is published by Theatre Communications Group, Inc., 355 Lexington Ave., New York, NY 10017-0217.

Mann, Emily.
Testimonies : four plays / Emily Mann.
Annulla : An autobiography : Still life :
Execution of justice : Greensboro : A requiem.
ISBN 1-55936-117-4
1. Vietnamese Conflict, 1961–1975–Influence–Drama. 2. Ku Klux Klan
(1915–)–North Carolina–Drama. 3. Milk, Harvey–Assassination–Drama.
4. Holocaust survivors–Drama.
I. Title.
PS3563. A5357T47   1997
812'.54–dc20   96–7092
CIP

Cover photo by Ken Collins
Cover design by Carol Devine Carson
Book design by Lisa Govan
Typesetting by The Typeworks

First Edition, February 1997

To all those people who trusted me with their stories

CONTENTS

INTRODUCTION

BY ATHOL FUGARD

I have three very vivid and cherished theatre memories of the work of Emily Mann—all of them as an audience member.

The first, which was also my introduction to her work, was Barney Simon's powerful production of *Still Life* at the Market Theatre in Johannesburg. I have a notebook entry of the conversation Barney and I had after the performance over a late night pot of tea at his home:

> Another challenging reunion with Barney—firstly his production of E.M.'s *Still Life* . . . powerful and very moving . . . and then a long talk about it and theatre in general afterward. In talking about Mann's work he used the word "testimony" several times—I made him check its dictionary definition: "To bear witness" according to the *OED* [*Oxford English Dictionary*]. A perfect definition of the challenge our [South Africa's] theatre faces at this moment in our country's history.

The year was 1983 and South Africa was moving into one of the darkest periods of the Apartheid era.

My note continues:

> Barney became very worked-up: "We can't be silent! We must give evidence! We are witnesses!" He said Mann's work had been a great provocation to him and had revitalized his sense of theatre's role in a time of crisis.

Then, about twelve years later, there was a young white woman, a high school student with notebook and pencil in her lap, sitting next to me during a matinee performance of *Having Our Say* in New York. One of those bonds of spontaneous friendship that sometime develop between strangers in a theatre audience brought us together as we both laughed and listened in silence to the wonderful story being told by the two women on stage.

In the course of our conversation during the second intermission she said to me: "We must never forget must we." I asked her what she meant.

"We've got to face the facts. We've got to know what happened, what it was like."

I was surprised. She was obviously an American. "Didn't you know?" I asked her.

She thought for a moment. "Yes and no. They teach you the history of the Civil Rights Movement at school, but those are just the facts. You don't really get what it felt like, what it meant to be the victim of prejudice."

"And that is what you are getting this afternoon?"

She nodded. "Yes, that and much more."

Before I could ask her what the "much more" was, the house lights dimmed and we were into the glorious third act.

Lastly, there is my own personal response at the end of the first workshopped reading of *Greensboro* in Princeton last year. In talking afterward to my American friends in that audience, I real-

ized that for all their anger and outrage at what Emily Mann's im-
peccably documented and gripping retelling of that story had re-
minded them of, there was an even deeper process at work. The
word that came immediately to mind was "healing." And once
again there was a compelling relevance to the situation in my own
country. South Africa was, and still is, involved in a heated and
passionate debate about the formation of a Commission for Truth
and Reconciliation—a commission that will be empowered to investigate and expose the crimes of our Apartheid era and, in so doing, hopefully create a spirit of reconciliation in the country.
Because without that spirit of reconciliation, unless we face up to
and come to terms with the lies behind us, no healing of the terrible wounds of our Apartheid past will take place.

I don't doubt for one moment that a great deal of good is going
to come from that commission (which is on the point of holding
its first hearings as I write these words). But I also do believe that
in any society trying to deal with evil and injustices in its past, like
my own country and America, the artist has a very significant role
to play. I would even go so far as to say that the work of artists will
ultimately have a much deeper and more lasting effect on the national psyche than any government-appointed commission.

I read somewhere that Confucius believed that by using only
words, the poet could remedy the injustices of the past, right the
wrongs, and judge and sentence the wrongdoers. I subscribe to
that belief and I point to the passionate and eloquent work of
Emily Mann in support of that conviction. More than any other
American writer of our time, the body of her work has demonstrated the central importance of theatre to the psychic well-
being and sanity of a society.

Athol Fugard
Port Elizabeth, South Africa
March 26, 1996

ACKNOWLEDGMENTS

There are many people who have contributed to the making of these plays. First and foremost, I must thank all those who entrusted their stories to me. Many of them do not wish their real names used and so I must simply say thank you.

For each play, I have thanked those who contributed to its making in the introduction to the play. But there are yet more people to thank: Irene Dische, for her friendship and support over nearly a quarter of a century; Nadine Strossen, for introducing me to the original Nadine of *Still Life;* the casts, crews and staffs of the various productions of the plays as they developed along the way; and most recently, the staff and crews of the Mc-Carter Theatre where I have premiered both *Having Our Say* and *Greensboro (A Requiem).* Special thanks to Janice Paran, dramaturg; Loretta Greco, associate director; my assistant, Grace Shackney; and Mara Isaacs, staff producer. Janice, Grace and Loretta were there for each step of the process. For their consummate professionalism and great patience, a special thanks to Steve Howe, master electrician; Cheryl Mintz, production stage manager; David York, production manager; and the McCarter house crew. And my most heartfelt thanks to my partner, managing director Jeff Woodward, who keeps us all on course. To Tom Lynch, who has solved the physical demands of many productions over the years, my many thanks. To Ming Cho Lee, Pat Collins, Jennifer Von Mayrhauser, Allen Lee Hughes, Baikida Carroll and the late Judy Dearing—I am indebted to you for your artistry, support and dedication.

Linda Hunt, Barbara Bryne, John Spencer, Mary McDonnell, Timothy Near, Gerry Bamman, Peter McNichol, Mary Alice and Gloria Foster all acted when I directed and helped the writer.

Stephen Wadsworth, Peter Kazaras, Joyce Carol Oates, Ray Smith, Leigh Bienen, Judith Rutherford James and Camille Cosby read manuscripts and gave their very good comments.

To my agent, George Lane, who has been with me since the first reading of *Still Life*, I thank you for believing in me from the very start.

From the very, very start, however, my father, the late Arthur Mann; my mother, Sylvia; my sister, Carol; and brother-in-law, Howard Helene, have been my greatest support.

And now, more recently, thanks to my son, Nick Bamman, who shares the computer with me, and to Gary Mailman, who shares my life.

PUBLISHER'S NOTE

We originally intended to include Emily Mann's adaptation of *Having Our Say: The Delany Sisters' First 100 Years*, but unfortunately one of the copyright holders declined participation in this volume. Anyone who wishes to read this wonderful play can do so by obtaining the acting edition published by the Dramatists Play Service.

ANNULLA

(AN AUTOBIOGRAPHY)

Overleaf: Linda Hunt as Annulla Allen in the New Theatre of Brooklyn production. Photo by Jessica Katz.

A Love Letter to Mother

Special thanks to the remarkable Timothy Near

An earlier version of the play, *Annulla Allen: Autobiography of a Survivor (A Monologue)*, premiered at the Guthrie Theatre's Guthrie 2 in 1977, in a production directed by the author and starring Barbara Bryne. The production was remounted for the Goodman Theatre the next year, and later recorded for "Earplay."

Annulla, An Autobiography was presented March 20–April 7, 1985, at the Repertory Theatre of St. Louis. Timothy Near directed. The set and costumes were designed by Arthur Ridley and the lighting was by Max DeVolder. The cast was as follows:

ANNULLA	Jacqueline Bertrand
YOUNG WOMAN'S VOICE	Jennifer Russell

The play was presented October 1988 in New York at the New Theatre of Brooklyn. Sets were designed by Marjorie Bradley Kellog and Diann Duthie, costumes by Jennifer Von Mayrhauser, lights by Don Holder and sound by Tom Gould. The author directed the following cast:

ANNULLA	Linda Hunt
YOUNG WOMAN'S VOICE	Karen Ludwig

PLAYWRIGHT'S NOTE

For the most part, these are Annulla Allen's own words told to me during the summer of 1974 in London, and my own words told to Timothy Near over a decade later.

During the voice-overs, lights change, and Annulla continues her activities. In Ms. Near's production, the sound of a ticking clock accompanied the Young Woman's Voice.

The play takes place in Annulla's North London kitchen. It is clean but untidy. A mammoth manuscript covers the kitchen table stage center. It is half typed/half written, and in terrible disorder.

The room is still. It is teatime. The kettle whistles on the stove.

YOUNG WOMAN'S VOICE: In 1974, the summer I left college, I went to England. That is where I met Annulla. Annulla is the aunt of the woman who was my roommate in college and is my dearest and closest friend. We got a grant to do oral histories of her family, a fascinating family, and I was going on that trip to find my grandmother's village, in Poland. My mother's mother's village—Ostroleka. We went first to London, Irene and I, and at that time she said to me, "Emily, before we go to Poland you must meet my father's sister, my aunt, my Aunt Annulla."

She lived in a flat in Hampstead Heath. We went for a visit. We went for tea.

(Annulla enters, carrying packages. She switches on the kitchen light and crosses to the stove.)

ANNULLA: Oh! How do you do? I am so sorry I am late. Oh, this kettle. Excuse me. I have just to put these packages down. *(Puts them down on the table. Taking off hat and coat)* I would have been earlier but I had to go shopping for my sister, Ada. She was hit by a milk truck six months ago. She says to me, "I will stay crippled for life now because you have no time for me." Pah! *(She looks up sweetly)* I am really very glad you came here for tea today, really. I expect it's because you have heard about my play.

Here it is. It is called *The Matriarchs.* I have boiled it down to just over six hours, but they tell me it has to be a bit more condensed, but you know I am a woman who has never any time. *(Crosses to cabinet and opens it to put away food. The closet is overstuffed and things fall)*

Oh, really this is too much! Oh, I am always doing things like this when I have visitors. *(Scrambles around, closes closet door)*

Oh, really, you know, my life is in terrible disorder. And this is so tragic, really, I have so much to do. *(Goes over to the sink and rinses out a cup. Crosses to stove and pours water over tea)*

Do you know, my brother who is a very eminent biochemist is always reproaching *me* about not being hygienic enough. *(Imitates brother in a loud voice)* "Don't you know there is bacteria there?" *(Indicating pot)* He says this is *poison.* Tea! Only metal is good. If you have tea in an old china cup and you put more in after six hours, this is dangerous. I never knew I lived dangerously. *(Sips)* Ach! This tea is terrible.

But, do you know, I think I will someday commit suicide.

My sister thinks that I should be at her *beck* and *call* since her accident. I am a woman who never has any time.

(She goes to the cabinet to get a plate and crosses to the table, putting biscuits on the plate) If you ask me what I am doing one day, I could not explain. Do you know, I don't know what I am doing? I remember when I was eleven, I felt already adult, we went on holiday to Heist, the whole family—the five children, the father and the mother, and the governess. And on the train, a man talked to us, to the children, and then said to my mother *(Laughing)* "I am telling you, Madame, one day you will conquer the world with your children." He was so impressed. I was eleven, Ada was nine-and-a-half, Czecha was thirteen or fourteen, Nunu was sixteen, Mania was . . . I don't remember. But that man was so impressed. He was an intellectual. "One day you will conquer the world with your children." We didn't conquer the world yet.

But can you imagine that family! Czecha was a concert pianist at the age of eleven, Ada was . . . a young ballet star. Mania was . . . Mania—och. You don't need to know about Mania. She's a happy woman. Married. Lives in Israel now. Very boring. Nunu was in Vienna teaching medicine as a young teenager. And then came the war. You know, he is a very eminent biochemist. Everyone was convinced that he would win the Nobel Prize. Then the Nazis destroyed his laboratory in Vienna in 1938 and he had to flee. *(Returns to the table and sits in center chair)*

Yes, I can tell you what it was like to live always in the shadow of tyrants. I have seen firsthand men's barbarism taken to its extreme with Hitler. You know, I just bought this Solzhenitsyn's *Archipelago*. You know, those of us who lived through it are not shocked by the Stalinists. It is common knowledge to us the barbarism of these men. If there were a global matriarchy, you know, there would be no more of this evil. I have all the answers in my play! I wanted to read you some of my play. The pages are not numbered. Just before you came I dropped it . . . It's all out of order. It's too much of a mess now, maybe later I will read parts of it to you. *(Stands at table and looks at her script)*

VOICE: I needed to go to someone else's relative in order to understand my own history because by this time my only living relative of that generation was my grandmother—my mother's mother—and she had almost no way to communicate complex ideas. She'd lost her language. Her first languages were Polish and Yiddish, but when she went to America she never spoke Polish again. My grandfather spoke English at work, but at home they spoke a kind of Kitchen Yiddish together—certainly not "the language of ideas." Her children first spoke Yiddish, but they wanted to become American, so as soon as they went to kindergarten, they only spoke English. So in the end, she read a Yiddish newspaper but spoke in broken Yiddish—half Yiddish, half English. She had *no fluent language.* This isn't uncommon among immigrants of her generation.

So I went to Annulla, who had the language.

ANNULLA *(Goes to the sink, dumps cup of tea, crosses to the stove and prepares new cup of tea)*: You know, it is funny, the police, you know—from immigration—they came to see me in London, asked me where I came from. I said, "L'vov, Galicia." He said, "Where?" I said, "Don't you know? It was Austria when I was born, and then it was Poland. Now it is Russia." "But," he said, "where was Poland before?" He didn't even know there was no Poland in 1900. I say this to you gently, but I want you to know that I mean it. How can people change if they don't know what happened? It is like in psychoanalysis. You must know what happened to you. Do you know, some people do not remember their childhoods at all? I remember almost nothing of my childhood, but I had such an unhappy childhood I want to forget it.

But I must tell you, I have been lucky in my life. I was telling my niece that I was pretending to be an Aryan all the time

I was in Germany. I was like the horseman. Do *you* know this
fable by Heine? No? Then I must tell you. A man, riding a
horse at night, a cold foggy night, is riding with no direction.
He is riding for miles and can't get to the place he wants to.
And in the morning, when the first light arrives, he realizes
he was riding all night on the thin ice of the Bodensee and he
didn't know it. And he was lucky, nothing happened to him.
That is how I felt in Vienna when my husband was in Dachau. Either or. Either they will find me out and kill me or I
would survive. It was the only chance. I was really ignorant
of the horror that could befall me because I had to be. My
cousin did the same thing in Poland, but she was found out.
She knew it was her only chance—she was looking also very
un-Jewish—and someone gave her away. An anti-Semitic
Pole, and she was sent to Auschwitz . . . *(Sits)* They did not
take the women on that first raid when my husband was
taken. They took only the men. They made a raid of all Jews
in Vienna and took all the men away in 1938, the Night of
Broken Glass. You have heard about this? . . . Kristallnacht.
The SS came to our house. I can't remember it was so fast.
And they were so crude! This Solzhenitsyn says in his book,
this *Gulag Archipelago,* and I quote: "That's what arrest is:
it's a blinding flash and a blow which shifts the present in-
stantly into the past and the impossible into omnipotent reality." *(Throws books down)* And that is how it was.

They never found out that I am Jewish. They thought that
I am Czech because of my accent, you see. And, in Vienna
you had hundreds of thousands of marriages between Aryan
women and Jews. And the Viennese Jews—and my husband
was Viennese—never married the Polish Jews. So they never
suspected. And, of course, I was so beautiful they couldn't
believe I could be a Jew. And I was so cheeky with them. I
must tell you this story . . . There was this Gestapo man at
headquarters—I knew there was one chance to save my husband's life—get the rubber stamp on this document so he

could leave the camp. The man said to me, *"Waren helfen Sie disen Jude? Why are you helping this Jew?"*

He wanted to show me what a big powerful man he was—of course, I had flirted with him a little to get my way. He said, "You just go upstairs and ask for the rubber stamp." So I went upstairs to that office and said, "Mr. So-and-So downstairs told me to tell you to give me that rubber stamp on this document." He said, "Are you Aryan?" I said, "Yes." And he gave it to me. This is how I went along.

Of course, I had no papers. I remember I went shopping into a Jewish shop one day. And they waited for me outside. They wanted to hang on me the placard for Aryan women who still shopped in Jewish shops. I tell the man that I am Jewish. I wasn't afraid then. Because it was *before* my husband was taken. He said *(Does loud voice)* "I don't believe it! Show me your passport!" I said *(Looks indignant)* "If I were not Jewish I would show you my passport. But I am a Jew and you took away all our passports." So he let me go. This was a very interesting time, living in the shadow of the Nazis. My son, though, he got such a trauma from this experience. *(Tea cup in hand)* He was taken by friends when he was eight years old to Sweden. And then it was too dangerous for him. He couldn't get back. And I couldn't get to him. But I knew by 1939 . . . I knew it was safer for him to stay there. In Sweden. Oh, this time away from him. It was a great grief. He grew up without me. They sent me a photo of him at school. Curly red hair. Fat little cheeks. A little Jewish boy, the only one. He looked out at me from that picture—"Mummileh, I am so lonely."

(Sips tea) Ach! This tea should be a farce. *(Goes to the sink to dump tea, then crosses to the stove, lights the burner to reheat the water)* I go on and on. It is not me who is interesting, it is my play. You know, it tells how there would be no more tyrants if the women ruled the world.

VOICE: We sort of knapsacked our way around London. We were still the knapsack generation. You know, skinny, tanned and freckled from too much hitchhiking, T-shirts, T-shirts with no bras, jeans and sandals, frizzy wild hair, uh . . . smoking constantly. You get the picture.

We were ecstatic to be in England. As a child I had traveled with my parents all over the world but had never gone to Ostroleka. We had never gone to Poland. When I asked my grandmother about it she'd say, "Why do you want to go there? They killed us there. Why—what do you want to know about that place?" But now I was on my own. I was young—And I wanted to know.

ANNULLA: You know, I knew what went on in Dachau. In 1938 I knew. My husband wrote me every month a letter. He was very sick when he was there—his legs swelled up. My friends who survived said he looked like an elephant. *(Prepares fresh teapot)* But it was because of the Nazis that he survived. B&M is the first antibiotic invented. They tried the drug on the prisoners because they dared not experiment on the Aryans. They tried it on the Jews first, you see? *(Returns to table and sits)* And they saved my husband's life. Can you imagine? *(Laughing)* There are times when I feel grateful for the strangest things. Do you know what I mean? Have you also?

Do you know I went to Dachau? For a visit. Yes. I did. It was the worst day of my life. You see, I was so indifferent to what would happen to me. One day, some man from the Gestapo came to see me and said, "I am going to buy your house. I will give you so-and-so marks for it. You have to sell it to me." I said, "But my husband is in Dachau." And he said, "Well, you'll have to get his signature." So I went to Dachau. I took a train from Munich to Dachau, spent the night in a hotel . . . can you imagine, a Jewish woman in Dachau in 1938 and I took a room in a hotel! The cheek. *(Laughing)*

And this solicitor who worked in the Dachau camp. He came back and told me, "I spoke to your husband . . . and got the signature. I'll tell you something. But it is confidential and *really* I am not allowed to tell you, but I will tell you. Your husband *will* come out . . . before the end of the year." And do you know, he came out on the thirty-first of December? Yes, you see, they were moved by the many steps I had taken. They couldn't understand. They asked me why do you not leave this Jewish husband? They asked me in Vienna, they asked me in Munich—I did not say it was because I am also Jewish. I said, "Because I love him."

You know, I got only inside the perimeter of Dachau. I saw through the barbed wire fence, but I did not see my husband—they told me later, the survivors, that they called my husband the saint. He gave the prisoners the strength to live. Oh, he was a good man, my husband. He was not very bright, I must tell you, but he was so kind, so tender. You know, I loved him very much. Those thirteen months while he was in Dachau and I was alone were horrible.

But this is when I became political. It was rage at what was happening, you know, and nobody did anything about it. Everyone, especially Americans, ask why? Why, if you *knew*, did no one *do* anything about it? Well, I will tell you. I don't think *you* would have done anything about it either. That is normal human nature. That you don't do anything about it. That is what is appalling about human nature. *(Crosses back to the table)* But I have found the solution for everything in my play. If the women with their hearts would start thinking, we could change everything within a year. But the women are not taking action. And that is the trouble. *(Sorting the manuscript, she shuffles through the pages)*

Here I will read a bit. Oh, really I can't find anything, it is all out of order. Ah! here is the beginning. Oh, no, what, what, what? Ah, here is something. No, it is really not applicable. Excuse me. *(Angry)* I have to start skinning this chicken for Ada's dinner. *(Puts books on one of the chairs. Takes out a chicken, a board and a very blunt old knife, and starts to skin the chicken, standing behind the table)*

I shall send this play off to the producers after I have edited a bit more, but I am a woman who never has any time, and sometimes I don't know why I bother. *(Throws down chicken, goes to her desk, piled high with papers. Types. Then reads)*

VOICE: Well, who knows if she would ever have been a writer or not, she was constantly interrupted—she was an immigrant from the earliest time in her life. She left L'vov in Galicia in her early teens, where her first language was what? Polish? Right. Then German. And then—and then Ukrainian. Then French with her governess, also Ruthenian, she spoke Ruthenian because the peasants who lived in the Carpathian Mountains near her summer home spoke Ruthenian. Then she went to Vienna, where she started using her German. Then to Germany. From Germany to Italy in her thirties. She learned Italian, and then escaped to England. Her seventh language is English. She loved England. And she thought it was "*the* civilized place to live." Prides herself on the fact that she has perfect English, which we know, of course, she doesn't. And then she tries to learn how to write in her seventh language . . .

ANNULLA: But I can understand you women not being able to take action when you feel a great grief. During those thirteen months when I was alone, posing as an Aryan every day, I lost myself. I couldn't work. I got those crying fits. You know, they are called *schreikrampf,* screaming spasms. I suddenly screamed without any reason. I would be doing something normal, something ordinary, like ironing a shirt, and then suddenly I would get this screaming fit. That grief was so deep. Because I never believed that he would come back. *(Pause)* I met him on the stairs. I was in a coffeehouse in Vienna with some other women. They telephoned me to the coffeehouse and said, "Come quickly, there is news from Gustav." They did not want to shock me too much by telling me he had come back.

So I came up the stairs, and he came towards me down the stairs. You know, I was stunned! I was standing there, I couldn't move. I didn't believe my eyes. I thought I would never see him again. But my husband was such a good soul with such a mild nature that not even the Nazis could have harmed him. *(A laugh)* It is six years since he died and there are times I feel how long it has been since I saw him. *(Gets up, washes her hands, starts to skin chicken again)* You know, if his mother had not died from cancer, he would have never have got married. He had a slight Oedipus condition, my husband. When his mother died, she died a year before we got married, he felt suddenly completely lost. I married him, you know, only because I got so bedazzled by sex. And at this time, you couldn't sleep with a man like now. That was not done. Not in our circle. That is why I couldn't write my thesis. I was too absentminded, distracted by this sex. In Vienna, don't forget the men were all killed off in the First World War. There was one man to ten women in the 1920s. "So, all right," I said, "I'll marry him." He was very nice to me. As he always was. And he was very tender . . . And he wanted to get married by hook or crook. *(Hits chicken; sits)* So, I got married. Just got married to get married. Then he grew on me. I fell in love gradually. And I loved him very much. Afterwards. Because I didn't know him. You know, we knew each other only four weeks when he proposed to me. And you know, there was a thunderstorm when he proposed to me. We were on the street, and I said, "Yes, all right, I'll marry you." And, there was this thunder and I got terribly frightened. Oh, my father wanted me to get married. I was a terrible nuisance at home. I was twenty-eight, I hated my mother. She hated me. It was high time I got married. And, how I resented my father. He had a compassion, a burning compassion for suffering, but he was very indifferent to his children. I liked him, but he didn't notice me. Actually, I pitied him because he had too many commitments. You see, he had a whole family who relied on him to support them. Ach, we were a tragic family. My mother often said, "We are like the Strindberg families . . . "

Do you know Strindberg? Where everybody is at odds with everybody else. Fantastic. Such tension. *The Road to Damascus* is a fantastic drama. You know, Strindberg is not appreciated in America. They like Ibsen. They play him on and on. But really there is very little in it. Ah, but Strindberg . . . You know why they can't play it? Because there are no actors of the stage who can play these people. It's like *Faust* by Goethe. All those tormented souls. Americans can't play this.

I wanted to be an actress, you know. I went for an audition—to the Vienna State Theatre—and the director said to me: "You might be quite good, you know, but you are much too small for the stage."

Ada is a Strindberg character. In Vienna she danced on the stage, the Viennese ballet. She was good, nothing special, but she was good. You wouldn't want to meet her . . . You know, ballet bores me to extinction. *(Puts chicken in pot)*

When I went to Vienna I wanted to work, to really take a job. And do you know they shooed me out? Do you know why? They found out my father was a millionaire. You know how? My father offered for sale to some other firm something or other. And this firm where I was working wanted to buy it, so they asked me. Are you any relation to Simon? I said, "Yes, that's my father." The next day they gave me notice. I am always connected to the wrong people. *(Puts lid on pot)*

But you know, then I went back to making my thesis, and I passed all my seminars and at last I thought I would settle down to do something *useful*, and then I got married! I wouldn't have finished that thesis anyway. It was on that Gautier. You probably never even heard of him. Very boring. So, I got married and my father died on the first day of our honeymoon. We left on the twenty-first of April and he died on April twenty-third at six o'clock in the morning. But do you know, from that day on, my mother became the best of mothers, and I became the best of daughters. Because we didn't need each other any more. We no longer lived in the same house. *(Gets onions)* Ach, you know I *abused* my mother. I called her names. I was so bitter about her. My mother was a tyrant. She wanted everyone to be according to her image. She couldn't stand otherwise. That is why my older sister, Czecha, was the way she was. I had a stronger personality than my sister. I could survive it. My sister could not survive it. They call it now schizophrenia is a person who tries to live in an unlivable world. And that world was unlivable for my sister. And she escaped from it, through schizophrenia. *(Sigh)*

My mother was a very bad mother really. She didn't take any notice of the younger children. Only Nunu and Czecha. They were her darlings. We got pushed away with nannies, with *Kindermadchen*. We never saw our mother and father. We were deprived children, completely deprived of love. *(Chops onions)*

You know, my father moved from L'vov to Vienna so that Czecha could be analyzed by Freud. In the end it was Adler who treated her. But she saw a few times Sigmund Freud. Oh yes—we're quite an interesting family.

When we moved back to the house in L'vov, Galicia, the three small children lived downstairs with our French governess and the others lived upstairs. Only I and Ada went to the same school. To *(Laughs)* a Catholic nun's school! We had to go to prayers every morning and kneel down. They didn't allow the Jewish religion there. But they accepted us. You know, they were fond of us, the Catholics. This is unusual, especially in L'vov where the anti-Semitism was horrid. *(Puts onions in pot)*

You know, when Ada left Vienna, she came to live with me and my family in London after the war in 1949. It was a terrible time. I gave her the bedroom. My husband slept in the dining room. I slept in the small room; my son was in the living room. I was so unhappy I got cancer. The doctor told me: happy people do not get cancer. Ada is very difficult to put up with. Where are the carrots? *(Goes to the fridge and gets out carrots; crosses to the table and cuts off the carrot tops)*

We have never been on very good terms with one another; I take care of her only out of a sense of duty. She was a very spoiled girl. She married that man only because he was very good-looking. Really good-looking. *(Gets a peeler from the cabinet drawer, crosses to the sink and scrapes the carrots)*

They met each other by him putting an advertisement in the paper that he was looking for a good-looking girl who can act, and he is a producer of Sasha, the only film company in Vienna. Ada went to see him for an audition. It turned out later that he was a *friend* of someone's at Sasha, and he gave him the room to interview people. He was a cheat. But Ada fell in love with him . . . a very unsavory business, I can tell you.

I wrote her letters every day. Ada, I warn you *(Crosses back to table)* don't marry that man. He's taking advantage of you. He wants your money. He has no job, he will never have a job, he embezzles money, and he lives in the your flat. *(Chops carrots)* He still lives in her flat with another woman which belongs to Ada which my mother left her when she went back to Poland. Ada could stay because she was married to an Aryan. We couldn't stay. So my mother went to Poland with my older sister where they were killed; they were shot by the Nazis, my mother and Czecha, before they got to the concentration camps. And Ada was left with the flat. And this man took it over and threw her out of it. We tried to get her a divorce after the war. We told Ada, "Look, go into the flat and claim your conjugal rights and your flat." And she said, "I'm not going to. I'm afraid of him." And that was that. She never wanted a divorce really, I think. She couldn't get married anymore. Ach, she had a very bad life. I don't think any man she was ever with really cared about her. *(Crosses to the trash with the carrot tops; scrapes carrots into pot)*

You know, it's difficult not to call Ada gruesome. She's terribly gruesome. A terribly gruesome person. She loves children, you know. She has missed something in life. *(Rinses cutting board, crosses back to the table; sits)* Some women are not suitable to be mothers, but she is. And that is the tragedy of it. You see, every time she would have no fathers for her children. So she had to get abortions. For a time, she lived with a Rumanian in the country. I never met him. She still writes letters to him. Or to his family. I think he died. I posted a letter just last week. I think she still loves him. He left her for a servant. *(Pause)* And she can't see why. After all, she was forty-two or forty-three when she met him. And when she tells you this story she says, "How can a man with his culture get himself a servant girl?" She couldn't understand that this servant girl attracted him immediately. She wouldn't understand that . . .

You know, my husband knew nothing about sex when I married him. He was thirty years old; he came to sex late in life, too. And he was wonderful. *(Laughs)* I remember he used to come home from work to have lunch with me in the first years we were married, and you know, I don't think he once had time for a meal. You know, I think for some it is better to be older. All of these young people are so impatient. And then they get bored so fast. My niece, though, is different. She has a lot of boyfriends. Intellectuals, athletes, politicians. Very good-looking. Do you know she is very politically aware for her age? She says that when I was in Berlin in 1919 there were huge workers' riots. You know, I was so frivolous that I can not even remember that. All I remember is that everyone spoke Russian to me. You know why, of course. There were one hundred thousand Russian emigrés from the revolution in Berlin. This is where I met the Pasternaks. I lived with Lydia, Boris's sister, during the Second World War in Oxford. Lydia is a wonderful woman. She has a Russian soul. But she never had any hope for my Women's Party. It was wartime, of course, and she was sure we would lose the war. Everyone thought we would lose the war in 1941. But even now, she cannot talk about politics. She lives like it is still *Dr. Zhivago*. I cannot talk to her at all anymore. But when I met them in Berlin, it was an interesting time. Of course, there were so many refugees and Jews there, the anti-Semitism didn't become obvious until they didn't accept us at university. This happened to a lot of Jews. You see, I started following the lectures. And after two or three months, they told me they had rejected my application because I was a foreigner. Do you know what my passport was? Ukrainian. Yes, I was Ukrainian for one year. You see, when the Russians had that war with Poland in 1918, they made Galicia a state of its own in the Ukraine. And since I was born there, I got a passport from them, the Provisional Ukrainian Government, which was established by the Communists. And with that passport I went to Berlin. Of course, they didn't accept me. My father had applied for Polish citizenship in 1918 because he had all his estates in Poland. He had to become Polish. The Poles were completely disorganized still. They were only one year old. There was no Poland before. But really I did not want to become Polish. The Poles butchered Jews, they always have. Everyone says: but if you speak Polish, you should want to become a Pole. But I say: no. This didn't matter to me. My mother tongue may have been Polish but I also spoke Ukrainian because the peasants spoke Ukrainian. They couldn't speak Polish. And, of course, I spoke German. *(Crosses to the stove and checks the chicken)*

Oh, that makes me think—I must tell you—I met a man in Switzerland last February. I was having coffee in a restaurant. He sat at my table only because everything was occupied, so it appeared. He started speaking German to me. He said, "You are not Swiss, are you?" I said, "No, I am not." He said, "What are you? You sound, what, Russian?" I said,

"No, I am not Russian either." He suddenly started talking
Russian to me. So I answered in Ukrainian because I could
understand what he was saying but I couldn't speak the
Russian. "You are not from Russia. You are from the
Ukraine." I said, "Yes." Then he went on speaking Russian
very fast to me. And I couldn't understand a word. So I think
he thought I was a Russian spy. *(Puts lid on pot)* Speaking of
spies. You know, I was photographed coming out of the tube
(Phone rings)—oh—here at Swiss Cottage station—excuse
me. *(Exits, audience hears part of angry conversation)*

Hello, what? Oh, really. This is too much. Oh, no, I'll
bring you my bread. Oh really—no! All right, all right.
(Hangs up the phone violently; enters angry)

That was my sister. I will commit suicide. She can do everything for herself. Now she rings me she hasn't any bread.
I come back at four o'clock. Now she rings me at five she
hasn't got any bread. I told her, "I'll give you my bread."
"No, I don't eat your bread. It must be Farmhouse or Sunblest." *(Goes to stove and stirs chicken)*

Ada is impossible! She wants me to sacrifice my life for
her now that she is sick. *(Adds spices to pot)*

VOICE: Annulla arranged for us to meet Ada. We came to tea one
day and Ada was at Annulla's, sitting regally at the dining
room table, her blond, blond hair done up in a French
twist—exquisitely dressed, with her leg elevated on Annulla's
best pillows—a little princess even in her seventies; and Annulla was serving her in an absolute rage. *(Laughs)*

ANNULLA *(Stirs pot)*: You know, they thought she would never
walk again. The first day when I asked the doctor, he said
she would be here for a very long time. Well, Ada decided it
would not be a very long time. She simply started getting out
of bed. She has a colossal willpower when she wants to *(Puts
lid on the pot)* . . . But Ada is a flighty woman. *(Goes to the
table and sits)*

While she was living with that husband of hers, she was
pregnant by another man whom I knew. And she had to

have an abortion. Ada told me her husband never found out why she was ill, but I knew. That other man proposed to me, I want you to know, to go over the border illegally. I was alone in Vienna. My son was already in Sweden. My husband had already left for England in April because the visa came. I had no visa, no place to go. The Nazis had taken my place already in Vienna. I was with Ada in the flat that husband of hers has now. "Look," this man said, "I'm going illegally over the Czech border. Why don't you come with me?" He was a Jew, by the way, who dared to wear the swastika, so he wasn't molested. I lived the same life he did—we both passed for Aryans—but I didn't wear the swastika. *(Thumps table emphatically)* This is the man that made Ada pregnant. The cheek of that man. He lost a job when the Nazis came. I can't remember what. He was some sort of intellectual . . . Ada made a human being out of him. He wasn't a *very* human being, but he was a normal man. That is to say, he wasn't mad. He lived on the earnings of a woman who was a cello player. She had a child by him, and they lived together and he wasted her money, spending her money on cardplaying at night. He was terrible, terrible man. I got out without him. I went with my typewriter to Italy. I just crossed the border myself. They tried to stop me. I said, "Leave me alone. I'm writing a novel." Then I was getting on the boat to go to England and they stopped me again. I *threw* my typewriter at the man—I was in such a rage. *(Pause)* I got to England. *(Crosses to the sink and pours out a cup of tea that has been sitting on the table. Pours fresh cup of tea, taking it back to the table)*

You know, I wanted to tell you: you Americans are not unresponsible for the Nazis, you know. And the English and the French. What they did to Germany, no country could take. The Germans are a very proud people and I am not surprised. It cost five million marks in 1923 for a loaf of bread. People used to go to bakeries with wheelbarrows full of money that was as valuable as rubbish. And it was not just the Depression. It was the reparations, that Treaty of Versailles. This is one of the reasons a Hitler could come about. And the stupid French. The French were responsible for it too. They said the Germans started the war. All right, but so in 1917, we didn't have anything to *eat*. I had a friend, an Aryan friend at school. She was fifteen years old and looked like a girl of eight: Because she had nothing to eat. Terrible injustice was done to people in Europe by those countries. Of course, we were a wealthy family, we didn't starve; but these people did. And the blockade. No food could come through. The anti-Semitism, this is complicated, but you know anti-Semitism has been ingrained in the German culture for the longest time. You know, I had a cousin of my uncle—a businessman. He saw he could buy whole buildings for practically nothing in 1923. So he did it. He bought up all these poor people's homes. For nothing. He was rich. They were starving—they had nowhere to live. And he was a Jew, so . . . People needed a catchword, you know, for the misery, and the Jews were the obvious target. They always are. I cannot even talk to you about the death camps . . . this whole affair, this whole Hitler affair . . . this whole war, made me start thinking about my Women's Party. I didn't know that people were so evil until I saw it with my own eyes. I didn't believe it that people could be so evil. *(Sips tea)*

I started thinking of founding my Women's Party as early as 1939. You know, I don't think very much of your America. You may think of founding a political party, but you need a lot of money to found a political party in the United States. You don't here. You can start a party like the Liberals. You know what one of them did? He went on television. Did you see this? And said, "Every person who voted Liberal (eight million voted Liberal in the last election) should send me a pound." And I sent him a pound to the House of Commons. And what do you think? I got a letter which cost three pence to post, and the secretary, and the paper to write on, and how much does he have left of the pound I sent him? This time I am going to send him two pounds.

Excuse me, I must start cleaning up for Ada's dinner. *(Goes to the cabinet and gets out a Tupperware container for the chicken)*

(Annulla puts on the radio; we hear Heifetz) Ah—Heifetz.

VOICE: I have a sense from my—both my father and mother—a sense of responsibility, history. Of course, I am the daughter of an historian, but I think most Jewish children do have this. I look at those old family pictures that people will look at and I know who everyone is. I know where they lived. I know the towns. I know every face. *(Pause)*

The Nazis *(Annulla is stopped by the word "Nazis")* came into Ostroleka and they said they wouldn't harm people if they would point out the Jews. So the neighbors who'd lived side by side with them for ever and ever, harmoniously, saved their own lives, I guess, and pointed everyone out. They were all herded into the town square. My great-grandfather unfortunately was a much-loved elder of the community, so he was . . . you know . . . taken by the beard and made to eat grass before they killed him and then the entire community was shot. And my mother remembers when my grandmother got the letter in America—telling her . . .

ANNULLA: Do you know that during the war people did nothing. They saw evil all around them and they didn't do anything. Of course, a Marx could have inspired people to make a revolution. It has to be a Marx. *(Packs up dinner into Tupperware container)*

But do you know that all of the main revolutions ended up with things becoming as they were before? Look at the French Revolution, how many people they sent to the guillotine and what happened after that. Look at the Russian Revolution. Look at any revolution you like. Everything gets worse. I have a special chapter in my play for the Chinese. They are not human anymore. It is my intuition only. I know nothing of what goes on inside China. But the Western people don't even see that Mao has made the Chinese not human anymore. They have been completely brainwashed. They are like you put on a tape recorder. And this cheek of that Mao! He entertains your Nixon. He was in Peking and they entertain him. Did you see this on television? With this ballet of a capitalist landlord and this girl. And this girl *shoots* the capitalist! This is tact for you. This is tact, and poor Nixon has to smile. This is politicians. And do you know on the corners of the street in Peking there are school-children while the workers are going to work, they read aloud Chairman Mao's thoughts? To the workers who pass them . . . They are brainwashed from *cradle* to *grave*. They cannot think anything for themselves.

Don't you have any women in America who can *talk*? You have a lot of millionairesses in their own rights in your country, my brother tells me. Widows. They must give this money for the party!

How many women do you have in your Congress? This is disgraceful. Have you no women who can rouse people? My play—I hope you like it—is not silly. Ada dragged me to Brecht's *Arturo Ui*. I was outraged. This moronic man, this Brecht, makes Hitler *funny*! Did he think no one in the audience had lived through it? You know, Brecht had not. He was in Hollywood. To make Hitler into a gangster, *this* shows ignorance. To make Nixon into a gangster, this I can understand. But anyone who had lived through Hitler would not do this.

But you Americans with your capitalism. It is a terrible, terrible system. Communism would be a better system if it had any humanity in it, if they could combine freedom and communism. But they cannot seem to do it. I don't know why; communism is better in the book . . . *(Crosses back to the table but remains standing)*

If I had not been an alien, I would have started my party. You see, only women know mother-love. It is the most powerful response in the world of a positive kind. Men have

strong feeling too, but they are violent. They should not be
allowed to rule. A woman's *natural* instinct is loving. Oh, I
go on and on. It will be clear when I finish my play. Oh, I
don't know what I am doing. I would have started my party
here, but you could not believe the anti-foreign feeling here
in England . . . *(Crosses to her easy chair)* My husband came
to England first. I couldn't get a visa. I had to get a domestic
servant card from my cousin. She sent me a visa to Italy. You
see, they wouldn't let anyone in who didn't want to work,
the English. They didn't like aliens. They still don't like
aliens. And when I hear that standard phrase: "Don't tell
bad things about Churchill. Be grateful he saved you from
Hitler!" He did not want to save us from Hitler. He wanted
to have domestic servants. I worked as a domestic servant
for three months and then I took a job as a children's maid
in Oxfordshire with a gentry family. And only because my
husband joined the English forces could I get permission to
drive a lorry. *(Puts on a sweater)*

I wanted to join the ATS—the Women's Auxiliary Territo-
rial Services. They were crying out for drivers because
hardly any girls knew how to drive at that time. And I came
with my international driver's license and said, "I would like
to join the ATS. I would like to join as a driver." "Oh, no,"
they said, "You are an enemy alien!" I said, "I am not an enemy alien. I have been cleared because my husband is in the
British *army*." They said, "You are still a foreigner. You can
only be an orderly." That means scrubbing floors. I said.
"Thank you very much. I'd rather not join." *(Annulla sits in
easy chair)*

VOICE: We got to Ostroleka. My grandmother had drawn us a map.
She marked where the family store had been, the synagogue.—She wanted us to find the graves. Well, we got to the
town—followed the map—we found the store, but it wasn't a
store anymore. The synagogue had been destroyed, never
rebuilt. There was no Jewish graveyard. We went to the town
hall and asked for the family records. We were told that

there was no record of any of the names we asked for. There were no records. No trace. Nothing.

ANNULLA: You know, my husband did not come back from Dunkirk. This was when my first neurosis came. My husband, you should have known him. He was the slowest man on earth. *(Laughing)* He missed all the boats. Everyone else was back on the sixth of June in 1940 except him. He didn't come back. I thought the worst that could, happened. He had already been in Dachau. He was a traitor, you see. They would have eaten him alive. I don't know what they would have done. I wrote a letter to Anthony Eden—he was a Secretary at the time. I said, "Where is my husband? If he falls into German hands, you can't imagine what will happen to him." And he wrote back, "He is not in German hands. He will come back. His unit is still in the harbor." So Gustav came back on the sixteenth of June. But this ten days was such a horror that two months later, I got this anxiety neurosis.

This was not the screaming. Anxiety neurosis is a terrible illness. You are afraid, but you do not know what you are afraid of. You can't eat, you can't sleep. I saw letters upside down, I had illusions. It is horrible. A doctor saw me and said, "No, she is not mad . . . it is a delayed reaction, an anxiety from those ten days." But do you know, my son arrived on the sixteenth of April 1942, and from that day on, the neurosis had gone. And the first words he said to me, I will never forget . . . He came running up to me, "Mummileh, Mummy have you grown small? You are very small." He forgot that he had grown four years. He was eight when he left and almost twelve when he returned. He's very tall now. I did not see him for four years. Oh, that time was a great grief. I don't think anyone who has not gone through this experience can really understand. My dreams. I always dreamed that Gustav was in a cage behind bars and he was telling me, "I am not in Dachau. I am dead. Don't you know. I am dead." I kept dreaming this over and over again. Do you have recurring dreams? Isn't it horrible? It was the worst time of my life, but it was like the year after my husband's death. You know, at his funeral I screamed again, just as I had when he went to Dachau. Now I knew he would never come back.

VOICE: My mother looks more beautiful and more alive than she's ever looked. She said such an interesting thing to me. She said, "I feel like I've finally figured out how to live and it's going to be over." And I know what she means. I remember being with her at her mother's funeral. And the tears just welled up in her eyes. And she said, "I can't believe it went by so fast." She was putting her mother into the ground, and she remembered sitting in the kitchen and talking to her about—you know—baking bread; five years old, remembered the smell, remembered every single moment of it and all of a sudden fifty years had passed. Her mother's life was over. And she looked at me and said, "There's no time."

ANNULLA: I have so much time now, I am alone. I write all of the time. That is why I wake up every day. *(Laughing)* Ada is a terrible nuisance . . .

Do you know, when my son was born, I sobbed uncontrollably. Every woman has this love in her. It may be sleeping but it can be awakened. I sobbed and sobbed when they gave him to me. The doctor said to me, "Why are you crying?" I said, "Because I am happy." He said, "People who are happy do not cry." I said, "I do." *(Laughs. Pause)*

But after all this—after Dachau, after Dunkirk—do you know how my husband died? He was sitting here, in the kitchen watching me fry an egg like I always did for him. I turned around to look at him and he had fallen over . . . dead. Yes . . . so . . . *(Gets up, crosses to table. Looks at manuscript)* It still needs some minor editing.

Excuse me, I have to go. *(Indignant)* I have to take dinner and Sunblest bread to Ada. *(Puts on coat)*

VOICE: I came back to America just before my grandmother died. I told her we went to Ostroleka. I think she actually was glad. I tried to get into Bucovina where my father's family came from, but it's no longer in Austria, it is in Russia and they wouldn't let us in. My family names on my mother's side are: Brum, Blum, Schleifer, Zimyevsky, Blut and Simon.

There is a wonderful fairy tale about a young girl who loans her relatives to another young girl who doesn't have any. You see? It's been fourteen years since I visited Annulla.

ANNULLA *(At a loss. Tentative, very vulnerable)*: I am so glad you could come to see me today. Really. But *it went by so fast.* Do you know, *everything* has gone by so fast . . . Thank you . . . It was so nice to meet you. Good-bye.

VOICE: Good-bye.

ANNULLA *(Gets to door. Turns back. Very difficult to say)*: Good-bye.

(Annulla exits.)

END OF PLAY

STILL LIFE

Overleaf: Mary McDonnell (Cheryl), John Spencer (Mark) and Timothy Near (Nadine) in American Place Theatre's production. Photo by Martha Holmes.

Still Life premiered at the Goodman Studio Theatre in October 1980. The same production was then produced by the Women's Project at American Place Theatre in New York in February 1981. Under the author's direction, the production won Obies for playwriting, direction, all three performances, as well as for best production. Set and costume design were by Tom Lynch and lighting design was by Annie Wrightson. The cast was as follows:

MARK	John Spencer
CHERYL	Mary McDonnell
NADINE	Timothy Near

The play has subsequently been performed around the world—at the Market Theatre in Johannesburg, at the Avignon and Edinburgh festivals, in London and Paris, and in major regional theatres and universities throughout the United States.

Still Life is about three people I met in Minnesota during the summer of 1978. It is about violence in America. The Vietnam War is the backdrop to the violence at home. The play is dedicated to the casualties of the war—all of them.

The play is a "documentary" because it is a distillation of interviews I conducted during that summer. I chose the documentary style to ensure that the reality of the people and events described could not be denied. Perhaps one could argue about the accuracy of the people's interpretations of events, but one cannot deny that these are actual people describing actual events as they saw and understood them.

The play is also a personal document. A specialist of the brain and its perceptions said to me after seeing *Still Life* that the play is constructed as a traumatic memory. Each character struggles with his traumatic memory of events and the play as a whole is my traumatic memory of their accounts. The characters speak directly to the audience so that the audience can hear what I heard, experience what I experienced.

I have been obsessed with violence in our country ever since I came of age in the 1960s. I have no answer to the questions I raise in the play but I think the questions are worth asking. The play is a plea for examination and self-examination, an attempt at understanding our own violence and a hope that through understanding we can, as Nadine says, "come out on the other side."

PRODUCTION NOTES

The actors speak directly to the audience. The rhythms are of
real people's speech, but may also at times have the sense of im-
provisation one finds with the best jazz musicians: the monologues should sometimes sound like extended riffs.

The play is written in three acts but this does not denote act
breaks. Rather, the acts represent movements and the play
should be performed without intermission. The ideal running
time is one and a half hours.

Mark

an ex-marine, Vietnam veteran, husband, artist, lover, father

Cheryl

his wife, mother of his children

Nadine

his friend, artist, mother of three, divorcee, a woman with many jobs and many lives, ten to fifteen years older than Mark and Cheryl

TIME

The present.

PLACE

The setting is a long table with ashtrays, water glasses, Mark's pictures and slides upon it. Behind it is a large screen for slide projection. The look is of a conference room or perhaps a trial room.

The director may also choose to create a space in which there are numerous locations, e.g., Mark's studio, Mark and Cheryl's living room, Nadine's office or a café.

NOTE: In the Paris production, the director, Jean-Claude Fall, created a surreal landscape. Palm trees backed by a brilliant blue cyclorama lined the upstage. On the downstage edge was a strip of sandy beach with a trunk containing Mark's "artifacts." Upstage of the strip of sand was a row of broken theatre chairs; upstage of that, and up a level, was an old 1950s style chair, home slide projector and screen. Instead of marking the breaks with silence, ear-splitting Algerian rock music punctuated the breaks.

ACT ONE

Mark snaps on slide of Cheryl: young, fragile, thin, hair flow-ing, quintessentially innocent.

MARK:

This is a picture of my wife before.

(Lights up on Cheryl, six months pregnant, heavy, rigid.)

This is her now.
She's been through a lot.

(Mark snaps on photographic portrait of himself. Face gentle. Halo of light around head.)

This is a portrait Nadine made of me.

(Lights up on Nadine.)

This is Nadine.

(Lights out on Nadine. Snaps on slide of marine boot and leg just below the knee.)

This is a picture of my foot.
I wanted a picture of it because if I ever lost it,
I wanted to remember what it looked like.

(He laughs. Fade-out.)

11

CHERYL:

    If I thought about this too much I'd go crazy.
So I don't think about it much.
I'm not too good with the past.
Now, Mark, he remembers.
That's his problem.
I don't know whether it's 1972 or 1981.
Sometimes I think about divorce.
God, I don't know.
Divorce means a lot of nasty things
like it's over.
It says a lot like
Oh yeah. I been there. I'm a divorcee . . . Geez.
You could go on forever about that thing.
I gave up on it. No.
You know, I wasn't willing to give up on it,
and I should have,
for my own damn good.

You look:
It's all over now,
it's everywhere.
There are so many men like him now.

You don't have to look far to see how
sucked in you can get.

You got a fifty-fifty chance.

III

NADINE:

When I first met Mark, it was the big stuff.
Loss of ego, we shared everything.

The first two hours I spent with him and what I
    thought
then is what I think now, and I know just about
    everything
there is to know, possibly.

He told me about it *all* the first week I met him.
We were discussing alcoholism.
I'm very close to that myself.
He said that one of his major projects
was to face all the relationships he'd been in
where he'd violated someone.
His wife is one.

He's so honest he doesn't hide anything.

He told me he beat her very badly.
He doesn't know if he can recover that relationship.

I've met his wife.
I don't know her.
I sometimes even forget . . .

He's the greatest man I've ever known.
I'm still watching him.

We're racing. It's very wild.
No one's gaming.
There are no expectations.
You have a foundation for a lifelong relationship.
He can't disappoint me.

Men have been wonderful to me,
but I've never been treated like this.
All these—yes, all these men—
businessmen, politicians, artists, patriarchs—none of
them, no one has ever demonstrated this to me.

He's beyond consideration.
I have him under a microscope.
I can't be fooled.
I know what natural means.
I know when somebody's studying.
I've been around a long time.
I'm forty-three years old.
I'm not used to being treated like this.

I don't know. I'm being honored, cherished, cared
    about.

Maybe this is how everybody's treated and I've missed
    out.

(Laughs.)

IV

MARK:

My biggest question to myself all my life was

How I would act under combat?
That would be who I was as a man.

I read my Hemingway.
You know . . .

The point is,
you don't *need* to go through it.

I would break both my son's legs
before I let him go through it.

CHERYL:

I'm telling you—
if I thought about this, I'd go crazy.
So I don't think about it.

MARK *(To Cheryl)*:

I know I did things to you, Cheryl.
But you took it.
I'm sorry.
How many times can I say I'm sorry to you?

(To audience)

I've, uh, I've, uh, hurt my wife.

NADINE:

He is incredibly gentle. It's madness to be treated this
way. I don't need it. It's great without it.

CHERYL:

He blames it all on the war . . . but I want to tell
you . . . don't let him.

MARK:

My wife has come close to death a number of times,
   but uh . . .

NADINE:

Maybe he's in awe of me.

CHERYL:

See, I read into things,
and I don't know if you're supposed to, but I do.
Maybe I'm too against his artist world,
but Mark just gets into trouble
when he's into that art world.

NADINE *(Laughing)*:

Maybe he's this way to his mother.

CHERYL:

One day I went into the basement to take my clothes
   out of the washer,
Jesus I have to clean out that basement,
and I came across this jar . . .

NADINE:

Especially from a guy who's done all these dastardly
   deeds.

CHERYL:

He had a naked picture of me in there,
cut out to the form,
tied to a stake with a string.
And there was all this broken glass,
and I know Mark.
Broken glass is a symbol of fire.

(Thinking)

What else did he have at the bottom?

NADINE:

I accept everything he's done.

CHERYL:

Yeah, there was a razor blade in there

and some old negatives of the blood stuff, I think.
I mean, that was so violent.
That jar to me, scared me.
That jar to me said:
Mark wants to kill me.
Literally kill me for what I've done.
He's burning me at the stake like Joan of Arc.
It just blew my mind.

NADINE:

Those jars he makes are brilliant, humorous.
He's preserving the war.
I'm intrigued that people think he's violent.
I know all his stories.
He calls himself a time bomb.
But so are you, aren't you?

MARK:

I don't know what it would be for women.
What war is for men.
I've thought about it. A lot.
I saw women brutalized in the war.
I look at what I've done to my wife.

CHERYL:

He keeps telling me: He's a murderer.
I gotta believe he can be a husband.

MARK:

The truth of it is, it's different
from what we've heard about war before.

NADINE:

He's just more angry than any of us.
He's been fighting for years.
Fighting the priests, fighting all of them.

MARK:

I don't want this to come off as a combat story.

CHERYL:

Well, a lot of things happened that I couldn't handle.

MARK:

It's a tragedy is what it is. It happened to a lot of
people.

CHERYL:

But not too, you know, not anything
dangerous or anything like that—
just crazy things.

NADINE:

I guess all my friends are angry.

CHERYL:

But, uh, I don't know.
It's really hard for me to bring back those years.

NADINE:

Mark's just been demonstrating it, by picking up
weapons,
leading a group of men.

CHERYL:

Really hard for me to bring back those years.

MARK:

My brother . . .
He has a whole bunch of doubts now,
thinking, "Well I wonder what I'd do
if I were in a fight."
And you don't *need* to go through that shit.
It's *bullshit*.
It just chews people up.

NADINE:

Leading a whole group into group sex, vandalism,
theft.
That's not uncommon in our culture.

MARK:

You go into a VFW hall, that's all men talk about.
Their trips on the war.

NADINE:

I don't know anyone who cares so much about his
parents.

He's trying to save them.
Like he sent home this bone of a man he killed, from
    'Nam.
It was this neat attempt to demand for them to listen,
about the war.

MARK:

I can't talk to these guys.
There's just no communication.
But we just . . . know.
We look and we know.

NADINE:

See, he's testing everyone all the time.
In very subtle ways.
He can't believe I'm not shocked.
I think that intrigues him.

CHERYL:

Oh. I don't know.
I want it suppressed as fast as possible.

NADINE:

He laughed at me once.
He'd just told a whole raft of stories.
He said: "Anyone who understands all this
    naughtiness
must have been pretty naughty themselves."
Which is a pretty simplistic way of saying we can all
    do it.

MARK:

I thought:
If I gave *you* the information,
I couldn't wash my hands of the guilt,
because I did things over there.
We all did.

CHERYL:

I would do anything to help suppress it.

MARK *(Quietly to audience)*:
We all did.

V

NADINE:

You know what war is for women?
A friend of mine sent me this line:
I'd rather go into battle three times than give birth
    once.
She said Medea said that.
I stuck it on my refrigerator.
I showed it to Mark. He laughed for days.

MARK:

When Cheryl, uh, my wife and I first met,
I'd just come back from 'Nam.
I was so frightened of her.
She had this long hair and she was really thin.
I just thought she was really, uh,
really American.

NADINE:

Do you know I never talked with my husband
about being pregnant?
For nine months there was something going on down
    there
and we never mentioned it. Ever.

MARK:

You know, it was like I couldn't talk to her.
I didn't know how to respond.

NADINE:

We completely ignored it.
We were obsessed with names.
We kept talking constantly about what we would
    name it.
I gained fifty pounds. It was sheer ignorance.
I was a good Catholic girl
and no one talked about such things.
I never knew what that part of my body was doing.

CHERYL:

It was my naivety.
I was so naive to the whole thing, that his craziness
had anything to do with where he'd been.
I mean, I was naive to the whole world
let alone somebody
who had just come back from there.

NADINE:

When the labor started, we merrily got in the car
and went to the hospital.
They put me immediately into an operating room.
I didn't even know what dilation meant.
And I couldn't.
I could not dilate.

CHERYL:

See, I'd hear a lot from his family.
I worked for his father as a dental assistant.
And it was all they talked about—Mark—so I had to
    meet the guy.

NADINE:

I was in agony, they knocked me out.

CHERYL:

And I saw, I mean, I'd open a drawer and I'd see these
    pictures—

NADINE:

My lungs filled up with fluid.

CHERYL:

. . . dead men. Men hanging. Things like that.
Pictures Mark had sent back.

MARK:

Yeah. I kept sending everything back.

NADINE:

They had to give me a tracheotomy.
My trachea was too small.
They went running out of the operating room to get

the right equipment.
Everyone thought I was going to die.

CHERYL:

Once he sent back a bone of a man he killed. To his
mother.

MARK:

To my brother, not my mother.

CHERYL:

Boy, did that lady freak.

NADINE:

My husband saw them burst out of the room in a
panic.
He thought I was gone.

CHERYL:

Now it doesn't take much for that lady to freak.
Very hyper. I think I'd've gone nuts.
I think I'd wanna take it
and hit him over the head with it.
You just don't do those things.
What the heck is happening to you? I'd say.
They never asked that though.
I don't think they wanted to know
and I think they were afraid to ask.

MARK:

I know. I really wanted them to ask.

CHERYL:

I think they felt the sooner forgotten, the better off
you'd be.

NADINE:

I remember leaving my body.

MARK:

I'll never forget that.

CHERYL:

They didn't want to bring up a bad subject.

MARK:

I came home from a war, walked in the door,

they don't say anything.
I asked for a cup of coffee,
and my mother starts bitching at me about drinking
coffee.

NADINE:

I looked down at myself on that operating table and
felt so free.

CHERYL:

Your mother couldn't deal with it.

NADINE:

They gave me a C-section.
I don't remember anything else.

CHERYL:

My memory's not as good as his.
It's like I put bad things in one half
and in time I erase them.

NADINE:

I woke up in the hospital room with tubes in my
throat,
stitches in my belly. I could barely breathe.
My husband was there. He said: Have you seen the
baby?
What baby, I said.

Can you believe it?

CHERYL:

That's why I say there's a lot of things, weird things,
that happened to us, and I just generally put them
under the title of weird things . . .
and try to forget it.
And to be specific, I'm real vague on a lot of things.

NADINE:

I never knew they were in there
and so I guess I didn't want them to come out.

CHERYL:

I mean, my whole life has turned around since then.

I mean, gosh, I got a kid and another one on the way.
And I'm thinking of climbing the social ladder.
I've got to start thinking about schools for them,
and I *mean* this, it's a completely
different life,
and I've had to . . .
I've *wanted* to change anyway.

It's really hard to bring these things back out.

NADINE:

For my second child, the same thing happened.
By the third time around
they had to drag me out of the car.
I thought they were taking me to my death for sure.

MARK:

Cheryl is amazing.
Cheryl has always been like chief surgeon.
When the shrapnel came out of my head,
she would be the one to take it out.

CHERYL:

It's no big deal.

NADINE:

So when people ask me about the birth of my
      children,
I laugh.

MARK:

Just like with Danny.
She delivered Danny herself.

NADINE:

My children were *extracted* from me.

CHERYL:

It's no big deal. Just like pulling teeth.
Once the head comes out, there's nothing to it.

V I

MARK:
　　　　I want to tell you what a marine is.

NADINE:	**CHERYL:**
I have so much to do.	See, I got kids now.
Just to keep going.	
	I can't be looking into
Just to keep my kids going.	myself.
I don't sleep at all.	I've got to be looking
	out.
When my kids complain	
about supper.	For the next five years
	at least.
I just say:	
I know it's crappy food.	When I'm ready to look
Well, go upstairs	in, look out.
and throw it up.	
	God, don't get into the
I was in a cafe today.	kid routine. It'll do
	it to you every time.
	Because you're getting
	their best interests
	mixed up with *your* best
	interests. And they
	don't go together.
I heard the funniest comment:	
	They go together because
	it *should* be your best
	interest, and *then their*
	best interest. So what
	are you gonna do to them
	in the meantime?
She must be married.	
She spends so much money.	You're talking head trips.

V I I

MARK:

There was this whole trip that we were really special.
And our training was really hard,
like this whole Spartan attitude.

CHERYL:

The war is the base of all our problems.
He gets crazy talking about it
and you can't get him to stop
no matter what he's doing to the people around him.

MARK:

And there was this whole thing too
I told Nadine about that really knocked me out.
There was this whole ethic:
You do not leave your man behind on the field.
I love that.

CHERYL:

Well, he's usually talking more than they can handle.

NADINE:

You know, we had two months of foreplay.

MARK:

I came to a point in there:
Okay, you're here, there's no escape, you're going to
    get taken,
it's all right to commit suicide.
And it was as rational as that.

We came across a hit at night, we got ambushed,
it was a black guy walking point, and you know,
bang, bang, bang.
You walk into it. It was a surprise.

Well, they got this black guy.
And they took his body and we found him about a
    week later . . .

CHERYL:

> People start getting really uncomfortable,
> and you can see it in his eyes,
> the excitement.

NADINE:

> The first time I met Mark,
> I'd gone to his shop to buy supplies.
> I didn't think anything about him at first.
> (I've never been attracted to younger men.)
> But he seemed to know what he was doing.

CHERYL:

> It's almost like there's fire in his eyes.

MARK:

> And they had him tied to a palm tree,
> and his balls were in his mouth.
> They'd opened up his stomach and it had been pulled
>   out.
> And I knew . . .

NADINE:

> I saw some of his work.

MARK:

> Nobody was going to do that to me.

NADINE:

> Some of the blood photography I think.

MARK:

> Better for me to rationalize suicide
> because I didn't want . . .
> that.
> I don't know.

CHERYL:

> It bothers me because it's better left forgotten.
> It's just stirring up clear water.

NADINE:

> We talked and I left. But I felt strange.

MARK:

> R. J. was my best friend over there.

He and I got into a whole weird trip.
We found ourselves competing against one another,
setting up ambushes,
getting people on *kills* and things,
being the best at it we could.

NADINE:

All of a sudden, he came out of the shop and said:
"You want a cup of tea?"
I was in a hurry,
(I'm always in a hurry)
but I said, "Sure," and we went to a tea shop.

(Laughs.)

MARK:

R. J. is dead.
He got killed in a bank robbery in Chicago.
(He was one of the few friends of mine who survived
    the war.)

NADINE:

Two hours later, we got up from the table.
I'm telling you, neither of us could stand up.
We were gasping for breath.

MARK:

See, I got all these people involved
in a Far East smuggling scam when we got back,
and then it all fell apart
and we were waiting to get arrested.

The smack got stashed in this car that was being held
in a custody lot.
Everyone was afraid to go get it.
So I decided to get it.
I did this whole trip Thanksgiving weekend.
I crawled in there,
stole the tires off the car

that were loaded with the smack.
I had R. J. help me.
We were doing the war all over again.
That was the last time I saw him alive.

NADINE:

We had said it *all* in two hours.
What I thought then is what I think now
and I think I know everything there is to know.

We must have looked pretty funny staggering out of
    there.

MARK:

I heard from one guy on a regular basis, maybe once
    a year.
He was green to Vietnam.
We were getting into
some real heavy contact that Christmas.
It was late at night, the VC went to us
while we were sleeping.
They just threw grenades in on us.
The explosion came, I threw this kid in a bush.
All I did was grab him down,
and he got a medical out of there.
But he feels I saved his life.

NADINE:

When we got out onto the street we said good-bye
but we both knew that our whole lives had changed.

CHERYL:

I know he has other women. I don't know who they are.
At this point I don't really care.
I have a child to think about
and just getting by every day.

NADINE:

We used to meet and talk.
We'd meet in the plaza and talk.
We'd go for rides in the car and talk.

CHERYL:

See, lots of times people break up.
And then the man goes on to the next one.
And you hear the guy say:
"Oh, my wife was crazy." Or something like that.
"She couldn't take it."

NADINE:

Sometimes we'd be driving,
we'd have to stop the car and get our breaths.
We were dizzy, we were gasping for breath,
just from being together.

CHERYL:

But the important question to ask is: *Why* is she
    crazy?

MARK:

So he wants to see me.
I haven't been able to see him.

CHERYL:

My brother is a prime example.
He nearly killed his wife a number of times.
She was a real high-strung person.
She snapped.
The family keeps saying, oh, poor Marge, she was so
    crazy.

MARK:

He was only in the bush maybe five, six weeks,
but it did something to him.
He spent two years, he wrote me a letter,
in a mental institution.
I don't know.

I knew he knew what I knew.

CHERYL:

My brother's now got one little girl
that *saw* her little brother
get shot in the head by his mother . . .

MARK:

I know who's been there.
And they know.

CHERYL:

And then saw her mother come after her.

MARK:

But in a sense we want to be as far away
from each other as possible.
It's become a *personal* thing. The guilt.
There *is* the guilt.
It's getting off on having all that power every day.
Because it was so nice.
I mean, it was power . . .

NADINE:

You know they're doing surveys now, medical
    research on this.

MARK:

I had the power of life and death.

NADINE:

They think something actually changes
in the blood or the lungs when you feel this way.

CHERYL:

I'm sorry. They were married too long
for it just to have been Marge.

MARK:

I'm sitting here now deep down thinking about it . . .

NADINE:

You watch. Soon there'll be a science of love,
and there should be.

CHERYL:

When someone goes so-called crazy in a marriage,
I always think:
It takes two.

MARK:

It's like the best dope you've ever had,
the best sex you've ever had.

NADINE:

It was like dying,
and it was the most beautiful feeling of my life.

CHERYL:

My brother's on to a new woman now.

MARK:

You never find anything better.
And that's not something
you're supposed to feel good about.

CHERYL:

If Mark and I split up, I pity the next one.

MARK:

I haven't told you what a marine is yet.

CHERYL:

Women should warn each other.

(Pause.)

NADINE:

Everything Mark did was justified.
We've all done it.
Murdered someone we loved, or ourselves.

MARK:

I mean, we were trained to do one thing.
That's the one thing about the marines.
We were trained to kill.

NADINE:

This is hard to say.
I have been in the jungle so long,
that even with intimates, I protect myself.
But I know that Mark felt good killing.
When he told me that I didn't bat an eye.
I understand.

CHERYL:

Look,
I think Mark and R. J. were close

only because they both got off on the war.
And I think they were the only two over there that
    did.
Doesn't it kill you when they get into this men-talk?
All men don't talk like that,
when they get together to reminisce.
They don't talk about getting laid and dope.
Imagine getting together with your best girlfriend
and talking about what it was like the night before in
    the sack.
That grosses me out.

NADINE:

I judge everyone so harshly
that it is pretty ironic
that I'm not moved by anything he tells me.
I'm not changed. I'm not shocked.
I'm not offended. And he must see that.

MARK:

I had the power of life and death.
I wrote home to my brother.
I wrote him, I told him.
I wrote:
I dug it. I enjoyed it.
I really enjoyed it.

NADINE:

I understand because I'm *convinced*
that I am even angrier than Mark.
I went off in a different direction, that's all.

CHERYL:

Now I don't think Mark and R. J. were rare.
I think the *degree* is rare.
I mean men would not be going on fighting like this
for centuries if there wasn't something besides
having to do it for their country.
It has to be something like Mark says.
I mean he said it was like orgasm.

He said it was the best sex he ever had.
You know where he can take that remark.
But what better explanation can you want?
And believe me, that is Mark's definition of glory.
Orgasm is *glory* to Mark.

MARK:

I talked with R. J. about it.
He got into a hit once at about 8:30 at night.
And there was this "person" . . .
laying down, wounded,
holding on to a grenade.
(It was a high contact.)
We watched R. J. walk over and he just shot . . .
the person . . .
in the face.

He knew it.

As incredibly civilized as we are in this room, these
     things go on.

NADINE:

Until you know a lot of Catholics
you can't understand what hate means.
I mean I'm a . . . I was a Catholic.
And Catholics have every right to hate like they do.
It requires a whole lifetime
to undo what that training does to them.

MARK:

It's getting hard to talk.
Obviously, I need to tell it,
but I don't want to be seen as . . .
a monster.

NADINE:

Just start talking to Catholics
who allow themselves to talk.
It's unspeakable what's been done to Catholic youths.

Every aspect of their life from their table manners
to their sexuality. It's just terrible.

MARK:

I'm just moving through society now.

(Pause.)

VIII

NADINE:

I mean my definition of sophistication
is the inability to be surprised by anything.

MARK:

I look at my face in a mirror,
I look at my hand, and I cannot believe . . .
I did these things.

CHERYL:

Mark's hit me before.

MARK:

See, I see the war now through my wife.
She's a casualty too.
She doesn't get benefits for combat duties.
The war busted me up, I busted up my wife . . .

CHERYL:

He's hit me more than once.

MARK:

I mean I've hit my wife.

NADINE:

Have you ever been drunk for a long period of time?

MARK:

But I was always drunk.

NADINE:

Well, I have.

MARK:

We were always drunk.

It would boil out,
the anger,
when we were drunk.

NADINE:

I used to drink a lot
and did vicious things when I was drunk.
And until you're there,
you don't *know*.

MARK:

When I was sober, I found out what I'd done to her.
It was . . . I just couldn't stop.

CHERYL:

I was really into speed—oh, how many years ago?
I'm not good with the past.
I mean Mark knows dates and years.
God I don't know.

MARK:

It's like . . .
I feel terrible about it.
The last time it happened
it was about a year ago now.
I made up my mind to quit drinking
because drinking's what's brought it on.

CHERYL:

We got into some kind of argument about speed.
And he pushed me down the stairs.
He hit me a couple of times.

NADINE:

Yeah it's there and it takes years.
My husband and I were
grooving on our fights.
I mean really creative.
And five years ago we got down to the count.
Where we were batting each other around.
Okay, I hit my husband. A lot.
See, I'm capable of it.

MARK:

> I dropped out of AA.
> I put the cork in the bottle myself.

NADINE:

> Okay—I really was drunk, really mad.
> And I beat him up and do you know what he said to
>   me?
> He turned to me after he took it and he said:
> "I didn't know you cared that much."
> It was the most incredible thing.
> And he stood there and held his face
> and took it
> and turned around in a state of glory and said:
> "I didn't think you cared."
> I'll never hit another person again.

CHERYL:

> I went to the hospital
> 'cause my ribs . . .
> I think, I don't know.
> I don't remember it real clearly.
> It had something to do with speed.
> The fact that I wasn't, I was,
> I wasn't rational.
> No, I must have really tore into him.
> I mean I can be nasty.
> So anyway that was hard because I couldn't go to
>   work
> for a couple of weeks.

NADINE:

> And I see Mark.
> The fact that he beat his wife.
> I understand it.
> I don't like it.
> But I understand it.

MARK:

> I've been sober so long now, it's terrifying.

See, I really got into photography while I was
     drunk.
Got involved in the art program at the U.
I mean I could be fine
and then the wrong thing would come up
and it would shut me off.

NADINE:

Don't distance yourself from Mark.

MARK:

I'd space out and start talking about the war.
See, most of these people
didn't have to deal with it.
They all dealt with the other side.

NADINE:

I was "antiwar," I marched, I was "nonviolent."

(Laughs.)

MARK:

I brought some photos.
This is a picture of some people who at one point in
     time
were in my unit. That is,
they were there at the time the photo was taken.
Some of them are dead, some of them made it
     home,

(Pause.)

some of them are dead now.

NADINE:

But I'm capable of it.

MARK:

After I was there, I could never move with people
who were against the war in a real way.

It took a part of our life.
I knew what it was and they didn't.

NADINE:

We all are.

MARK:

They could get as pissed off as they wanted to
I didn't fight with them.
I didn't bitch with them.
I just shut up. Excuse me.

(Looks at audience. Sees or thinks he sees that they're on the other side. Moment of murderous anger. He shuts up and exits.)

I X

CHERYL:

I'm scared knowing that I have to keep my mouth
   shut.
I don't know this for a fact, but I mean
I fantasize a lot.
I have to.
I've got nothing else to do.
See, I've got no real line of communication at all, on
   this issue.
If I ever told him I was scared for my life, he'd freak
   out.
If I ever said anything like that, how would he react?
Would he get angry?
What do you think? Do I want to take that chance?

I got too much to lose.
Before, you know, when we were just single together,
I had nothing to lose. I have a little boy here.

And if I ever caught Mark hurting me
or that little boy again, I'd kill him.
And I don't wanna be up for manslaughter.

Danny means more to me than Mark does.
Only because of what Mark does to me.
He doesn't realize it maybe, but he squelches me.

God, I'm scared.
I don't wanna be alone for the rest of my life
with two kids. And I can't rob my children of what
little father they could have.

NADINE:

I've always understood
how people could hurt each other
with weapons.

If you've been hurt to the quick,
and a weapon's around, WHAP.

I signed my divorce papers because
last time he came over, I knew if
there'd been a gun around, I'd've
killed him.

(Mark enters.)

X

MARK:

I'm sorry.
I don't think you understand.
Sure, I was pissed off at myself that I let myself go.
Deep down inside I knew I could have stopped it.

I could just have said:
I won't do it.
Go back in the rear, just not go out,
let them put me in jail. I could have said:
"I got a toothache," gotten out of it.
They couldn't have forced me.
But it was this duty thing.
It was like:
You're under orders.
You have your orders, you have your job,
you've got to *do* it.

Well, it was like crazy.
At night, you could do anything . . .
It was free-fire zones. It was dark, then
all of a sudden, everything would just burn loose.
It was beautiful . . . You were given all this power to
    work outside the law.
We all dug it.

But I don't make any excuses for it.
I may even be trying to do that now.
I could have got out.
Everybody could've.
If *everybody* had said *no*,
it couldn't have happened.
There were times we'd say:
let's pack up and go, let's quit.
But jokingly.
We knew we were there.
But I think I knew then
we could have got out of it.

NADINE:

Oh,
I'm worried about men.

MARK:

> See, there was a point, definitely, when I was
> genuinely interested in trying to win the war.
> It was my own area.
> I wanted to do the best I could.
> I mean I could have played it really low-key.
> I could have avoided things, I could have made
> sure
> we didn't move where we could have contacts.

NADINE:

> I worry about them a lot.

MARK:

> And I watched the younger guys.
> Maybe for six weeks there was nothing.
> He'd drift in space wondering what he'd do under
> fire.
> It only takes once.
> That's all it takes . . .
> and then you dig it.

NADINE:

> Men are stripped.

MARK:

> It's shooting fireworks off, the Fourth of July.

NADINE:

> We took away all their toys . . . their armor.
>
> When I was younger, I'd see a man in uniform
> and I'd think:
> What a hunk.
> Something would thrill in me.
> Now we look at a man in uniform—
> a Green Beret, a marine—
> and we're embarrassed somehow.
> We don't know who they are anymore.
> What's a man? Where's the model?

All they had left was being Provider.
And now with the economics, they're losing it all.
My father is a farmer.
This year, my mother learned to plow.
I talked to my father on the phone the other night
    and I said:
Hey, Dad, I hear Mom's learning how to plow.
Well, sure, he said.
She's been a farmer's wife for forty, fifty years.
Yes. But she's just learning to plow now.
And there was a silence
and then he said:
That's a feminist issue I'd rather not discuss
at the moment.

So. We don't want them to be the Provider,
because we want to do that ourselves.
We don't want them to be heroes,
and we don't want them to be knights in shining
    armor, John Wayne—
so what's left for them to be, huh?

Oh, I'm worried about men.
They're not coming through.
(My husband)
How could I have ever gotten married?

They were programmed to fuck,
now they have to make love.
And they can't do it.
It all comes down to fucking versus loving.

We don't like them in the old way anymore.
And I don't think they like us, much.
Now that's a war, huh?

ACT TWO

MARK:

This is the photo I showed you.
Of some guys in my unit.

We were south-southwest of Da Nang—
we were in that whole triangle, not too far
from where My Lai was.
Near the mountains, near the coast.

Everybody knew about My Lai.
But it wasn't different from what was going on.
I mean, the grunts did it all the time.

This fellow up there, that's Michele.
He ended up in the nuthouse,
that's the fellow I pulled out of the bush.

This is the machine gunner.
The kid was so good
he handled the gun like spraying paint.
This kid was from down South.
Smart kid.
He got hit in the head, with grenade shrapnel.
He's alive, but he got rapped in the head.
That was the end of the war for him.

NADINE:

I don't know what it is with Mark.
I have a lot of charming friends
that are very quiet, like him—
but they don't have his power.

CHERYL:

You know what Mark's power is:
He's got an imagination that just doesn't quit.

NADINE:

It got to be coincidental when we'd been somewhere
    together
and someone said: You know your friend Mark,
I liked the way he was so quiet.

MARK:

There were no two ways about it . . .

CHERYL:

He's got an imagination that, that embarrasses me . . .

MARK:

People who were into it really got a chance to know.

CHERYL:

Because I am conservative.

MARK:

You knew that you were killing something.
You actually knew it, you saw it, you had the body.
You didn't take wounded. That was it.
You just killed them.
And they did the same to you.

NADINE *(Laughing)*:

I told him his face is a dangerous weapon.

He ought to be real responsible with it.

CHERYL:

All his jars . . .

NADINE:

I think we'd only known each other for a week and I
said:

You should really have a license for that face.

MARK:

That's my friend, that's R. J.

My friend R. J. used to carry a machete.

I don't know why he never did it.

But he always wanted to cut somebody's head off.

NADINE:

You know why they went crazy out there?

It's that totally negative religion.

It makes you fit to kill.

Those commandments . . .

MARK:

He wanted to put it on a stick and put it in a village.

NADINE:

Every one of them

"Thou shalt not."

MARK:

It was an abuse of the dead.

We got very sacred about taking the dead.

NADINE:

Take an infant and start him out on the whole world
with

Thou shalt not . . .

and you're perpetually in a state of guilt

or a state of revolt.

MARK:

There's a whole Buddhist ceremony.

R. J., everybody—got pissed off.
He wanted to let them know.

CHERYL:

But he's got an imagination . . .

MARK:

I never saw our guys rape women. I heard about it.

CHERYL:

And it's usually sexually orientated somehow.

MARK:

But you never took prisoners, so you'd have to get
involved with them while they were dying
or you'd wait until they were dead.

CHERYL:

Everything Mark does is sexually orientated.

MARK:

The Vietnamese got into that.
There was this one instance I told you about
where R. J. shot the person in the face . . .
it was a woman.

CHERYL:

I don't know why we got together.

MARK:

The Vietnamese carried that body back.
It took them all night long to work that body over.

CHERYL:

When I think back on it, he was weird, off the war.

MARK:

It was their spoils.
They could do what they wanted.

NADINE:

So you send these guys out there
all their lives they've been listening
to nuns and priests
and they start learning to kill.

(Mark snaps on picture of him with medal. Full dress.)

MARK:

This is a picture of my first Purple Heart.

NADINE:

Sure Mark felt great. I understand that.
His senses were finally alive.

CHERYL:

His Purple Hearts never got to me.
I was never impressed with the fighting man,
I don't think.

MARK:

A lot of people bullshitted that war
for a lot of Purple Hearts.
I heard about a guy who was in the rear
who went to a whorehouse.
He got cut up or something like that.
And he didn't want to pay the woman
or something like that.
He ended up with a Purple Heart.

CHERYL:

Well, drugs helped, a lot.
We didn't have much in common.

MARK:

I don't know. We were out in the bush.
To me, a Purple Heart meant it was something
    you got
when you were wounded and you bled.
You were hurt during a contact.
I didn't feel anything getting it.
But I wanted a picture of it.

CHERYL:

I mean, I've got to get that basement cleaned
    out.

MARK:

Actually, I was pissed off about getting that medal.

CHERYL:

My little boy's getting curious.

MARK:

> There were South Vietnamese who were sent out
> with us, fought with us.

CHERYL:

> He goes down and sees some of that crap down there
> Mark's saved . . .

MARK:

> They didn't really give a shit.

CHERYL:

> Never throws anything away.

MARK:

> If things got too hot you could always
> count on them running.
> Jackasses.

CHERYL:

> Mark's a packrat

MARK *(Holds up a belt)*:

> I'm a packrat. I never throw anything away.
> This belt is an artifact.
> I took it off of somebody I killed.
> It's an NVA belt.
> I sent it home. I think it was kind of a trophy.
>
> This is the man's blood.
> That's a bullet hole.
> This particular fellow had a belt of grenades
> that were strapped to his belt.
> See where the rust marks are?

CHERYL:

> Everything he's done,
> everything is sexually orientated in some way.
> Whether it's nakedness or violence—it's all
> sexually orientated.
> And I don't know where this comes from.

(Mark searches for more slides.)

He can take those slides
and you know where he can put 'em.
Right up his butt.
I mean he's just,
he'll go down there
and dig up old slides.
I won't do that for him anymore.
I will not,
no way.

MARK:

Here's a picture of me . . .

(He snaps on picture of him and some children.)

CHERYL:

He asked if he can take pictures of Danny and I . . .

MARK:

And some kids. God I *loved* those kids.

CHERYL:

I think that's why I'm so against the artist world.
I just can't handle his work a lot of it.
It's because he's done that to me.

MARK:

Everybody hated them.
You couldn't trust 'em.

The VC would send the kids in with a flag.
I never saw this, I heard about it,
the kid would come in asking for C-rations,
try to be your friend, and they'd be maybe wired
with explosives or something
and the kid'd blow up.
There was a whole lot of weirdness . . .

CHERYL:

Mark's got this series of blood photographs.
He made me pose for them.

There's a kitchen knife sticking into me,
but all you can see is reddish-purplish blood.
It's about five feet high.
He had it hanging in the shop! In the street!
Boy, did I make him take it out of there.

MARK:

I really dug kids. I don't know why.

(More pictures of kids.)

I did a really bad number . . .
It went contrary, I think,
to everything I knew.
I'm not ready to talk about that yet.

CHERYL:

You just don't show people those things.

MARK:

These are some pictures of more or less dead bodies
    and things.

*(He snaps on pictures of mass graves, people half
blown apart, gruesome pictures of this particular war.)*

I don't know if you want to see them.

*(Five slides. Last picture comes on of a man, eyes to-
wards us, the bones of his arm exposed, the flesh torn,
eaten away. It is too horrible to look at. Mark looks at
the audience, or hears them.)*

Oh, Jesus.
Yeah . . .
We have to be patient with each other.

(He snaps the pictures off.)

CHERYL:

You know. I don't think . . .

MARK:

You know, I get panicky
if there's any element of control taken away from me.
(I don't like to be alone in the dark.
I'm scared of it. I'm not armed.)

I don't like fireworks.
If I can control them, fine.
I don't like them when I can't control them.

I've had bad dreams
when my wife's had to bring me back out.
Nothing like jumping her, though.
I've heard about vets killing their wives in their sleep.
But this is personal—for me,
the gun was always the instrument, or a grenade.
I never grabbed somebody and slowly killed them.
I've never choked them to death or anything.
I've never beaten anybody up, well . . .

I never killed
with my bare hands.

(Pause.)

I I

CHERYL:

You know, I don't think that
men ever really protected women
other than war time.

NADINE:

Listen, nobody can do it for you.
Now maybe if I weren't cunning and conniving and manipulative and courageous,
maybe I wouldn't be able to say that.

MARK:

It's still an instinctive reaction to hit the ground.

NADINE:

I'll do anything as the times change to protect my stake in life.

CHERYL:

And war's the only time man really goes out and protects woman.

MARK:

You know—when I got back, I said I'd never work again.
That's what I said constantly, that'd I'd never work again, for anyone.

NADINE:

I have skills now.
I remember when I didn't have them.
I was still pretty mad, but I wasn't ready.

MARK:

I was *mad.*
I figured I was *owed* a living.

NADINE:

I'm stepping out now, right?

CHERYL:

I know my mother protected my father all through his life.
Held things for him, only because she knew it would hurt him.

MARK:

And then I got in a position where I couldn't work because after I got busted and went to prison, no one would hire me.

I did the whole drug thing from a real
thought-out point of view.
I was really highly decorated, awards,
I was wounded twice.
I really looked good.

CHERYL:

That's where I get this blurting out when I'm drunk.
Because I'm like my mother—
That's the only time my mother would really let my
father know what's going on in this house.
(When he's not around seven days a week is when
    she's had a couple.)
Otherwise she was protecting him all the time.
Excuse me. I'm going to get another drink.

(She exits.)

MARK:

I knew I could get away with a lot.
I knew I could probably walk down the streets
and kill somebody and I'd probably get off.
Simply because of the war.
I was convinced of it.

NADINE:

I could have ended my relationship
with my husband years ago.
I sometimes wonder why I didn't.
And I don't want to think it was because of the
    support.

MARK:

I thought about killing people when I got back.

NADINE:

I've been pulling my own weight
for about eight years now.
Prior to that, I was doing a tremendous amount of work
that in our society is not measurable.

(Cheryl enters, angry.)

CHERYL:

My house is not my home.
It's not mine.

NADINE:

I kept a house.
I raised my children.

CHERYL:

Now, if it were mine I'd be busy at work.

NADINE:

I was a model mother.

CHERYL:

I'd be painting the walls,
I would be wallpapering the bedroom.
I would be making improvements.
I would be . . . linoleum the floor.
I can't do it.
Because it's not mine.

MARK:

I thought of killing people when I got back.
I went to a party with a lady, Cheryl, you know,
later we got married—
She was into seeing people who were into LSD.
And I had tried a little acid this night,
but I wasn't too fucked-up.
And we went to this party.

NADINE:

I tried to explain to Mark
that Cheryl may not always want from him what she
    wants right now:
looking for him to provide, looking for status.

CHERYL:

And Mark will never be ready to have the
    responsibility
of his own home. Never. Never.

MARK:

> And there was this big guy.
> I was with a friend of mine who tried to rip him off,
> or something like that.
> He said, the big guy said:
> Get the fuck out of here
> or I'll take this fucking baseball bat
> and split your head wide open.

CHERYL:

> And I'm being stupid to ever want it from Mark.

MARK:

> I started to size up what my options were . . .

NADINE *(Shaking her head)*:

> Looking for him to provide, looking for status.

MARK:

> In a split second, I knew I could have him.
> He had a baseball bat,
> but there was one of these long glass Coke bottles.
> I knew . . . Okay, I grabbed that.
> I moved toward him, to stick it in his face.
> I mean, I killed him.
> I mean in my mind.
> I cut his throat and everything.

CHERYL:

> Because your own home means upkeep.
> Means, if there's a drip in the ceiling
> you gotta come home and take care of it.

NADINE:

> But between us, I can't understand why a woman her
>   age,
> an intelligent woman,
> who's lived through the sixties and the seventies,
> who's living now in a society where women have
>   finally been given permission
> to drive and progress and do what they're entitled to do
> . . . I mean, how can she think that way?

MARK:

My wife saw this and grabbed me.
I couldn't talk to anybody the rest of the night.
I sat and retained the tension and said:
"I want to kill him."
They had to drive me home.
It was only the third time I'd been out with my wife.

CHERYL:

That fucking dog in the backyard
—excuse my French—
That dog is so bad. I mean,
there are cow pies like this out there.

(Demonstrates size.)

And when I was three months pregnant and alone
     here—
when Mark and I—
when I finally got Mark to get out of here—
I came back to live
because I just could not go on living at my
     girlfriend's,
eating their food and not having any money and
—and I came back here
and I had to clean up that yard.

MARK:

It wasn't till the next day that I really got shook by it.
My wife said,
"Hey, cool your jets."
She'd say, "Hey, don't do things like that.
You're not over there anymore.
Settle down, it's all right."

CHERYL:

I threw up in that backyard picking up dog piles.
That dog hasn't been bathed since I took her over to
this doggie place and paid twenty dollars

to have her bathed.
And that was six months ago. That dog has flies.

You open the back door
and you always get one fly from the fricking dog.
She's like garbage. She . . . she . . .

MARK:

I think my wife's scared of me.
I really do.
She'd had this really straight upbringing.
Catholic.
Never had much . . . you know.
Her father was an alcoholic and her mother was too.
I came along and offered her
a certain amount of excitement.

CHERYL:

My backyard last year was so gorgeous.
I had flowers.
I had tomatoes.
I had a whole area garden.
That creeping vine stuff all over.
I had everything.
This year I could not do it with that dog back there.

MARK:

Just after I got back, I took her up to these races.
I had all this camera equipment.
I started running out on the field.
I started photographing these cars zipping by at
ninety miles an hour.

NADINE:

What's important to me is my work.
It's important to Mark too.

MARK:

She'd just gotten out of high school.
She was just, you know, *at that point*.
She was amazed at how I moved through space.

NADINE:

We talk for hours about our work.

MARK:

'Cuz I didn't take anybody with me.

NADINE:

We understand each other's work.

MARK:

I moved down everybody's throats verbally.
First of all it was a physical thing.
I was loud.
Then I'd do these trips to out-think people.

NADINE:

His jars are amazingly original. Artifacts of the war.
Very honest.

MARK:

I'd do these trips.

NADINE:

You should see the portrait Mark did of himself.

MARK:

I had a lot of power, drugs,
I was manipulating large sums of money.

NADINE:

He has a halo around his head.

(Laughs.)

MARK:

She became a real fan.

NADINE:

And the face of a devil.

CHERYL:

That dog grosses me out so bad.
That dog slimes all over the place.
My kid, I don't even let him out in the backyard.
He plays in the front.

That's why his bike's out front.
I'll take the chance of traffic before I'll let him out
to be slimed over by that dog.

NADINE:

She decided to have that child.

MARK:

Later on, it got into this whole thing.
We lived together and with this other couple.

NADINE:

It's madness.
Everyone was against it.

MARK:

It was a whole . . . I don't know whether I
directed it . . . but it became this *big* . . .
sexual thing . . . between us . . . between them . . .
between groups of other people . . .
It was really a fast kind of thing.
Because no one really gave a shit.

CHERYL:

Oh, shut up!

NADINE:

His theory is she's punishing him.

MARK:

I don't know why I was really into being a stud.

NADINE:

Now no man has ever been able to lead *me* into
    sexual abuse.

MARK:

I wasn't that way before I left, so I don't know.
Maybe it was like I was trying to be like all the other
    people.

NADINE:

See, she participated. She had the right to say no.

CHERYL:

That dog jumps the fence, takes off.

I have to pay twenty dollars
to get her out of the dog pound.
She is costin' me so damn much money that I hate her.
She eats better than we do.
She eats better than we do.

NADINE:

She must have thought it would be fun.
And wow! That was that whole decade
where a whole population of people that age thought
    that way.

CHERYL:

My Danny is getting to the age where there's gotta be
    food.
I mean he's three years old.
He goes to the freezer he wants ice cream there.
He goes in the icebox there's gotta be pop.
I mean it's not like he's an infant anymore.

NADINE:

Every foul thing I've ever done,
I'm not uncomfortable about it.
And I don't blame anyone in my life.

CHERYL:

These things have to be there.
And it's not there.

NADINE:

I don't blame anyone.
I'm sorry, maybe you have to be older
to look back and say that.

CHERYL:

But there's always a bag of dog food in the place.
Anyways I run out of dog food,
Mark sends me right up to the store.
But I run out of milk I can always give him Kool-Aid
for two or three days.
Yeah—that's the way it is though.
We haven't been to the grocery store in six months

for anything over ten dollars worth of groceries at a
    time.
There is no money.

III

MARK:

You'd really become an animal out there.
R. J. and I knew what we were doing.

That's why a lot of other kids really got into trouble.
They didn't know what they were doing.

We knew it, we dug it, we knew
we were very good.

IV

CHERYL:

I'd turn off to him.
Because I knew that it was hard for me to accept—
you know what he . . . what happened and all that.
And it was hard for me to live with, and him being
drunk and *spreading* it around to others.

(To Mark)

How long has it been since anything like that
    happened?

MARK:

Well, last July I hurt you.

CHERYL:

Yeah, but Danny was what a year and half so
    everything was pretty . . .

MARK:

He was exposed to it.
My wife, uh, Cheryl, left one night.

CHERYL:

Don't.

MARK:

She left with, uh, she had a person come over and
    pick her up and take her away.
I walked in on this.
I was drunk. Danny was in her arms.
I attacked this other man and . . .
I did something to him.
I don't know.
What did I do to him?
Something.

CHERYL:

You smashed his car up with a sledge hammer.

MARK:

I, uh, Dan saw all that.

CHERYL:

He was only six months old though.

MARK:

No. Dan I think he knows a lot more than we
    think.
He saw me drunk and incapable of walking up the
    steps.
Going to the bathroom
half on the floor and half in the bowl.
He's a sharp kid.
Cheryl and I separated this spring.
And he really knew what was going on.

NADINE:

Christ, I hate this country.
I hate all of it.
I've never really said it before.

MARK:

> I come in and apologize when I think about the
>   incidents
> that I've done in the past now that I'm sober,
> and I feel terribly guilty.
> I've exploited Cheryl as a person, sexually . . .
> it wasn't exactly rape, but . . .

CHERYL:

> I can't deal with *that* at all.
> But I find that if I can at least put it out of my mind
>   it's easier.
>
> If I had to think about what he's done to me, I'd
> have been gone a long time ago.

NADINE:

> I have yet to be out of this country, by the way.
> And I'm criticizing it as if I think it's better
>   everywhere else.

MARK:

> See, I wanted to get back into the society and
> I wanted to live so much life, but I couldn't.
> I was constantly experimenting.

CHERYL:

> It was awful . . .
> He'd pick fights with people on the streets.
> Just about anyone. It was like a rage.
> He'd just whomp on the guy.
> Not physically but he would become very obstinate,
> very mean and cruel. In bars, handling people . . .
>
> *(To Mark)*
>
> You have to be *nice* to people to have them accept
>   you.

MARK:

> I don't know.
> I was afraid.
> I thought people were . . . uh . . . I mean
> I was kind of paranoid.
> I thought everybody knew . . .
> I thought everybody knew what I did over there,
> and that they were against me.
> I was scared. I felt guilty and a sense of . . .

CHERYL:

> I can't talk to you.

NADINE:

> He's trying to judge himself.
> One time we were together after a
> long period of incredible, sharing times.
> I said: "You're so wonderful."
> And he started to cry.

MARK *(To Nadine)*:

> I've done terrible things.

NADINE *(To Mark)*:

> I know.

> *(Long pause.)*

> Christ, I hate this country.

> I can remember everything.
> Back to being two years old,
> and all these terrible things they taught us.
> I can't believe we obeyed them *all*.

MARK *(Very quiet)*:

> I had two cousins who went through Vietnam.
> One was a truck driver and got through it.
> My other cousin was in the Army.
> His unit, about one hundred men were climbing up a
>   hill.

They were all killed except for him and another guy.
And they were lying there.
The VC were going around putting bullets
into people's heads.
Making sure they were dead.
And he had to lay there wounded faking he was dead.
He and I never talked.
Ever.
Someone else communicated his story to me,
and I know he knows my story.

(Pause.)

V

CHERYL:

I feel so sorry for Margie, my brother's wife.
I told you about.
You wonder why there's so much more lesbianism
    around now?
Look at the men!
You can see where that's turned a lot of women the
    other way.

NADINE:

He possibly is overpowering.
I don't know. She was proud to be his woman.
So he said frog, and they all jumped.
Well, that's terrific.
It cost him a lot
to have that power where he abused it.

CHERYL:

Christ!
Mark pushed me into that, once, too.
We were doing this smack deal,
he brought this woman into our room.

He wanted me to play with her.
He wanted me to get it on with her, too.
It just blew my mind.
I mean it just blew me away.

NADINE:

I know, I know, I know . . .
But I see when he talks about his wife,
I feel encouraged that there are men that can be that
    way.
He has never, ever said an unkind word about her.
God, I mean it's incredibly civilized
the way he talks about her.
In fact, had he ever said anything foul about her,
it would have grated on me.
Maybe he just knows what I require.
But I have yet to hear him say
anything bad about anyone;
even those terrible people he had to deal with
in the jungle.

MARK:

I saw my cousin at his dad's funeral last
    December.

CHERYL:

Now it's so complex
every time I look . . .
Oh, God . . . every time I look
at a piece of furniture,
it reminds me of something.

MARK:

Wherever we moved,
we knew where the other was.
Something radiates between us.

NADINE:

I think he's quite superior.
I really do.
I think he's got it all figured out.

MARK:

Our eyes will meet, but we can't touch.

NADINE:

I think he's gonna make it.

(Nervous)

I wonder how you perceive him.

MARK:

There's no difference between this war and World
    War II.
I'm convinced of that.

Maybe it was different in that it was the race thing.

(Admitting)

We referred to them as zips, or dinks, or gooks.
But I don't think I would have had any trouble
    shooting anything.

We weren't freaks out there.
Guys in World War II cracked up, too.

We're their children.
I would like to play you a song.

*(Mark turns on tape. In the original production he
played "No More Genocide," by Holly Near.)*

ACT THREE

Mark snaps on slide of him and R. J.

MARK:

This is a picture of me and R. J.
We look like a couple of bad-asses.
It was hot. Shit, I miss him.
We were so close.
We talked about everything.
We talked about how each of us lost our
virginity, we talked about girls.

CHERYL *(Agitated)*:

My girlfriend across the street told me
how babies were made when I was ten years old.
I just got sick. I hated it.

MARK:

> We talked about fights, getting back on the streets,
> drugs.

CHERYL:

> From that moment on,
> I had a model:
> I wanted kids . . .

MARK:

> We talked about getting laid . . .

CHERYL:

> But I didn't want the husband that went along with it.
> I still feel that way.

MARK:

> We talked about how we would be inseparable
> when we came home.
> We never would have, even if he hadn't died.
> We knew too much about each other.

CHERYL:

> And this spooks me because I said this
> when I was ten years old.
>
> *(New slide.)*

MARK:

> This is the place, the Alamo.
> That's where the rocket came in and
> killed a man . . . uh . . .
>
> *(Indicates in the picture.)*
>
> We got hit one night.
> Some several people were sleeping, this fellow . . .
>
> *(Picture of him.)*
>
> A rocket came in and blew his head off.

NADINE:

I said to Mark:
"You're still pissed off because they let you go.
Even assholes stopped their kids from going.
Your good Catholic parents sent you to slaughter."

MARK:

It was near dawn.
We moved his body out of there.
We put his body on a rice-paddy dike.
I watched him. He was dead and he was
very close to me and I don't know.

NADINE:

His parents pushed him into going.
They believed all those terrible clichés.

MARK:

I didn't want him to lay in that place where he died.
I didn't want him laying in the mud.
And I think I was talking to him.
I was crying, I don't know.

NADINE:

Do you know, to this day his father
will not say the word Vietnam.

MARK:

His dog came out and started . . .
The dog was eating him.
I just came out and fired at the dog.
I got him killed.

(Snaps picture.)

Later, I took that picture.

NADINE:

But his father talked to everyone but Mark about the
    war.
He's got his medals on his wall.

MARK:

> I don't know.
> It became a sacred place. It was "the Alamo."
> That's what we named it.
> I shot the dog because it was desecrating.
> The dog was eating our friend . . .
> I would have done anything, if I could have,
> if I could have kept flies off of him, even.

NADINE:

> His father's ashamed of himself.
> When you let your son go to war
> for all the wrong reasons,
> you can't face your son.

MARK *(Crying)*:

> I just wanted him . . .
> He coulda gone home the next day.
> The war was over for him.
> I wanted him to get home.

> *(Pause.)*

I I

CHERYL:

> I want to go home.
> To the church, to my family.
> The sixties are over.

NADINE:

> The sixties . . .
> You know, a lot of us went through that whole
> decade pretending to ourselves we were pacifists.

MARK:

> I wanted to get home so bad.

CHERYL:

> Well, I mean I'm gonna have another kid.
> I'm gonna have to take him to the Cathedral to be

baptized 'cuz our wedding wasn't blessed.
It wasn't in a church.
We had to get married and we had to do it fast.
In South Dakota.
In the clothes we'd been in for three days.

NADINE:

As if we didn't know what violence was.

MARK:

You know, the biggest thing I had to adjust to
coming home was I didn't have my gun.

CHERYL:

My dad had just died so I didn't really care.
My dad and I were really close.
He was the only one who mattered . . .

MARK:

I mean, that gun was mine.

CHERYL:

I don't know why I'm remembering all this
all of a sudden . . .

MARK:

I knew every part of it.

NADINE:

God, we hated those vets.

MARK:

The barrel burned out of it.
You know, I had a new barrel put in,
but I mean that gun was mine.
I took that gun everywhere I went.
I just couldn't live without that gun.

NADINE:

All that nonsense about long hair, flowers and love.

CHERYL:

I mean, my family just dug my father's hole
and put him right in there.

NADINE:

And the women were exempt!

They were all supposed to be Mother Earths making
 pots.

CHERYL:

My brother's wife went nuts and shot her two-year-
 old son and killed him.
I told you.
I mean—all the things we did to him.
He had to come and get me out of jail
at three in the morning and he's not—
he wasn't a strong man.
So my father just jumped into that bottle
and nobody could get him out of it.

NADINE:

I think I knew then what I know now.

MARK:

When I got on the plane coming home
I was so happy. I didn't miss my gun then.
It was my birthday.

NADINE:

I don't know.

MARK:

I turned twenty-one.
I did my birthday coming home.

NADINE:

Oh, Jesus.

MARK:

I did my birthday across the dateline.
I was incredibly happy.
We hit Okinawa.
R. J. was there.
We saw all these guys who were just going over.

NADINE:

I only hope I would have done exactly what Mark
 did.

MARK:

All these guys were asking us how it was.

We were really getting off on the fact
that we were done.
These guys were so green and fat.
We were brown, we were skinny.
We were animals.

NADINE:

I think he survived
because he became an animal.
I hope I would have wanted to live that bad.

CHERYL:

I used to stay up all night with my dad.
I was doing a lot of speed then
and I used to stay up all night with him and talk.
I'd be sewing or something like that at the kitchen
    table
and he'd be sittin' there drinking and bitching.

MARK:

I don't know why I couldn't talk to my parents when I
    got back.

NADINE:

We just can't face that in ourselves.

MARK:

I told my dad everything when I was over there.

CHERYL:

My dad was an intelligent, common-sense-type man.
He had no college education, but judging
    characters . . .

NADINE:

Oh, God.

CHERYL:

Oh, God.

MARK:

The only way I could cry was to write to my dad.
"God, Dad. I'm really scared. I'm really terrified."

CHERYL:

Oh, God. He could pick out people.

MARK:

> When I sent somebody out and they got killed,
> I could tell my dad.

CHERYL:

> My dad told me: "Stay away from Mark."

MARK:

> I got into L.A. . . . , called:
> "Hey, I'm back. I'm back."
> My dad said: "Oh, great. We're so relieved.
> I'm so happy." My mother cried, she was happy.
> I said: "I'm going to buy a hamburger."

CHERYL:

> He told me: "Mark can't communicate, his style of
>   dress is weird, the war . . ."

MARK:

> I just got on this stool going round and round.
> "Hey, I'm back."
> No one wanted anything to do with me.
> Fuckin' yellow ribbons.
> I thought I was tired.

NADINE:

> The problem now is knowing what to do with what
>   we know.

CHERYL:

> My dad said:
> "I want you to forget him.
> Just forget him.
> Get out of this now, while you can."

MARK:

> I waited around until 3 A.M.,
> caught a flight, got out here.
> 6:30 in the morning.
> Beautiful, beautiful day.
> Got my stuff, threw it over my shoulder,
> and started walking.

CHERYL:

> I saw Mark occasionally, anyway.
> Shortly after that, my dad had a stroke.
> You know, my dad and I are identical.

MARK:

> I walked in the door and set everything down.
> I was home.
> My dad looked at me, my mom looked at me.
> I sat down. Said:
> "Could I have some coffee?"
> That's when my mother started raggin' on me
> about drinking coffee.
> The whole thing broke down.

NADINE:

> Oh, God . . .

CHERYL:

> My sister had a baby when she was seventeen.
> They put her in a home, you know, the whole route.
> Shortly after that, I was five years younger than her,
> I was just starting to date.

MARK:

> "Well," my mom said, "you better get some sleep.
> I've got a lot to do."
> I said: like I don't want to sleep.
>
> I got incredibly drunk.

CHERYL:

> I remember—I'd come home from a date.
> The only time I saw my father was late at night.
> He would take a look at me and say:
> "Well, I hope you learned from your sister
> that the only way to stay out of trouble
> is to keep your legs crossed."

MARK:

> My mom and dad had to go out that night.

I thought, well, I'd sit down
and talk with them at dinner.
They were gone.

CHERYL:

End of conversation.

MARK:

We didn't see each other that day.
We never really did see each other.

CHERYL:

I mean, he got his point across . . .
more or less.

MARK:

I had no idea what was going on.
This was 1970.
My hair was short.
I got really crazed out on junk and stuff.
Then when I was totally avoiding going home
somewhere in that I wanted to . . .
I really wanted bad to . . .
communicate with a woman.

NADINE:

You know, all Mark did was—
He brought the war back home
and none of us could look at it.

MARK:

I wanted to fuck my brains out.

CHERYL:

God, I was naive.
I was naive as they come.
And to sit here and say that now knowing what I know
and what I've been through
just gives me the creeps.

MARK:

No one wanted anything to do with me.

NADINE:

We couldn't look at ourselves. We still can't.

CHERYL:

> Because I am so far from being naive.
> I mean, just the idea if I ever divorced Mark . . .
> I don't think I could ever find anyone who
> could handle my past.
> I mean, I have a hard time relating to it myself.

III

NADINE:

> Oh, God.
> I'm worried about us.
> I keep this quiet little knowledge with me every day.
> I don't tell my husband about it
> I don't tell my kids,
> or Mark.
> Or anyone.
> But something has fallen apart.
> I'm having trouble being a mother.
> How can you believe in sending your children to
>   special classes
> when you know it doesn't matter?
> Oh,
> I worry, I worry,
> I worry one of my daughters
> will be walking down the street
> and get raped or mugged by someone who is angry or
>   hungry.
> I worry I have these three beautiful daughters (pieces
>   of life)
> who I have devoted my whole life to,
> who I've put all my energy into—bringing up—raising—
> and then somebody up there goes crazy one day
> and pushes the "go" button and
> phew! bang, finished, the end.

I worry that my daughters won't want to give birth
because of my bad birthing experience.
And I worry that they *will* want to give birth.

I worry that—
Well, one of my daughters does blame me
for the divorce
because I have protected them from knowing
what kind of man their father really is.

(I worry that I worry too much about all this
and I worry that I really don't worry enough about it
    all.)
I worry so much it makes me sick.

I work eighteen hours a day just to pay the bills.
This year, I work on the feminist caucus,
I do my portraits, run my magazine, organize civic
    events.
I hold two jobs and more.
I invited my dear, sweet, ninety-one-year-old uncle
to come die at my house.

I go to recitals, shopping, graduation,
I don't go through the ritual
of getting undressed at night.
I sleep with my shoes on.
My husband's alcoholism has ruined us.
(Forty-five thousand dollars in debt.)

I don't dare get angry anymore.
Can you imagine what would happen,
if I got angry?
My children . . .

(Can't go on.)

MARK:

My wife means so much to me.
I don't want to jeopardize what she's giving to me.
I don't want to jeopardize her.

It's like the Marine Corps.
Cheryl is like a comrade. She's walking wounded
    now.
You don't leave a comrade on the field.

NADINE:

It's all out of control.

MARK:

Sometimes I think Nadine loses sight of things.
Sometimes, I think she's way ahead of me.

NADINE:

I don't know what I'm doing.

MARK:

I can't talk to you about Nadine.

NADINE:

Oh, men. I have to take care of them.
And they're all cripples.
It's so depressing.

MARK:

It's like I know that I'm carrying a time bomb
and there are times that I just don't know
if I'll go off.
I don't know that in the end
I won't destroy myself.

NADINE:

And yet, there's that little voice inside me
that reminds me that even though it's hopeless
I have little children that can't survive without me.

MARK:

Maybe because I just can't comprehend war.
War that's political enough in terms of
what you have and what you get out of it.

NADINE:

>I guess I could possibly be the most
>vulnerable person of all of us.
>But I've also built up all these other devices
>which will overrule that.

MARK:

>I need to tell you what I did.
>My wife knows it.
>She's come through times
>when I got to the very edge of suicide.
>She's helped me through a couple of times
>that without her help . . .
>I'd be dead.
>Now, I've been very honest with Nadine
>except when she asked me about suicide.
>I couldn't tell her that.

NADINE:

>I couldn't even think about suicide.

IV   THE SPAGHETTI STORY

CHERYL:

>I hate to cook.
>Probably because he likes to cook.
>I hate to cook.
>I don't know how to cook,
>and I hate it.
>
>Mark does this spaghetti dinner once a year.
>Has he ever told you about that?
>Holy Christ!

MARK:

>Excuse me.
>
>*(Leaves.)*

CHERYL:

Every day before Thanksgiving
Mark does a spaghetti dinner, and this
is a traditional thing.
This is the one traditional bone Mark has in his body,
and I'd like to break it.

He has twenty to forty-five people come to this thing.
He makes ravioli, lasagna, spaghetti, meatballs,
three different kinds of spaghetti sauce:
shrimp, plain, meat sauce.
Oh, he makes gnocchi! He makes his own noodles!
And it's good.
He's a damn good cook for Italian food.
But you can imagine what I go through
for three weeks for that party
to feed forty people.
Sit-down dinner.
He insists it's a sit-down dinner.
So here I am running around
with no time to cook with him.
I'm trying to get enough shit in my house
to feed forty people sit-down dinner.
We heated the porch last year
because we did not have enough room to seat forty
    people.
And I run around serving all these slobs,
and this is the first year he's really charged anyone.
And we lose on it every year.
I mean, we lose, first year we lost three hundred dollars.
This dinner is a five-hundred-dollar deal.
I'm having a baby this November,
and if he thinks he's having
any kind of spaghetti dinner,
he can get his butt out of here.
I can't take it.

Pizzas! He makes homemade pizzas.
You should see my oven.
Oh my God! There's pizza shit everywhere.
Baked on.
And when it's over with,
he just gets up and walks out.
He's just done.
The cleanup is no big deal to him.
He won't even help.
He rolls up the carpets for this dinner.
People get smashed!
He's got wine everywhere, red wine.
It has to be red so if it gets on my rugs,
my rugs are ruined and my couch is ruined.
I've just said it so many times I hate it.
He knows I hate it.

My brother brought over some speed
to get me through that night.
My brother, Jack, who is a capitalist—
intelligent—makes me sick.
Never got into drugs. Was too old.
Missed that whole scene.
But he now has speed occasionally
on his bad day, you know, drink, two drinks one
    night,
speed to get him through the day.
Businessman.

He brought me some speed to get me through the
    night
'cause he knew what a basket case I'd be.

And then Mark goes and invites my family.
And they're the last people I want to see at this.
Sure, they love it.

I mean, they all sit around and they
stuff themselves to death.
I'm not kidding!
It is one big stuffing feast.

The first time, the first spaghetti dinner we had was
right after Danny was born.
Danny's baby book got torn up.
I had to start a whole new one.
Mark's crazy friends.
Drunk.
Broken dishes everywhere.
I'm not kidding.
It's just a disaster.

Spaghetti on the walls.
Spaghetti pots dropped in the kitchen.
Spaghetti all over the sink.

That's why I ask him.
I go: "Why?"
"It's traditional. I have to do this every year."
It was three years ago he started.
Tradition, my ass.

I'm telling you.
I mean, he wonders why I can't sleep with him
        sometimes.
Because I just work up such a hate for him inside
        that . . .

(Mark enters.)

I'm a perfectionist.
My house has to be this way,
and before I go to sleep,

I'll pick up after him.
I'm constantly picking up after him.
Christ Almighty!
In the morning, if he comes in late,
he's read the newspaper
and there's newspaper all over the room.
He *throws* it when he's done with it.
I've broken toes on his shoes.
I broke *this* toe on his shoe.
He always leaves his shoes right out in walking space.
Every morning I trip on
either his tennis or his good shoes.
Whichever pair he doesn't have on.
He's so inconsiderate of other people.
He's so selfish, he's so self-centered.
And this is what I tell him.
I'm just tired of it.
He's so selfish.
Because this spaghetti dinner just ruins me.
Baby or no baby,
it just completely ruins me.
And he's showing off his,
his wonderful cooking that he does once a year.
And I suppose this is why I hate cooking.

V

Mark shows us slide of wounded children.

MARK:

This is a picture of some kids who were hurt.
I used to take care of them,
change their bandages and shit.
I loved these kids.

Oh, God . . .

VI

CHERYL:

What am I gonna do? I mean,
someday Danny's gonna have to see Mark
for what he is.
And that just scares the piss right out of me.

NADINE:

How do you tell your children their father is an asshole?

CHERYL:

I don't wanna be here when Mark tells Danny
about the war.
I don't trust him.

NADINE:

How could I tell my children that their father is
in town and hasn't called?

CHERYL:

I don't trust what he's gonna tell the kid.
And the way I wanna bring the kid up,
you can't tell him anything.

NADINE:

You can't tell your kids
they can't have something they want
because their father has squandered their money.

CHERYL:

You're just better off not saying anything.

NADINE:

What'm I going to do,
tell them he's off somewhere getting drunk
and has forgotten all about them?

CHERYL:

I'm just, you know,
when that sort of thing comes along,
I live from day to day.

NADINE:

The counselors tell me and my lawyers tell me

that I should stop protecting them from him.
But it's hard enough, don't you think?
They hurt enough already.

CHERYL:

Later on, you know—
there might not be a war going on.
I might not have to deal with that.
And maybe someday *I* can explain to him.

NADINE:

One time I told them he was in town
because I couldn't find a way
to cover up the fact that I knew.
They were depressed for weeks.
I have to protect them.

CHERYL *(Angry)*:

See, why do I have to do all this????
And I do.
I find myself doing everything.
Covering for him . . .

NADINE:

I don't protect Mark.
He doesn't need it.
He judges himself all the time,
he's devoted to his son.

CHERYL:

Sure Mark plays with him.
But when it comes to discipline,
that kid's a little brat,
I mean he is.
And Mark's never around when it comes to discipline.

NADINE:

He works hard at his shop. He is supporting his family.

CHERYL:

He's never around.

NADINE:

He is working his way back into society.

He's beginning to believe in himself
and do his work.

CHERYL:

I'm past the sixties.
I want to go back to the Church.
And Mark just will not understand the importance of
    this for me.
I mean, when there's no father around,
the Church shows some order, you know.

NADINE:

He told me he's discovering
who he always thought he was.
I think of him as an artist
and a lifelong friend.

VII

Mark is holding the picture he has framed of the children.

MARK:

I'm terrified . . .
I have a son . . .
There's another child on the way . . .
I'm terrified for what I did now . . .

CHERYL:

The war is the base of all our problems.

MARK:

It's guilt . . .
it's a dumb thing . . .
it makes no sense logically . . .
but I'm afraid there's this karma I built up
of hurting . . .
there are children involved . . .
like it's all going to balance out
at the expense of my kids.

CHERYL:

> I get so scared when he says that.
> I mean, I never did anything.

MARK:

> There's no logic to it but it's there.
> I try . . .
> I'm really intense with my boy.
>
> I think what we're beginning to see here is
> that it was a different world I was in.
> I'd like to be real academic about this . . .
> closed case . . .
> but this is an ongoing struggle.

NADINE:

> Mark!

MARK:

> I don't know.
> I just don't know.
> Sometimes I look at a news story.
> I look at something someone goes to prison for here,
> I think about it.
> There's no difference.
> It's just a different place.
> This country had all these rules and regulations
> and then all of a sudden they removed these things.
>
> Then you came back and try to make your life
> in that society where you had to deal with them.
> You find that if you violate them,
> which I found,
> you go to jail,
> which I did.
> I sit back here sometimes and watch the news,
> watch my mother,
> watch my father.
> My parents watch the news and say:

"Oh my God somebody did that!
Somebody went in there . . . and started shooting . . .
and killed all those people.
They ought to execute him."
I look at them.
I want to say,
"Hell, what the fuck,
why didn't you ever listen . . .
You want to hear what I did?"
It's real confusion.
I'm guilty and I'm not guilty.
I still want to tell my folks.
I need to tell them what I did.

VIII

CHERYL:

There was a time when a man would confess to me,
"I'm a jerk,"
at a private moment
and I would smile
sweetly
and try to comfort him.

Now I believe him.

IX   THE CONFESSION

MARK:

I . . . I killed three children, a mother and father in
    cold blood.

(Crying.)

CHERYL:

> Don't.

MARK:

> I killed three children, a mother and father . . .

> *(Long pause.)*

NADINE:

> Mark.

MARK:

> I killed them with a pistol in front of a lot of people.

> I demanded something from the parents and then
> systematically destroyed them.
> And that's . . .
> that's the heaviest part of what I'm carrying around.
> You know about it now, a few other people know
>   about it,
> my wife knows about it, Nadine knows about it,
> and nobody else knows about it.
> For the rest of my life . . .

> I have a son . . .
> He's going to die for what I've done.
> This is what I'm carrying around;
> that's what this logic is about with my children.

> A friend hit a booby trap.
> And these people knew about it.
> I knew they knew.
> I knew that they were working with the VC
>   infrastructure.
> I demanded that they tell me.
> They wouldn't say anything.
> I just wanted them to confess before I killed them.
> And they wouldn't.

So I killed their children
and then I killed them.

I was angry.
I was angry with all the power I had.
I couldn't beat them.
They beat me.

(Crying.)

I lost friends in my unit . . .
I did wrong.
People in the unit watched me kill them.
Some of them tried to stop me.
I don't know.
I can't. . . . Oh, God . . .

A certain amount of stink
went all the way back to the rear.
I almost got into a certain amount of trouble.

It was all rationalized,
that there was a logic behind it.
But they knew.
And everybody who knew had a part in it.
There was enough evidence,
but it wasn't a very good image to put out
in terms of . . .
the marines overseas, so nothing happened.

I have a child . . .
a child who passed through the age
that the little child was.
My son . . . my son
wouldn't know the difference between a VC and a
    marine.

The children were so little.

I suppose I could find a rationalization.

All that a person can do is try and find words
to try and excuse me,
but I know it's the same damn thing
as lining Jews up.
It's no different
than what the Nazis did.
It's the same thing.

I know that I'm not alone.
I know that other people did it, too.
More people went through more hell than I did . . .
but they didn't do this.

I don't know . . .
I don't know . . .
if it's a terrible flaw of *mine*,
then I guess deep down I'm just everything that's bad.

I guess there is a rationale that says
anyone who wants to live that bad
and gets in that situation . . .

(Long pause.)

but I should have done better.
I mean, I really strove to be good.
I had a whole set of values.
I had 'em and I didn't.
I don't know.

I want to come to the point
where I tell myself that I've punished myself enough.

In spite of it all,
I don't want to punish myself anymore.
I knew I would want to censor myself for you.

I didn't want you to say:
What kind of a nut, what kind of a bad person is he?
And yet, it's all right.
I'm not gonna lie.

My wife tries to censor me . . .
from people, from certain things.
I can't watch war shows.
I can't drive.
Certain things I can't deal with.
She has to deal with the situation,
us sitting around, a car backfires,
and I hit the deck.

She knows about the graveyards, and R. J. and the
        woman.
She lives with all this still hanging out.
I'm shell-shocked.

X

NADINE:

Well, I'm going to look forward to the rest of my life
because of what I know.
I can't wait to test myself.
See, I guess I've known what it is to feel hopeless
politically.
And I've known what it is to plunge
personally.
But Mark has become a conscience for me.
Through him—I've come to understand the violence

in myself . . . and in him, and in all of us.
And I think if we can stay aware of that,
hold on to that knowledge,
maybe we can protect ourselves
and come out on the other side.

MARK *(Mumbling)*:

I'm just a regular guy.
A lot of guys saw worse.

NADINE:

If anything I'm on a continuum now.

MARK:

See, I didn't want to see people
going through another era of
being so ignorant of the fact that war kills people.

NADINE:

And I don't know if it's cynicism or just experience,
but I'm sure I'm never gonna plunge
in the old way again.
I'm not saying that trying to sound tough.
I know about that. I know all about that.

MARK:

I feel protective of our children.
Once you're out there, you know there is no justice.
I don't want the children to die.

NADINE:

But I have no old expectations anymore.
And when you have none,
you're really free.
And you don't ever plunge.
What do you plunge for?

MARK:

It will happen again.

NADINE:

I'm just going to work so hard because of what I
    know.
I do every day.

Did I tell you about not going to sleep at night
because I can't bear to stop thinking about it all?
I'm just going to be so busy for whatever's left.
(But I'm not mad at anyone.)
I don't blame anyone.
I've forgiven everyone.
God, I feel my house is in order at last.

MARK:

I *dedicate* . . . this evening to my friends . . .
I'd like a roll call for my friends who died.

NADINE:

There's one other thing.
When we all sit around together
with our friends
and we tell women
that no man can do it for you,
we all know it's true,
but I guess for some of us
it never works that way.
At this point in my life,
this curtain has dropped.

MARK:

Anderson, Robert.

NADINE:

And we see . . .

MARK:

Dafoe, Mark.

NADINE:

We need them—to be here, questioning themselves
and judging themselves—and us—like Mark.

MARK:

Dawson, Mark.

NADINE:

I love Mark.

MARK:

Fogel, Barry.

NADINE:

Well, . . . so . . .
The material has been turning over and over.

MARK:

Grant, Tommy.

NADINE:

Where is it at now?

MARK:

Gunther, Bobby.

NADINE:

You see.

MARK:

Heinz, Jerry.

NADINE:

What do you see, just a cast of characters?

MARK:

Jastrow, Alan.
Lawrence, Gordon.
Mullen, Clifford.

*(Roll call continues through Cheryl's speech, ending
with a conscious decision on Mark's part to name R. J.
among the casualties of Vietnam.)*

X I

CHERYL:

The men have it all.

MARK:

Nelson, Raymond.

CHERYL:

They've had it for the longest time.

MARK:

Nedelski, Michael.

CHERYL:

There's another thing I believe.
There's a lot more people
that are messed up because of the way we were
        brought up.

MARK:

Nevin, Daniel.

CHERYL:

Not brought up, but the things we've been through
since we were brought up.

MARK:

O'Brien, Stephen.

CHERYL:

So I think our generation,

MARK:

Rodriguez, Daniel.

CHERYL:

the hippie generation, shortly before and after,
are gonna be the ones that suffer.

MARK:

Rogers, John.

CHERYL:

Because ninety percent of the men never
        straightened out.

MARK:

Ryan, John.

CHERYL:

But what I also believe
is that for every woman that has her beliefs,
there's a man that matches.

MARK:

Sawyer, Steven.

CHERYL:

Whether you find him or not,
is, is like finding a needle in a haystack.

With our population,
I mean, that's the odds you have.

MARK:

Simon, Jimmy.

CHERYL:

And there's the Women's Libs.
And there's a man for them too.

MARK:

Skanolon, John.

CHERYL:

See, what we're doing is crossing.
We're meeting the men
that should be with the other ones.
And I truly believe that,
that there is an equal balance.
Even though our group is so fucked-up.
And we are.

MARK:

Spaulding, Henry.

CHERYL:

You'll look, you'll go in college campuses now
and it's completely back the way it was . . .
and it should stay there.

MARK:

Stanton, Ray.

CHERYL:

I don't wanna see that shit come back.
I didn't even get that involved in it.
I got involved in it in my own little niche.
But I didn't, you know, get into it
in the school matter.
I went two years and I had it up to here.
And sure I would like to have gone on to school,
but I was competing with Mark.
And I'm not,
I do not like competing with someone.

MARK:

Vechhio, Michael.

CHERYL:

I'm a happy-go-lucky person.
I used to be anyway, before I met Mark,
where you couldn't depress me on the worst day.
And I had a good day every day of my life.

MARK:

Walker,

(Pause.)

CHERYL:

And that is the way life was gonna be for me.

MARK:

R. J.

(Pause.)

X I I

*Mark points to his photograph of two grapefruits, an orange,
a broken egg, with a grenade in the center on a dark background. Also some fresh bread, a fly on the fruit. From far
away it looks like an ordinary still life.*

MARK:

My unit got blown up.
It was high contact.
We got hit very, very hard.
The Marine Corps sends you
this extra food, fresh fruit, bread,
a reward
when you've had a heavy loss.

What can I say?
I am still alive—my friends aren't.
It's a still life.
I didn't know what I was doing.

(The women's eyes meet for the first time as lights go down.)

END OF PLAY

EXECUTION
OF JUSTICE

Overleaf: Will Marchetti (the Cop) in the Berkeley Rep/San Jose Rep/Eureka Theatre Company production. Photo by Ken Friedman.

This play is dedicated to Oskar Eustis, dramaturg,
who understood the trials

Many thanks to the Eureka Theatre and artistic director
Tony Taccone, who risked the verdict

ACKNOWLEDGMENTS

The author thanks the John Simon Guggenheim Memorial Foundation for its fellowship to research and write the play.

Thanks to the following people for their help and information: Scott Smith and the Harvey Milk Archives, Harry Britt, Rob Epstein and Richard Schmiechen, Supervisor Carol Ruth Silver, Russ Cone, Gene Marine, Corey Busch, Gwenn Craig, Randy Shilts, Mike Weiss, Daniel Nicoletta, Jim Denman, Mel Wax, Marilyn Waller, Warren Hinckle, Bill Bathurst, Edward Mycue, Joseph Freitas, Jim Nicola and New Playwrights' Theatre, Stuart Ross, Bonnie Ayrault, Bill Block.

Special thanks to Jon Jory, Julie Crutcher and Actors Theatre of Louisville; Stan Wojewodski and Center Stage; Susan Gregg, David Feldshuh and Theatre Cornell; Tom Creamer, M. Burke Walker and The Empty Space; Doug Wager and Arena Stage; Sharon Ott and Berkeley Repertory Theatre; Liviu Ciulei, Mark Bly, Michael Lupu and The Guthrie Theater; Gail Merrifield Papp; Lester and Marjorie Osterman, Mortimer Caplin, Richard C. Norton and Christopher Stark, Broadway producers.

PRODUCTION HISTORY

Execution of Justice was commissioned by San Francisco's Eureka Theatre in 1982, and developed over the next eighteen months in collaboration with dramaturg Oskar Eustis, artistic director Anthony Taccone and the company's actors. A co-winner of Actors Theatre of Louisville's 1984 Great American Play Contest, the play received its premiere there in March of that year, under the direction of Eustis and Taccone.

The play was presented on Broadway at the Virginia Theatre in March 1986. Sets were designed by Ming Cho Lee, costumes by Jennifer Von Mayrhauser, lights by Pat Collins and sound by Tom Morse. The author directed the following cast:

DAN WHITE	John Spencer
MARY ANN WHITE	Mary McDonnell
COP	Stanley Tucci
SISTER BOOM BOOM	Wesley Snipes

Chorus of Uncalled Witnesses

JIM DENMAN, White's Jailer	Christopher McHale
YOUNG MOTHER	Lisabeth Bartlett
MILK'S FRIEND	Adam Redfield

GWENN CRAIG, Vice President of
the Harvey Milk Democratic Club   Isabell Monk
HARRY BRITT, City Supervisor
and Milk's successor   Donal Donnelly
JOSEPH FREITAS, D.A.   Nicholas Hormann
MOURNER   Nicholas Hormann

Trial Characters
THE COURT   Nicholas Kepros
COURT CLERK   Lisabeth Bartlett
DOUGLAS SCHMIDT, defense attorney   Peter Friedman
THOMAS F. NORMAN, prosecuting attorney   Gerry Bamman
JOANNA LU, TV reporter   Freda Foh Shen
PROSPECTIVE JURORS   Josh Clark, Suzy Hunt
JUROR #3/FOREMAN   Gary Reineke
BAILIFF   Jeremy O. Caplin

Witnesses for the People
CORONER STEPHENS   Donal Donnelly
RUDY NOTHENBERG, Deputy Mayor,
Moscone's friend   Earle Hyman
BARBARA TAYLOR, reporter   Marcia Jean Kurtz
OFFICER BYRNE, Department of Records   Isabell Monk
WILLIAM MELIA, civil engineer   Richard Riehle
CYR COPERTINI, secretary to the Mayor   Suzy Hunt
CARL HENRY CARLSON, aide to Harvey Milk   Nicholas Hormann
RICHARD PABICH, assistant to Harvey Milk   Wesley Snipes
FRANK FALZON, Chief Inspector of Homicide   Jon DeVries
EDWARD ERDELATZ, inspector   Stanley Tucci

Witnesses for the Defense
DENISE APCAR, aide to White   Lisabeth Bartlett
FIRE CHIEF SHERRATT   Gary Reineke
FIREMAN FREDIANI   Jeremy O. Caplin
POLICE OFFICER SULLIVAN   Stanley Tucci
CITY SUPERVISOR LEE DOLSON   Richard Riehle

PSYCHIATRISTS:

DR. JONES	Earle Hyman
DR. SOLOMON	Marcia Jean Kurtz
DR. BLINDER	Donal Donnelly
DR. LUNDE	Gary Reineke
DR. DELMAN	Jon DeVries

In Rebuttal for the People

CAROL RUTH SILVER, City Supervisor	Marcia Jean Kurtz
DR. LEVY, psychiatrist	Gary Reineke
RIOT POLICE	Jeremy O. Caplin, Josh Clark, Jon DeVries, Richard Riehle, Stanley Tucci
ACTION CAMERAMAN	Richard Howard

1975

San Francisco is in flux. The great port that had sprung up to handle the Gold Rush, that had built thousands of ships and processed millions of servicemen in two world wars, is in decline. Piers that once held freight now hold tourist attractions. Tourism becomes a billion-dollar-a-year industry. Downtown develops as a corporate headquarters, and white-collar jobs open up. Blue-collar jobs are lost, are outnumbered by service-industry jobs. Working-class neighborhoods, both black and Irish Catholic, deteriorate. Some are torn down as downtown and superhighways expand. Some fill up with Asian and Hispanic immigrants. Others undergo gentrification. San Francisco's homosexual community grows strong and becomes a mecca for thousands of gays from across the country, long attracted to the city by its "open" reputation. Many settle in one of the city's changing neighborhoods, along Castro Street.

Office seekers adapt to the realignment of political power.

Two young women try to kill President Ford.

November 4, 1975

A coalition of racial minorities, labor rank and file, and neighborhood activists breaks down the decades-long control of City Hall by the Irish political machine. George Moscone is elected mayor.

Among the new mayor's appointments is the Reverend Jim Jones, whom Moscone names chairman of the city's Housing Authority.

1976

An attempt is made, with a bomb, to kill Supervisor Dianne Feinstein.

November 2, 1976

Voters approve a new system for electing the Board of Supervisors, San Francisco's equivalent of a city council; the city is divided into eleven districts, each of which will select its own supervisor.

1977

An attempt is made, with a bomb, to kill District Attorney Joseph Freitas.

Spring 1977

Dan White decides to run for supervisor from District 8, a heavily Catholic working-class neighborhood in southeast San Francisco. White is a native San Franciscan, a high school sports star, a Vietnam vet, an ex-police officer and a fireman. A prime issue in White's campaign is his opposition to the Youth Campus, a home for juvenile offenders located in his district.

Harvey Milk, a small businessman and leader of the Castro Street gay community, will run for supervisor in District 5. Milk is a native New Yorker and part of the recent gay migration to San Francisco, having settled in the city in 1972.

November 8, 1977

Harvey Milk, "The Mayor of Castro Street," wins a seat on the Board of Supervisors. He is the first openly gay elected official in the United States. Dan White, who in his campaign had pledged to "eradicate the malignancies which blight our beautiful city," also wins election to the board.

March 1978

A Board of Supervisors committee, chaired by White, meets to consider Milk's first legislative proposal: a ban on all forms of discrimination against gays in the city. The committee votes 3-0 to recommend approval to the full board. The following Monday, the board considers whether to approve the Youth Campus. White believes he has Milk's support to give him the 6-5 majority he needs to close the Youth Campus. When the vote is taken, however, Milk votes for the Youth Campus, and the issue White had campaigned on is defeated by one vote. When the gay rights legislation is brought up before the entire board a week later, White is the one supervisor to vote against it.

Fall 1978

Harvey Milk campaigns statewide against the Briggs Initiative, a ballot proposition championed by archconservative State Senator John Briggs. It would ban homosexuals from teaching in California schools. Dan White contributes $100 to Milk's anti-Briggs campaign, saying "Everyone has the right to earn a living."

Harassed by press investigations into irregularities at the People's Temple, Jim Jones moves his congregation to Jonestown, the jungle refuge he is building in Guyana.

Tuesday, November 7

The Briggs Initiative is defeated. Another initiative sponsored by Briggs, Proposition 7, passes. Proposition 7 enacts a tougher death penalty and includes a clause invoking an automatic death penalty for anyone convicted of murdering a public official in an effort to prevent that official from carrying out his public duties. Milk and Moscone strongly oppose Proposition 7. White supports its passage.

Friday, November 10

Dan White resigns from the Board of Supervisors. He cites financial difficulties as the reason. Upon his election he had been forced to resign from the Fire Department; the supervisor's salary is only $9,600. The previous spring he had sought extra income by signing a lease to operate a fast-food stand, the Hot Potato.

Harvey Milk extracts a promise from Mayor Moscone that White's replacement will be sympathetic to the needs of the gay community.

Tuesday, November 14
Challenged by his disappointed aides and supporters, White reconsiders his decision. He calls Moscone and asks for his resignation back.

Wednesday, November 15
Moscone meets with White and tells him that as long as there are no legal impediments he will consider the resignation rescinded. He adds that if there is a legal question, he will simply reappoint White to the board. White goes to the city attorney's office to ask about the legal question and overhears a phone call from Harvey Milk asking the same information.

Congressman Leo Ryan arrives in Guyana to investigate a constituent's charges that his grandson is being held in Jonestown against his will.

Thursday, November 16
Dan White appears at a public rally organized to oppose his reappointment to the board. He fails to win the crowd to his side and is booed off the stage. Hearing of this, Moscone begins to have second thoughts about reappointing White.

Saturday, November 18
The city attorney tells Moscone that White cannot rescind his resignation, it's up to the mayor to reappoint him. Moscone tells White he needs concrete proof of support for White from the citizens of District 8.

Sunday, November 19
Congressman Ryan is killed in Guyana and the first news of the massacre reaches San Francisco.

Tuesday, November 21
Moscone meets with Don Horanzey, a candidate backed as a replacement for White. White's aides seek a temporary restraining order to prevent the mayor from appointing someone else.

The body count in Guyana tops five hundred. Rumors of a People's Temple hit squad are given credence by the police. Security measures are implemented at City Hall.

Thursday, November 23
Thanksgiving. Moscone receives two death threats connected with the People's Temple.

Friday, November 24
Dianne Feinstein, president of the Board of Supervisors, meets with the city attorney, who tells her that White intends to take his seat when the board convenes on Monday the 27th. Feinstein says that although she favors White regaining his seat, she will not recognize him unless he has been reappointed by the mayor. That evening, Moscone learns that the restraining order has been turned down in court. He is free to appoint whom he wants.

The body count in Guyana is up to 780.

Saturday, November 25
Moscone offers Horanzey the District 8 seat on the Board of Supervisors. Horanzey asks for time to consider. White hears the rumor that someone will be appointed to his seat on Monday.

Sunday, November 26
The morning paper puts the body count in Guyana at 910.

Horanzey calls Moscone to accept the seat. Moscone tells him to be at City Hall for a press conference at 10:30. When the board convenes at 2:00 Horanzey will be sworn in. The mayor tells his press secretary to send telegrams to the other candidates informing them they have not been selected. White's name is not on the list, and the press secretary assumes the mayor will call White personally. Moscone neglects to do this.

That evening, White receives a phone call from KCBS News asking for his reaction to Moscone's decision to appoint someone else to his seat.

Monday, November 27
Dan White enters the mayor's office in City Hall and shoots George Moscone four times. He reloads his gun, enters the supervisors' office, and shoots Harvey Milk five times. He meets his wife Mary Ann at St. Mary's Cathedral, then surrenders to the police. That evening a tremendous crowd moves down Market Street from the Castro District in a candlelight procession and gathers outside City Hall.

Dianne Feinstein, as president of the Board of Supervisors, becomes acting mayor.

May 1, 1979
The trial of Dan White, on two counts of first-degree murder, begins.

May 21, 1979
Dan White is convicted on two counts of the reduced charge of voluntary manslaughter. Maximum sentence: seven years and eight months. A mob of thousands, led by the city's gay community, attacks City Hall, shattering windows and burning police cars; 150 are injured. Later that night, the police riot on Castro Street, clubbing down homosexuals on the sidewalks and in the gay bars.

November 1979
Dianne Feinstein is elected mayor of San Francisco.

1980
Voters repeal district elections for the Board of Supervisors and reinstate citywide, at-large elections.

The California penal code is amended to prevent arguing the "diminished capacity" defense, which attorney Douglas Schmidt used in the trial of Dan White.

January 6, 1984
Dan White is paroled from Soledad Prison. He begins life outside in Los Angeles.

October 21, 1985
Dan White is found dead of carbon monoxide poisoning at his wife's home in San Francisco.

Adapted from Tom Creamer's notes for The Empty Space program, incorporating additional facts from Warren MacIsaac's notes for the Center Stage program.

Witnesses for the People
STEPHENS, the coroner
RUDY NOTHENBERG, Deputy Mayor
BARBARA TAYLOR, KCBS reporter
OFFICER BYRNE, policewoman in charge of records
WILLIAM MELIA, JR., civil engineer
CYR COPERTINI, appointment secretary to the mayor
CARL HENRY CARLSON, aide to Milk
RICHARD PABICH, assistant to Milk
FRANK FALZON, Chief Inspector of Homicide
EDWARD ERDELATZ, inspector

Witnesses for the Defense
FIRE CHIEF SHERRATT
POLICE OFFICER SULLIVAN
CITY SUPERVISOR LEE DOLSON
FIREMAN FREDIANI
PSYCHIATRISTS JONES, BLINDER, SOLOMON, LUNDE, DELMAN
DENISE APCAR, aide to White

In Rebuttal for the People
CAROL RUTH SILVER, City Supervisor
DR. LEVY, psychiatrist

Characters on Tape
DIANNE FEINSTEIN, City Supervisor, later Mayor
GEORGE MOSCONE, Mayor
HARVEY MILK, City Supervisor

People of San Francisco, Jurors, Cameramen, Mourners, Rioters, Riot Police

(The play can be performed by as few as 18 actors.)

TIME

1978 to the present.

PLACE

San Francisco.

AUTHOR'S NOTE

The words come from trial transcript, interview, reportage, the street.

ACT ONE

A bare stage. White screens overhead.

Screen: Images of San Francisco, punctuated with images of Milk and Moscone. Hot, fast music. People enter. A maelstrom of urban activity.

Screen: Without warning, documentary footage of Dianne Feinstein (almost unable to stand):

FEINSTEIN *(Taped voice)*: As president of the Board of Supervisors, it is my duty to make this announcement: Mayor George Moscone . . . and Supervisor Harvey Milk . . . have been shot . . . and killed.

(Gasps and cries. A long moment.)

The suspect is Supervisor Dan White.

(The crowd in shock. They cannot move. Then they run. In the chaos, Mary Ann White enters, trying to hail a cab; exits. Screen: A crucifix fades up. Shaft of light. A church window. Dan White prays. Audio: Hyperrealistic sounds of mumbled Hail Marys; of high heels echoing, moving fast; of breathing hard, running. Mary Ann White enters, breathless. Dan White looks up. She approaches him.)

WHITE: I shot the Mayor and Harvey.

(Mary Ann White crumples. Lights change.)

CLERK: This is the matter of the People versus Daniel James White.

(Amplified gavel. Lights change.)

COP *(Quiet)*:
>Yeah, I'm wearing a "Free Dan White" T-shirt.
>You haven't seen what I've seen—
>my nose shoved into what I think stinks.
>Against everything I believe in.
>There was a time in San Francisco when you knew a
>>guy
>by his parish.

(Sister Boom Boom enters. Nun drag; white face, heavily made up; spike heels.)

>Sometimes I sit in church and I think of those
>>disgusting drag queens dressed up as nuns and
>>I'm a cop,
>and I'm thinkin',
>there's gotta be a law, you know,

because they're makin' me think things I don't want
   to think
and I gotta keep my mouth shut.

(Boom Boom puts out cigarette.)

Take a guy out of his sling—fist-fucked to death—
they say it's mutual consent, it ain't murder,
and I pull this disgusting mess down, take him to the
   morgue,
I mean, my wife asks me, "Hey, how was your day?"
I can't even tell her.
I wash my hands before I can even look at my kids.

*(The cop and Boom Boom are very aware of each other but
never make eye contact.)*

BOOM BOOM: God bless you one. God bless you all.
COP: See, Danny knew—he believes in the rights of minorities. Ya
   know, he just felt—we are a minority, too.
BOOM BOOM: I would like to open with a reading from the Book of
   Dan. *(Opens book)*
COP:

We been workin' this job three generations—my
   father was a cop—
and then they put—Moscone, Jesus, Moscone put this
N-Negro-loving, faggot-loving chief telling us what to
   do—
he doesn't even come from the neighborhood,
he doesn't even come from this city!
He's tellin' us what to do in a force that knows what
   to do.
He makes us paint our cop cars faggot blue—
he called it "lavender gloves" for the queers,
handle 'em, treat 'em with "lavender gloves," he
   called it.

He's cuttin' off our balls.

The city is stinkin' with degenerates—

I mean, I'm worried about my kids, I worry about my
wife,

I worry about me and how I'm feelin' mad all the
time.

You gotta understand that I'm not alone—

It's real confusion.

BOOM BOOM: "As he came to his day of reckoning, he feared not
for he went unto the lawyers and the doctors and the jurors,
and they said, 'Take heart, for in this you will receive not life
but three to seven with time off for good behavior.'" *(Closes
book reverently)*

COP:

Ya gotta understand—

Take a walk with me sometime.

See what I see every day . . .

BOOM BOOM: Now we are all faced with this cycle.

COP:

Like I'm supposed to smile when I see two bald-
headed,

shaved-head men with those tight pants and muscles,

chains everywhere, French kissin' on the street,

putting their hands all over each other's asses,

I'm supposed to smile,

walk by, act as if this is *right*??!!

BOOM BOOM: As gay people and as people of color and as women
we all know the cycle of brutality which pervades our culture.

COP: I got nothin' against people doin' what they want, if I don't
see it.

BOOM BOOM: And we all know that brutality only begets more
brutality.

COP: I mean, I'm not makin' some woman on the streets for
everyone to see.

BOOM BOOM: Violence only sows the seed for more violence.

COP: I'm not . . .

BOOM BOOM: And I hope Dan White knows that.

COP: I can't explain it any better.

(Pause.)

BOOM BOOM: Because the greatest, most efficient information gathering and dispersal network is the Great Gay Grapevine.

COP: Just take my word for it—

BOOM BOOM: And when he gets out of jail, no matter where Dan White goes, someone will recognize him.

COP:
> Walk into a leather bar with me some night—
> they—they're—
> there are queers who'd agree with me—it's disgusting.

BOOM BOOM: All over the world, the word will go out. And we will know where Dan White is.

COP: The point is: Dan White showed you could fight City Hall.

(Pause.)

BOOM BOOM:
> Now we are all aware, as I said,
> of this cycle of brutality and murder.
> And the only way we can break that horrible cycle is
>   with
> love, understanding and forgiveness.
> And there are those who were before me here today—
>   gay brothers and sisters—
> who said that we must somehow learn
> to love, understand and forgive
> the sins that have been committed against us
> and the sins of violence.
> And it sort of grieves me that some of us are not
> understanding and loving and forgiving of Dan White.
> And after he gets out,
> after we find out where he is . . .

(Long, wry look)
I mean, not, y'know,
with any malice or planning . . .
(Long look)
You know, you get so depressed and your blood sugar
    goes up
and you'd be capable of just about *anything!*
(Long pause. Smiles)
And some angry faggot or dyke who is not
understanding, loving and forgiving—
is going to perform a horrible act of violence and
    brutality
against Dan White.
And if we can't break the cycle before somebody gets
    Dan White,
somebody will get Dan White
and when they do,
I beg you all to
love, understand and *for-give. (Laughs)*

(Lights fade to black.)

CLERK: This is the matter of the People versus Daniel James
White and the record will show that the Defendant is present with his counsel and the District Attorney is present and
this is out of presence of the jury.

(Courtroom being set up. TV lights.)

JOANNA LU *(On camera):* The list of prospective witnesses that the
defense has presented for the trial of the man who killed the
liberal mayor of San Francisco, George Moscone, and the
first avowedly gay elected official, City Supervisor Harvey
Milk, reads like a Who's Who of city government *(Looks at
list)* . . . Judges, congressmen, current and former supervisors, and even a state senator. The D.A. has charged White

with two counts of first-degree murder, invoking for the first time the clause in the new California capital punishment law that calls for the gas chamber for any person who has assassinated a public official in an attempt to prevent him from fulfilling his official duties. Ironically, Harvey Milk and George Moscone vigorously lobbied against the death penalty while Dan White vigorously supported it. This is Joanna Lu at the Hall of Justice.

(Gavel. Spotlight on clerk.)

CLERK: Ladies and gentlemen, this is the information in the case now pending before you: the People of the State of California, Plaintiff, versus Daniel James White, Defendant. Action Number: 98663, Count One.

(Gavel. Lights up. Trial in progress. Screen: "Jury Selection.")

COURT: Mr. Schmidt, you may continue with your jury selection.
SCHMIDT: Thank you, Your Honor.
CLERK: It is alleged that Dan White did willfully, unlawfully and with malice aforethought murder George R. Moscone, the duly elected Mayor of the City and County of San Francisco, California.
SCHMIDT: Have you ever supported controversial causes, like homosexual rights, for instance?
JUROR 1 *(Woman)*: I have gay friends . . . I, uh . . . once walked with them in a Gay Freedom Day Parade.
SCHMIDT: Your Honor, I would like to strike the juror.
JUROR 1: I am str . . . I am heterosexual.
COURT: Agreed.

(Gavel.)

CLERK: The Defendant Daniel James White is further accused of a crime of felony to wit: that said Defendant Daniel James

White did willfully, unlawfully and with malice afore-thought, murder Harvey Milk, a duly elected Supervisor of the City and County of San Francisco, California.

SCHMIDT: With whom do you live, sir?

JUROR 2: My roommate.

SCHMIDT: What does he or she do?

JUROR 2: *He* works at the Holiday Inn.

SCHMIDT: Your Honor, I ask the court to strike the juror for cause.

COURT: Agreed.

(Gavel.)

CLERK: Special circumstances: it is alleged that Daniel James White in this proceeding has been accused of more than one offense of murder.

JUROR 3: I worked briefly as a San Francisco policeman, but I've spent most of my life since then as a private security guard.

SCHMIDT: As you know, serving as a juror is a high honor and re-sponsibility.

JUROR 3: Yes, sir.

SCHMIDT: The jury serves as the conscience of the community.

JUROR 3: Yes, sir. I know that, sir.

SCHMIDT: Now, sir, as a juror you take an oath that you will apply the laws of the state of California as the judge will instruct you. You'll uphold that oath, won't you?

JUROR 3: Yes, sir.

SCHMIDT: Do you hold any views against the death penalty no matter how heinous the crime?

JUROR 3: No, sir. I support the death penalty.

SCHMIDT: Why do you think Danny White killed Milk and Moscone?

JUROR 3: I have certain opinions. I'd say it was social and political pressures . . .

SCHMIDT: I have my jury.

COURT: Mr. Norman?

(No response. Fine with him. Gavel.)

LU *(On camera)*: The jury has been selected quickly for the Dan
    White trial. It appears the prosecution and the defense want
    the same jury. Assistant D.A. Tom Norman exercised only
    three out of twenty-seven possible peremptory challenges.
    By all accounts, there are no blacks, no gays and no Asians.
    One juror is an ex-policeman, another the wife of the
    county jailer, four of the seven women are old enough to be
    Dan White's mother. Most of the jurors are working- and
    middle-class Catholics. Speculation in the press box is that
    the prosecution feels it has a law-and-order jury. In any
    case, Dan White will certainly be judged by a jury of his
    peers. *(Turns to second camera)* I have with me this morn-
    ing District Attorney Joseph Freitas, Jr.

(TV lights on Freitas.)

May we ask sir, the prosecution's strategy in the trial of Dan
    White?
FREITAS: I think it's a clear case. . . . We'll let the facts speak for
    themselves . . .

(Falzon enters, sits at prosecutor's table.)

CLERK: And the Defendant, Daniel James White, has entered a
    plea of not guilty to each of the charges and allegations con-
    tained in this information.

*(White enters. Mary Ann White enters with infant in arms,
    sees him. They sit.)*

COURT: Mr. Norman, do you desire to make an opening statement
    at this time?
NORMAN: I do, Judge.
COURT: All right. You may proceed.

(Lights change. Screen: "Act One: Murder." Gavel. Screens go to white.)

NORMAN *(Opening statement, prosecution)*: Your Honor, members of the jury—and you *(Takes in audience)* must be the judges now, counsel for the defense:

(To audience) Ladies and Gentlemen: I am Thomas F. Norman and I am the Assistant District Attorney, and I appear here as trial representative to Joseph Freitas, Jr., District Attorney. Seated with me is Frank Falzon, Chief Inspector of Homicide for San Francisco.

George R. Moscone was the duly elected Mayor of San Francisco.

(Screen: Portrait of Moscone.)

Harvey Milk was the duly elected Supervisor or City Councilman of District 5 of San Francisco.

(Screen: Portrait of Milk.)

The defendant in this case, Mr. Daniel James White, had been the duly elected Supervisor of District 8 of San Francisco, until for personal reasons of his own he tendered his resignation in writing to the mayor on or about November the 10th, 1978, which was approximately seventeen days before this tragedy occurred.

Subsequent to tendering his resignation he had the feeling that he wanted to withdraw that resignation, and that he wanted his job back.

George Moscone, it appears, had told the accused that he would give him his job back or, in other words, appoint him back to the board if it appeared that there was substantial support in District Number 8 for that appointment.

Material was received by the mayor in that regard, and in the meantime, Mr. Daniel James White had resorted to the courts in an effort to withdraw his written resignation.

It appears that those efforts were not met with much success.

(Screen: "The Defense, Douglas Schmidt.")

SCHMIDT: Ladies and Gentlemen, the prosecutor has quite skill-fully outlined certain of the facts that he believes will be supportive of his theory of first-degree murder.

I intend to present *all* the facts, including some of the background material that will show, not so much *what* happened on November 27th, but *why* those tragedies occurred on November 27th.

The evidence will show, and it's not disputed, that Dan White did, indeed, shoot and kill George Moscone and I think the evidence is equally clear that Dan White did shoot and kill Harvey Milk.

Why then should there be a trial?

The issue in this trial is properly to understand *why* that happened.

(Lights. Screen: "Chief Medical Examiner and Coroner for the City and County of San Francisco.")

STEPHENS *(Holding photo)*: In my opinion and experience, Counsel, the larger tattoo pattern at the side of the Mayor's head is compatible with a firing distance of about one foot, and the smaller tattoo pattern within the larger tattoo pattern is consistent with a firing distance of a little less than one foot.

That is: The wounds to the head were received within a distance of one foot when the mayor was already on the floor incapacitated.

(Norman looks to jury. Screen: Image of figure shooting man in head from a distance of one foot, leaning down. Lights.)

SCHMIDT: Why? . . . Good people, fine people, with fine back-
grounds, simply don't kill people in cold blood, it just doesn't
happen, and obviously some part of them has not been presented thus far. Dan White was a native of San Francisco. He
went to school here, went through high school here. He was
a noted athlete in high school. He was an army veteran who
served in Vietnam, and was honorably discharged from the
army. He became a policeman thereafter, and after a brief
hiatus developed, again returned to the police force in San
Francisco, and later transferred to the fire department.

He was married in December of 1976, and he fathered his
son in July 1978.

Dan White was a good policeman and Dan White was a
good fireman. In fact, he was decorated for having saved a
woman and her child in a very dangerous fire, but the complete picture of Dan White perhaps was not known until
sometime after these tragedies on November 27th. The part
that went unrecognized was—for the past ten years Daniel
White was suffering from a mental disease. The disease that
Daniel White was suffering from is called "depression,"
sometimes called "manic depression."

(Lights.)

NORMAN: Doctor, what kind of wound was that in your opinion?
STEPHENS: These are gunshot wounds of entrance, Counsel.

The cause of death was multiple gunshot wounds . . . particularly the bullet that passed through the base of the supervisor's brain. This wound would cause instant or almost
instant death. I am now holding People's 30 for identifica-
tion. In order for this wound to be received, Counsel . . . the
supervisor's left arm has to be in close to the body with the
palm up. The right arm has to be relatively close to the body
with the palm turned away from the body and the thumb in
towards the body.

NORMAN: Can you illustrate that for us?

STEPHENS: Yes, Counsel. The left arm has to be in close to the body and slightly forward with the palm up. The right hand has to be palm away with the thumb pointed towards the body and the elbow in slightly to the body with the arm raised. In this position, all of these wounds that I have just described in People's 30 and 29 line up.

(Freeze. Lights.)

SCHMIDT *(Talking to jury)*: Dan White came from a vastly different lifestyle than Harvey Milk, who was a homosexual leader and politician. Dan White was an idealistic young man, a working-class young man. He was deeply endowed with and believed very strongly in the traditional American values, family and home, like the district he represented. *(Indicates jury)* Dan White believed people when they said something. He believed that a man's word, essentially, was his bond. He was an honest man, and he was fair, perhaps too fair for politics in San Francisco.

(Screen: White campaigning, American flag behind him. Audio: Rocky theme song, crowd response throughout his speech.)

WHITE *(To crowd)*: Do you like my new campaign song?
CROWD *(Audio; cheering)*: Yeah!
WHITE *(To camera; TV lights)*: For years, we have witnessed an exodus from San Francisco by many of our family members, friends and neighbors. Alarmed by the enormous increase in crime, poor educational facilities and a deteriorating social structure, they have fled to temporary havens . . . In a few short years these malignancies of society will erupt from our city and engulf our tree-lined, sun-bathed communities that chide us for daring to live in San Francisco. That is, unless we who have remained can transcend the apathy which has caused us to lock our doors while the tumult rages un-

checked through our streets. Individually we are helpless. Yet you must realize there are thousands and thousands of angry frustrated people such as yourselves waiting to unleash a fury that can and will eradicate the malignancies which blight our beautiful city. I am not going to be forced out of San Francisco by splinter groups of radicals, social deviates and incorrigibles. UNITE AND FIGHT WITH DAN WHITE.

(Crowd cheers. Lights change. Screens go to white.)

SCHMIDT: I think Dan White saw the city deteriorating as a place for the average and decent people to live.

COURT: Mr. Nothenberg, please be seated.

SCHMIDT: This irony is . . . that the young man with so much promise in seeking the job on the Board of Supervisors actually was destined to construct his downfall. After Dan White was elected he discovered there was a conflict of interest if he was a fireman and an elected official. His wife, Mary Ann, was a schoolteacher and made a good salary. But after their marriage, it was discovered that the wife of Dan White had become . . . pregnant and had to give up her teaching job. So the family income plummeted from an excess of $30,000 to $9,600, which is what a San Francisco supervisor is paid. I believe all the stress and the underlying mental illness culminated in his resignation that he turned in to the mayor on November 10th, 1978.

(Screen: "Mr. Nothenberg, Deputy Mayor." Lights.)

NORMAN: Would you read that for us?

NOTHENBERG: "Dear Mayor Moscone: I have been proud to represent the people of San Francisco from District 8 for the past ten months, but due to personal responsibilities which I feel must take precedent over my legislative duties, I am resigning my position effective today. I am sure that the next representative to the Board of Supervisors will receive as much support from the People of San Francisco as I have. Sincerely, Dan White." It is so signed.

SCHMIDT *(To jury)*: Some days after November the 10th pressure was brought to bear on Dan White to go back to the job that he had worked so hard for, and there was a one-way course that those persons could appeal to Dan White, and that was to appeal to his sense of honor: Basically—Dan you are letting the fire department down, letting the police department down. It worked. That type of pressure worked, because of the kind of man Dan White is.

He asked the mayor for his job back.

NORMAN: Mr. Nothenberg, on or about Monday the 27th of November last year, do you know whether Mayor Moscone was going to make an appointment to the Board of Supervisors, particularly for District Number 8?

NOTHENBERG: Yes, he was.

SCHMIDT: The mayor said: We have political differences, but you are basically a good man, and you worked for the job and I'm not going to take you to fault. The letter was returned to Dan White.

NORMAN: Do you know whom his appointee to District 8 was going to be?

NOTHENBERG: Yes, I do.

NORMAN: Who was that please?

NOTHENBERG: It was going to be a gentleman named Don Horanzey.

SCHMIDT: As I said, Dan White believed a man's word was his bond. *(He moves down to the jury)*

Mayor Moscone had said: If there was any legal problem he would simply reappoint Dan White. Thereafter it became: Dan White there is no support in District 8 and unless you can show some broad-base support, the job will not be given to you, and finally, the public statement coming from the mayor's office: It's undecided. But you will be notified, prior to the time that any decision is made. They didn't tell Dan White. But they told Barbara Taylor.

(Lights change.)

TAYLOR *(Audio; on phone)*: I'm Barbara Taylor from KCBS. I'd like to speak to Dan White.

WHITE *(Audio)*: Yuh.

TAYLOR *(Audio)*: I have received information from a source within the mayor's office that you are not getting that job. I am interested in doing an interview to find out your reaction to that . . . Mr. White?

(Long pause. Spotlight on White.)

WHITE *(Audio)*: I don't know anything about it.

(Audio: Click, busy signal. Lights change.)

TAYLOR *(Live)*: The Mayor told me: "The only one I've talked to who is in favor of the appointment of Dan White is Dan White."

NORMAN: Thank you, Miss Taylor.

SCHMIDT: After that phone call, Denise Apcar, Dan's aide, told Dan White that there were going to be supporters down at City Hall the next morning to show support to the mayor's office. In one day they had collected eleven hundred signatures in District 8 in support of Dan White.

But the next morning, Denise called Dan and told him the mayor was unwilling to accept the petitioners.

(Screen: "Denise Apcar, Aide to Dan White.")

APCAR: Yes. I told Danny—I don't remember my exact words—that the mayor had "circumvented the people."

NORMAN: Did you believe at that time that the mayor was going to appoint someone other than Dan White?

APCAR: Oh, yes.

NORMAN: At that time, were your feelings such that you were angry?

APCAR: Definitely. Well the mayor had told him . . . and Dan always felt that a person was going to be honest when they said something. He believed that up until the end.

NORMAN: You felt and believed that Mr. Milk had been acting to prevent the appointment of Mr. Dan White to his vacated seat on the Board of Supervisors?

APCAR: Yes. I was very much aware of that.

NORMAN: Had you expressed that opinion to Mr. White?

APCAR: Yes.

NORMAN: Did Mr. White ever express that opinion also to you?

APCAR: He wasn't down at City Hall very much that week so I was basically the person that told him these things.

(Pause.)

NORMAN: Did you call Mr. White and tell him that you had seen Harvey Milk come out of the mayor's office after you had been informed the mayor was not in?

APCAR: Yes, I did. Then he called me back and said, "Denise, come pick me up. I want to see the mayor."

NORMAN: When you picked him up, did he do anything unusual?

APCAR: Well . . . he didn't look at me and normally he would turn his body a little bit towards the driver and we would talk, you know, in a freeform way, but this time he didn't look at me at all. He was squinting hard. He was very nervous, he was agitated. He was blowing a lot. He was rubbing his hands, blowing into his hands and rubbing them like he was cold, like his hands were cold. He acted very hurt. Yes. He was, he looked like he was going to cry. He was doing everything he could to restrain his emotion.

NORMAN: Did you ever describe him as acting "all fired up"?

APCAR: Yes, yes I—I believe I said that.

NORMAN: Did he mention at that time that he also was going to talk to Harvey Milk?

APCAR: Yes, he did.

NORMAN: Did he ever say he was going to "really lay it on the mayor"?

APCAR: It's been brought to my attention I said that, yes.

NORMAN: When you were driving Mr. White downtown, was there some discussion relative to a statement you made. "Anger had run pretty high all week towards the mayor playing pool on us, dirty, you know?"

APCAR: I believe I was describing my anger. At the time I made those statements I was in shock and I spoke freely and I'm sure I've never used those terms before.

NORMAN: When you made those statements it was forty minutes after noon on November 27th, was it not?

APCAR: Yes.

NORMAN: Miss Apcar— When you were driving Mr. White to City Hall did you know he was carrying a loaded gun?

APCAR: No. I did not.

NORMAN: Thank you.

(Lights.)

SCHMIDT: Dan White went to City Hall and he took a .38 caliber revolver with him, and that was not particularly unusual for Dan White.

Dan White was an ex-policeman, and as a policeman one is required to carry, off-duty, a gun, and as an ex-policeman—well, I think it's common practice.

And additionally, remember, there was the atmosphere created by the Jonestown People's Temple tragedy,

(Screens flood with Jonestown imagery. Music.)

which had occurred a few days before November 27th, and at that time there were rumors that there were hit lists that had been placed on public officials in San Francisco. Assassination squads. And in hindsight of course we can all realize the fact did not happen, but at the time there were nine hundred bodies laying in Guyana to indicate, that indeed, people were bent on murder.

(Screen: "Officer Byrne, Department of Records." Lights.)

NORMAN: Officer Byrne, do persons who were once on the police force who have resigned their positions, do they have a right to carry a concealed firearm on their person?

SCHMIDT: And I think it will be shown that Jim Jones himself was directly allied to the liberal elements of San Francisco politics and not to the conservative elements.

BYRNE: No, a resigned person would not have that right.

SCHMIDT: And so, it would be important to understand that there were threats directed towards conservative persons like Dan White.

NORMAN: Officer, have you at my instance and request examined those particular records to determine whether there is an official permit issued by the Chief of Police to a Mr. Daniel James White to carry a concealed firearm?

BYRNE: Yes, I have.

NORMAN: What have you found?

BYRNE: I find no permit.

NORMAN: Thank you.

(Lights.)

SCHMIDT: Yes, it's a violation of the law to carry a firearm without a permit, but that firearm was *registered* to Dan White.

NORMAN: Mr. Melia, please be seated.

SCHMIDT: Upon approaching the doors on Polk Street, White observed a metal-detection machine.

Knowing that he did not know the man that was on the metal-detection machine, he simply went around to the McAllister Street well, where he expected to meet his aide.

He did not find Denise Apcar there. She'd gone to put gas in her car. He waited for several moments, but knowing that it was imminent, the talk to the mayor, he stepped through a window at the Department of Public Works.

(Screen: Slide of windows with man in front demonstrating procedure.)

Which doesn't require any physical prowess, and you can step through those windows, and the evidence will show that though now they are barred, previously it was not uncommon for people to enter and exit there. They are very large windows, and are large, wide sills,

(Screen shows windows he stepped through—small, high off the ground, now barred.)

and it's quite easy to step into the building through these windows.

(Screen: Slide of man in three-piece suit trying to get leg up. Screen: "William Melia, Jr., Civil Engineer.")

MELIA: At approximately 10:35 I heard the window open. I heard someone jump to the floor and then running through the adjoining room. I looked up and caught a glance of a man in a suit running past the doorway of my office into the City Hall hallway.

NORMAN: What did you do?

MELIA: I got up from my desk and called after him: "Hey, wait a second."

NORMAN: Did that person wait or stop?

MELIA: Yes, they did.

NORMAN: Do you see that person here in this courtroom today?

MELIA: Yes, I do.

NORMAN: Where is that person?

MELIA: It's Dan White. *(Pause)* He said to me: "I had to get in. My aide was supposed to come down and let me in the side door, but never showed up." I had taken exception to the way he had entered our office, and I replied: *"And you are?"* And he replied: "I'm Dan White, the city supervisor." He said, "Say, I've got to go," and with that, he turned and ran out of the office.

NORMAN: Did you say that he ran?

MELIA: Right.

(Pause.)

NORMAN: Mr. Melia—had you ever seen anyone else enter or exit through that window or those windows along that side?

MELIA: Yes, I had. It was common for individuals that worked in our office to do that.

NORMAN: Were you alarmed when you learned that a supervisor crawled or walked through that window, or stepped through that window?

MELIA: Was I alarmed?

NORMAN: Yes.

MELIA: Yes. I was . . . alarmed.

(Norman looks to jury.)

SCHMIDT *(Annoyed)*: I think it's significant at this point—also because the fact that he crawled through the window *appears* to be important—it's significant to explain that people *often climb through that window,* and indeed, on the morning of the 27th, Denise had the key to the McAllister Street well door.

So, Dan White stepped through the window, identified himself, traveled up to the second floor.

(Screen: "Mrs. Cyr Copertini, Appointment Secretary to the Mayor.")

And then approached the desk of Cyr Copertini and properly identified himself, and asked to see the mayor.

(Lights.)

CYR: I am the appointment secretary to Mayor Feinstein.

NORMAN: In November of last year and particularly on November 27th what was your then occupation?

CYR: I was appointment secretary to the elected Mayor of San Francisco, George Moscone. *(She is deeply moved)*

NORMAN: Mrs. Copertini—were you aware that there was anything that was going to happen that day of November 27th of interest to the citizens of San Francisco, uh . . . I mean, such as some public announcement?

(Pause.)

CYR: . . . There was to be a news conference to announce the new supervisor for the eighth district, at 11:30.

NORMAN: Mrs. Copertini, at approximately 10:30 A.M. when you saw Mr. Daniel White, he appeared in front of your desk . . . do you recall what he said?

CYR: He said, "Hello, Cyr. May I see the mayor?" I said. "He has someone with him, but let me go check with him." I went in to the mayor and told him that Supervisor White was there to see him. He was a little dismayed. He was a little uncomfortable by it and said: "Oh, all right. Tell him I'll see him, but he will have to wait a coupla minutes."

I asked the mayor, "Shouldn't I have someone in there with him," and he said: "No, no, I'll see him alone."

I said, "Why don't you let me bring Mel Wax in?" And he said: "No, no, I'll see him alone." And then I went back.

NORMAN: Who was Mel Wax?

CYR: The press secretary.

NORMAN: When you went out to your office, did you then see Mr. Daniel White?

CYR: Yes. I said it will be a few minutes. He asked me how I was and how things were going. Was I having a nice day.

NORMAN: Was there anything unusual about his tone of voice?

CYR: No. I don't think so. He seemed nervous . . .

I asked him would he like to see the newspaper while he was waiting? He said, no, he wouldn't, and I said: "Well, that's all right. There's nothing in it anyway unless you want to read about Caroline Kennedy having turned twenty-one."

And he said: "Twenty-one? Is that right." He said: "Yeah, that's all so long ago. It's even more amazing when you think that John John is now eighteen."

(Lights change. Funeral mass: Gregorian chant; boys' choir. Pause.)

DENMAN: The only comparable situation I ever remember
CYR: It was about that time he was admitted to the mayor's office.

(Pause.)

DENMAN: was when JFK was killed.
NORMAN: Did you tell Mr. Daniel White that he could go in?
CYR: Yes.
DENMAN: I remember that in my bones, in my body.
NORMAN: Did he respond in any way to that?
DENMAN: Just like this one
CYR: He said: "Good girl, Cyr."
NORMAN: Good girl, Cyr?
CYR: Right.
DENMAN: when Camelot all of a sudden turned to hell.
NORMAN: Then what did he do?
CYR: Went in.

(Pause.)

NORMAN: After he went in there did you hear anything of an unusual nature that was coming from the mayor's office?
CYR: After a time I heard a . . . commotion.

(Lights change.)

YOUNG MOTHER: I heard it on the car radio, I literally gasped.

NORMAN: Explain that to us, please.

YOUNG MOTHER: I wanted to pull over to the side of the road and scream.

CYR: Well, I heard—a series of noises—a group and then one—

YOUNG MOTHER: Just scream.

CYR: I went to the window to see if anything was happening out in the street,

YOUNG MOTHER: Then I thought of my kids.

CYR: and the street was rather extraordinarily calm.

DENMAN: I noticed when I walked outside that there was an unusual quiet.

CYR: For that hour of the day there is usually more—there wasn't really anything out there.

DENMAN: I went to the second floor and started walking toward the mayor's office.

YOUNG MOTHER: I wanted to get them out of school and take them home,

NORMAN: Could you describe these noises for us?

YOUNG MOTHER: I wanted to take them home and *(Makes a hugging gesture)* lock the door.

CYR: Well, they were dull thuds rather like—

DENMAN: And there was this strange combination of panic and silence that you rarely see,

CYR: I thought maybe it was an automobile door that somebody had tried to shut, by, you know, pushing, and then finally succeeding.

DENMAN: it was like a silent slow-motion movie of a disaster.

NORMAN: Do you have any recollection that you can report with any certainty to us as to how many sounds there were?

CYR: No. As I stood there I—I thought I ought to remember—

(She breaks down.)

DENMAN: There was this hush and aura, people were moving with strange faces,

(Cyr sobs.)

as if the world had just come to an end.

MOSCONE'S FRIEND: George loved this city, and felt what was wrong could be fixed.

NORMAN: Do you want a glass of water?

(Cyr sobs.)

DENMAN: And I asked someone what had happened and he said: "The mayor has been shot."

CYR: I ought to remember that pattern in case it is something, but I—

MOSCONE'S FRIEND: He knew—it was a white racist town. A Catholic town. But he believed in people's basic good will.

(Cyr sobs.)

COURT: Just a minute. Do you want a recess?

MOSCONE'S FRIEND: He never suspected, I bet, Dan White's psychotic behavior.

NORMAN: Do you want a recess?

MOSCONE'S FRIEND: That son of a bitch killed someone I loved. I mean, I loved the guy.

CYR: No, I'm all right.

COURT: Are you sure you are all right?

CYR: Yes.

YOUNG MOTHER: I just thought of my kids.

(Long pause.)

MOSCONE'S FRIEND: I loved his idealism. I loved his hope.

CYR: Then what happened was Rudy Nothenberg left to tell the press that the conference would start a few minutes late.

MOSCONE'S FRIEND: I loved the guy.

CYR: And then he came back to me right away and said: "Oh, I guess we can go ahead. I just saw Dan White leave."

MOSCONE'S FRIEND: I loved his almost naive faith in people.

CYR: So then he went into the mayor's office and said: "He isn't here." And I said: "Well, maybe he went into the back room."

MOSCONE'S FRIEND: I loved his ability to go on.

CYR: Then he just gave a shout saying: "Gary, get in here. Call an ambulance. Get the police."

MOSCONE'S FRIEND: See, I got too tired to stay in politics and do it. George and I were together from the beginning. Me, Phil Burton, Willy Brown. Beatin' all the old Irishmen.

DENMAN: I heard right away that Dan White had done it.

MOSCONE'S FRIEND: But George believed, as corny as this sounds, that you do good for the people. I haven't met many of those and George was one of those. Maybe those are the guys that get killed. I don't know.

(Pause. Cyr crying.)

NORMAN: All right. All this you told us about occurred in San Francisco, didn't it?

(Pause.)

CYR *(Deeply moved)*: Yes.

SCHMIDT: Dan White, as it was quite apparent at that point, had *cracked* because of his underlying mental illness . . .

(Screen: "Carl Henry Carlson, Aide to Harvey Milk.")

CARLSON: I heard Peter Nardoza, Dianne Feinstein's aide, say "Dianne wants to see you," and Dan White said: "That'll have to wait a couple of minutes, I have something to do first."

NORMAN: I have something to do first?

CARLSON: Yes.

(Pause.)

NORMAN: Do you recall in what manner Mr. White announced himself?

SCHMIDT: There were stress factors due to the fact that he hadn't been notified,

CARLSON: He appeared at the door, which was normally left open. Stuck his head in and asked: "Say, Harv, can I see you for a minute?"

SCHMIDT: and the sudden emotional surge that he had in the mayor's office was simply too much for him

NORMAN: What did Harvey Milk do at that time if anything?

CARLSON: He turned around.

SCHMIDT: and he cracked.

CARLSON: He turned around

SCHMIDT: The man cracked.

CARLSON: and said "Sure," and got up and went across the hall . . .

SCHMIDT: He shot the mayor,

CARLSON: to the office designated as Dan White's office on the chart.

SCHMIDT: reloaded his gun, basically on *instinct*, because of his police training,

NORMAN: After they went across the hall to Mr. White's office . . .

SCHMIDT: and was about to leave the building at that point and he looked down the hall,

NORMAN: Would you tell us what next you heard or saw?

SCHMIDT: he saw somebody that he believed to be an aide to Harvey Milk.

CARLSON: A few seconds later, probably ten, fifteen seconds later, I heard a shot, or the sound of gunfire.

SCHMIDT: He went down to the supervisors' area to *talk* to Harvey Milk.

COURT: Excuse me. Would you speak out. Your voice is fading a bit.

SCHMIDT: At that point, in the same state of rage, emotional upheaval with the stress and mental illness having cracked this man

STEPHENS *(Demonstrates as he speaks)*: The left arm has to be close to the body and slightly forward with the palm up.

SCHMIDT: *ninety seconds* from the time he shot the mayor, Dan White shot and killed Harvey Milk.

CARLSON: After the shot, I heard Harvey Milk scream. "Oh, no." And then the first—the first part of the second "no" which was then cut short by the second shot.

STEPHENS: The right hand has to be palm away with the thumb pointed towards the body and the elbow in slightly to the body with the arm raised.

NORMAN: How many sounds of shots did you hear altogether, Mr. Carlson?

CARLSON: Five or six. I really didn't consciously count them.

STEPHENS: In this position all of these wounds that I have just described in People's 29 and 30 line up.

(Pause.)

CARLSON: A few moments later the door opened, the door opened and Daniel White walked out, rushed out, and proceeded down the hall.

NORMAN: Now, Mr. Carlson, when Daniel White first appeared at the office of Harvey Milk and he inquired of Harvey Milk, "Say, Harv, can I see you for a minute?" could you describe his tone of voice in any way?

CARLSON: He appeared to be very normal, usual friendly self. I didn't, I didn't feel anything out of the ordinary. It was just very typical Dan White.

(Lights change.)

GWENN: I'd like to talk about when people are pushed to the wall.

SCHMIDT: Harvey Milk was against the reappointment of Dan White.

GWENN: In order to understand the riots, I think you have to understand that the Dan White verdict did not occur in a vacuum.

SCHMIDT: Basically, it was a political decision. It was evident there was a liberal wing of the Board of Supervisors, and there was a smaller conservative wing, and Dan White was a conservative politician for San Francisco.

(Screen: "Richard Pabich, Legislative Assistant to Harvey Milk." Lights.)

PABICH: My address is 542-A Castro Street.

GWENN: I don't think I have to say what their presence meant to us, and what their loss meant to us—

NORMAN: What did you do after you saw Dan White put the key in the door of his old office, Room 237?

GWENN: The assassinations of our friends Harvey and George were a crime against us all.

PABICH: Well, I was struck in my head, sort of curious as to why he'd been running.

GWENN: And right here, when I say "us," I don't mean only gay people.

PABICH: And he was—it looked like he was in a hurry. I was aware of the political situation.

GWENN: I mean all people who are getting less than they deserve.

PABICH: I was aware that Harvey was taking the position to the mayor that Mr. White shouldn't be reappointed. Harvey and I had talked earlier that it would be a significant day.

(Lights. Subliminal music.)

MILK'S FRIEND: After Harvey died, I went into a depression that lasted about a year, I guess. They called it depression, anyway. I thought about suicide, well, I more than thought about it.

SCHMIDT: Mr. Pabich, Mr. Milk had suggested a replacement for Dan White, hadn't he?

PABICH: He had, to my understanding, recommended several people, and basically took the position that Dan White should not be reappointed.

MILK'S FRIEND: I lost my job. I stayed in the hospital for, I would guess, two months or so. They put me on some kind of drug that . . . well, it helped, I guess. I mean, I loved him and it was . . .

SCHMIDT: Was he requesting that a homosexual be appointed?

PABICH: No, he was not. *(He stares at Schmidt, stunned)*

(Lights change.)

MILK'S FRIEND: Well, he was gone and that couldn't change.

SCHMIDT: I have nothing further. Thank you.

MILK'S FRIEND: He'd never be here again, I knew that.

COURT: All right. Any redirect, Mr. Norman?

NORMAN: No. Thank you for coming, Mr. Pabich.

GWENN: It was as if Dan White had given the go-ahead. It was a free-for-all, a license to kill.

MILK'S FRIEND: I had this recurring dream. We were at the opera, Harvey and I.

(Pabich with Joanna Lu. TV lights.)

PABICH *(On camera)*: It's over. Already I can tell it's over. He asked me a question, a clear queer-baiting question, and the jury didn't bat an eye.

MILK'S FRIEND: I was laughing. Harvey was laughing.

PABICH *(On camera)*: Dan White's going to get away with murder.

LU *(On camera)*: Mr. Pabich . . .

MILK'S FRIEND: Then Harvey leant over and whispered: When you're watching *Tosca*, you know you're alive. That's when I'd wake up.

(Pabich rushes out, upset.)

GWENN: I remember the moment I heard Harvey had been shot— *(She breaks down)*

MILK'S FRIEND: And I'd realize—like for the first time all over again—he was dead.

(Blackout. Hyperrealistic sounds of high heels on marble, echoing, moving fast. Mumbled Hail Marys. Lights up slowly on Schmidt, Norman.)

SCHMIDT: From here I think the evidence will demonstrate that Dan White ran down to Denise's office, screamed at his aide to give him the key to her car.

And he left, went to a church, called his wife, went into St. Mary's Cathedral, prayed, and his wife got there, and he told her, the best he could, what he remembered he had done, and then they walked together to the Northern Police Station where he turned himself in; asked the officer to look after his wife, asked the officer to take possession of an Irish poster he was carrying . . .

(Screen: Cover of Uris book Ireland: A Terrible Beauty. *Desolate, haunting.)*

and then made a statement, what best he could recall had occurred.

(Lights. Falzon rises from his seat at prosecutor's table.)

FALZON: Why . . . I feel like hitting you in the fuckin' mouth. . . . How could you be so stupid? How?

WHITE: I . . . I want to tell you about it . . . I want to, to explain.

FALZON: Okay, if you want to talk to me, I'm gonna get my tape recorder and read you your rights and do it right.

NORMAN: The People at this time move the tape-recorded statement into evidence.

(Screen: "The Confession.")

FALZON: Today's date is Monday, November 27th, 1978. The time is presently 12:05. We're inside the Homicide Detail, Room 454, at the Hall of Justice. Present is Inspector Edward

Erdelatz, Inspector Frank Falzon and for the record, sir, your full name?

WHITE: Daniel James White.

(Lights.)

FALZON: Would you, normally in a situation like this, ah . . . we ask questions, I'm aware of your past history as a police officer and also as a San Francisco fireman. I would prefer. I'll let you do it in a narrative form as to what happened this morning if you can lead up to the events of the shooting and then backtrack as to why these events took place. *(Looks at Erdelatz)*

WHITE: Well, it's just that I've been under an awful lot of pressure lately, financial pressure, because of my job situation, family pressure because of ah . . . not being able to have the time with my family. *(Sobs)*

FALZON: Can you relate these pressures you've been under, Dan, at this time? Can you explain it to Inspector Erdelatz and myself.

WHITE: It's just that I wanted to serve

(Falzon nods.)

the people of San Francisco well and I did that. Then when the pressures got too great, I decided to leave. After I left, my family and friends offered their support and said, whatever it would take to allow me to go back into office—well, they would be willing to make that effort. And then it came out that Supervisor Milk and some others were working against me to get my seat back on the board. He didn't speak to me, he spoke to the city attorney but I was in the office and I heard the conversation.

I could see the game that was being played, they were going to use me as a *scapegoat*, whether I was a good supervisor or not, was not the point. This was a political opportunity and they were going to degrade me and my family and the job that I had tried to do an', an' more or less *hang me out to dry*. And I saw more and more evidence of this during the week when the papers reported that ah . . . someone else was going to be reappointed. The mayor told me he was going to call me before he made any decision, he never did that. I was troubled, the pressure, my family again, my, my son's out to a babysitter.

FALZON: Dan, can you tell Inspector Erdelatz and myself, what was your plan this morning? What did you have in mind?

WHITE: I didn't have any devised plan or anything, it's, I was leaving the house to talk, to see the mayor and I went downstairs, to, to make a phone call and I had my gun down there.

FALZON: Is this your police service revolver, Dan?

WHITE: This is the gun I had when I was a policeman. It's in my room an' ah . . . I don't know, I just put it on. I, I don't know why I put it on, it's just . . .

FALZON: You went directly from your residence to the mayor's office this morning?

WHITE: Yes, my, my aide picked me up but she didn't have any idea ah . . . you know that I had a gun on me or, you know, and I went in to see him an', an' he told me he wasn't going to, intending to tell me about it. Then ah . . . I got kind of fuzzy and then just my head didn't feel right and I, then he said: "Let's go into the, the back room and, and have a drink and talk about it."

FALZON: Was this before any threats on your part, Dan?

WHITE: I, I never made any threats.

FALZON: There were no threats at all?

WHITE: I, I . . . oh no.

FALZON: When were you, how, what was the conversation, can you explain to Inspector Erdelatz and myself the conversation that existed between the two of you at this time?

WHITE: It was pretty much just, you know, I asked, was I going to be reappointed. He said, no I am not, no you're not. And I

said, why, and he told me, it's a political decision and that's
the end of it, and that's it.

FALZON: Is this when you were having a drink in the back room?

WHITE: No, no, it's before I went into the back room and then he
could obviously see, see I was obviously distraught an' then
he said, let's have a drink an' I, I'm not even a drinker, you
know I don't, once in a while, but I'm not even a drinker.
But I just kinda stumbled in the back and he was all, he was
talking an' nothing was getting through to me. It was just
like a roaring in my ears an', an' then em . . . it just came to
me, you know, he . . .

FALZON: You couldn't hear what he was saying, Dan?

WHITE: Just small talk that, you know, it just wasn't registering.
What I was going to do now, you know, and how this would
affect my family, you know, an', an' just, just all the time
knowing he's going to go out an', an' lie to the press an', an'
tell 'em, you know, that I, I wasn't a good supervisor and
that people didn't want me an' then that was it. Then I, I just
shot him, that was it, it was over.

FALZON: What happened after you left there, Dan?

WHITE: Well, I, I left his office by one of the back doors an', I was
going down the stairs and then I saw Harvey Milk's aide an'
then it struck me about what Harvey had tried to do an' I
said, well I'll go talk to him. He didn't know I had, I had
heard his conversation and he was all smiles and stuff and I
went in and, you know, I, I didn't agree with him on a lot of
things, but I was always honest, you know, and here they
were devious. I started to say you know how hard I worked
for it and what it meant to me and my family an' then my
reputation as, as a hard worker, good honest person and he
just kind of smirked at me as if to say, too bad an' then, an'
then, I just got all flushed an', an' hot, and I shot him.

FALZON: This occurred inside your room, Dan?

WHITE: Yeah, in my office, yeah.

FALZON: And when you left there did you go back home?

WHITE: No, no, no I drove to the, the Doggie Diner on, on Van

Ness and I called my wife and she, she didn't know, she . . .

FALZON: Did you tell her Dan?

(Sobbing.)

WHITE: I called up, I didn't tell her on the phone. I just said she was work . . . see, she was working, son's at a baby-sitter, shit. I just told her to meet me at the cathedral.

FALZON: St. Mary's?

(Sobbing.)

WHITE: She took a cab, yeah. She didn't know. She knew I'd been upset and I wasn't even talking to her at home because I just couldn't explain how I felt and she had no, nothing to blame about it, she was, she always has been great to me but it was, just the pressure hitting me an' just my head's all flushed and expected that my skull's going to crack. Then when she came to the church, I, I told her and she kind of slumped and she, she couldn't say anything.

FALZON: How is she now do you, do you know is she, do you know where she is?

WHITE: I don't know now. She, she came to Northern Station with me. She asked me not to do anything about myself, you know that she, she loved me and she'd stick by me and not to hurt myself.

FALZON: Is there anything else you'd like to add at this time?

WHITE: Just that I've been honest and worked hard, never cheated anybody or, you know, I'm not a crook or anything an' I wanted to do a good job, I'm trying to do a good job an' I saw this city as it's going, kind of downhill an' I was always just a lonely vote on the board and try to be honest an', an' I just couldn't take it anymore an' that's it.

FALZON: Inspector Erdelatz?

ERDELATZ: Dan, right now are you under a doctor's care?

WHITE: No.

ERDELATZ: Are you under any medication at all?

WHITE: No.

ERDELATZ: When is the last time you had your gun with you prior to today?

WHITE: I guess it was a few months ago. I, I was afraid of some of the threats that were made an', I, I, just wanted to make sure to protect myself you know this, this city isn't safe you know and there's a lot of people running around an' well I don't have to tell you fellows, you guys know that.

ERDELATZ: When you left your home this morning Dan, was it your intention to confront the mayor, Supervisor Milk or anyone else with that gun?

WHITE: No, I, I, what I wanted to do was just, talk to him, you know, I, I ah, I didn't even know if I was going to be reappointed or not be reappointed. *Why do we do things, you know, why did I, I don't know.* No, I, I just wanted to talk to him that's all an' at least have him be honest with me an' tell me why he was doing it, not because I was a bad supervisor or anything but, you know, I never killed anybody before. I never shot anybody . . .

ERDELATZ: Why did . . .

WHITE: . . . I didn't even, I didn't even know if I wanted to kill him. I just shot him, I don't know.

ERDELATZ: What type of gun is that you were carrying, Dan?

WHITE: It's a .38, a two-inch .38.

ERDELATZ: And do you know how many shots you fired?

WHITE: Uh . . . no I don't, I don't. I, I out of instinct when I, I reloaded the gun ah . . . you know, it's just the training I guess I had, you know.

ERDELATZ: Where did you reload?

WHITE: I reloaded in my office when, when I was I couldn't out in the hall.

(Pause.)

ERDELATZ: And how many bullets did you have with you?

WHITE: I, I, I don't know, I ah . . . the gun was loaded an', an', I had some ah . . . extra shots you know, I just, I, 'cause, I kept the gun with, with a box of shells and just grabbed some.

ERDELATZ: Inspector Falzon?

FALZON: No questions. Is there anything you'd like to add, Dan, before we close this statement?

WHITE: Well it's just that, I never really intended to hurt anybody. It's just this past several months, it got to the point I couldn't take it and I never wanted the job for ego or, you know, perpetuate myself or anything like that. I was just trying to do a good job for the city.

FALZON: Inspector Erdelatz and I ah . . . appreciate your cooperation and the truthfulness of your statement.

(Lights change. White sobbing. Mary Ann White sobbing, jurors sobbing. Falzon moved.)

NORMAN: I think that is all. You may examine.

COURT: Do you want to take a recess at this time?

SCHMIDT: Why don't we take a brief recess?

COURT: Let me admonish you ladies and gentlemen of the jury, not to discuss this case among yourselves nor with anyone else, nor allow anyone to speak to you about the case, nor are you to form or express an opinion until the matter has been submitted to you.

(House lights up. Screen: "Recess.")

ACT TWO

IN DEFENSE OF MURDER

Audience enters. Screen: Documentary images of Milk and Moscone.

MOSCONE *(On video)*: My late father was a guard at San Quentin, and who I was visiting one day, and who showed to me, and then explained the function of, the uh, the uh death chamber. And it just seemed inconceivable to me, though I was pretty young at the time, that in this society that I had been trained to believe was the most effective and efficient of all societies, that the only way we could deal with violent crime would be to do the ultimate ourselves, and that's to governmentally sanction the taking of another person's life.*

*Monologues by Milk and Moscone excerpted from *The Times of Harvey Milk*, a film by Robert Epstein and Richard Schmeichen.

MILK *(On video)*: Two days after I was elected I got a phone call—
the voice was quite young. It was from Altoona, Pennsylva-
nia. And the person said, "Thanks." And you've got to elect
gay people so that that young child, and the thousands upon
thousands like that child, know that there's hope for a better
world. There's hope for a better tomorrow. Without hope,
they'll only gaze at those blacks, the Asians, the disabled, the
seniors, the us'es, the us'es. Without hope, the us'es give up.
I know that you cannot live on hope alone. But without it,
life is nor worth living. And you, and you, and you, gotta
give 'em hope. Thank you very much.*

*(Lights up. Courtroom. Falzon on witness stand. Dan White
at defense table sobbing. Mary Ann White behind him, sobbing. Five jurors sobbing.)*

WHITE *(Audio)*: Well, it's just that I never really intended to hurt
anybody. It's just this past several months, it got to the point
I couldn't take it and I never wanted the job for ego or, you
know, perpetuate myself or anything like that. I was just trying to do a good job for the city.
FALZON *(Audio)*: Inspector Erdelatz and I ah . . . appreciate your
cooperation and the truthfulness of your statement.

(Falzon switches tape off.)

NORMAN: I think that is all. You may examine.

*(Lights change. Screen: "Inspector Frank Falzon, Witness for
the Prosecution." Screen: "Act Two: In Defense of Murder.")*

SCHMIDT: Inspector Falzon, you mentioned that you had known
Dan White in the past, prior to November 27th, 1978?
FALZON: Yes, sir, quite well.
SCHMIDT: About how long have you known him?

FALZON:

>According to Dan, it goes way back to the days
>we attended St. Elizabeth's Grammar School together,
>   but
>we went to different high schools.
>I attended St. Ignatius, and he attended Riordan.
>He walked up to me one day at the Jackson
>   Playground,
>with spikes over his shoulders, glove in his hand,
>and asked if he could play on my team.
>I told him it was the police team,
>and he stated that he was a new recruit at Northern
>   Station,
>wanted to play on the police softball team,
>and since that day Dan White and I
>have been very good friends.

SCHMIDT: You knew him fairly well then, that is fair?

FALZON: As well as I know anybody, I believed.

SCHMIDT: Can you tell me, when you saw him first on November
27th, 1978, how did he appear physically to you?

FALZON:

>Destroyed. This was not the Dan White I had known,
>   not at all.
>That day I saw a shattered individual,
>both mentally and physically in appearance,
>who appeared to me to be shattered.
>
>Dan White, the man I knew
>prior to Monday, the 27th of November, 1978,
>was a man among men.

SCHMIDT: Knowing, with regard to the shootings of Mayor
Moscone and Harvey Milk, knowing Dan White as you did,
is he the type of man that could have premeditatedly and
deliberately shot those people?

NORMAN: Objection as calling for an opinion and conclusion.

COURT: Sustained.

SCHMIDT: Knowing him as you do, have you ever seen anything in his past that would lead you to believe he was capable of cold-bloodedly shooting somebody?

NORMAN: Same objection.

COURT: Sustained.

SCHMIDT: Your Honor, at this point I have anticipated that maybe there would be some argument with regard to opinions not only as to Inspector Falzon, but with a number of other witnesses that I intend to call, and accordingly I have prepared a memorandum of what I believe to be the appropriate law. *(Shows memo)*

COURT: I have no quarrel with your authorities, but I think the form of the questions that you asked were objectionable.

SCHMIDT: The questions were calculated to bring out an opinion on the state of mind and—I believe that a lay person, if he is an intimate acquaintance, surely can hazard such an opinion. I believe that Inspector Falzon, as a police officer, has an opinion.

COURT: Get the facts from this witness. I will let you get those facts, whatever they are.

SCHMIDT: All right, we will try that. Inspector Falzon, again, you mentioned that you were quite familiar with Dan White; can you tell me something about the man's character, as to the man that you knew prior to the—prior to November 27th, 1978?

NORMAN: Objection as being irrelevant and vague.

COURT: Overruled. *(To Falzon)* Do you understand the question?

FALZON: I do, basically, Your Honor.

COURT: All right, you may answer it.

NORMAN: Well, your Honor, character for what?

COURT: Overruled. *(To Falzon)* You may answer it.

FALZON:
> The Dan White that I knew prior to Monday,
> November 27, 1978,
> was a man who seemed to excel in pressure situations,

and it seemed that the greater the pressure, the more
    enjoyment that Dan had,
exceeding at what he was trying to do.

Examples would be in his sports life,
that I can relate to,
and for the first time in the history of the State of
    California,
there was a law enforcement softball tournament held
    in 1971.

The San Francisco Police Department entered
that softball tournament along with other major
    departments,
Los Angeles included,
and Dan White was not only named on the All-Star
    Team
at the end of the tournament,
but named the most valuable player.

He was just outstanding under pressure situations,
when men would be on base and that clutch hit was
    needed.

At the end of the tournament, a dinner was held,
the umpires were invited,
and one individual had umpired baseball games for
    over thirty years,
made the comment that Dan White
was the best ballplayer he had ever seen participate
in any tournament in South Lake Tahoe.

Another example of Dan White's attitude toward
    pressure
was that when he decided to run for the District 8
    supervisor's seat,

and I can still vividly remember the morning
he walked into the Homicide Detail and sat down to—
announced that he was gong to run for City
    Supervisor,

I said: "How are you going to do it, Dan?
Nobody heard of Dan White. How are you going to go
    out there,
win this election?"

He said: "I'm going to do it the way the people want
    it to be done,
knock on their doors, go inside, shake their hands,
let them know what Dan White stands for."

And he said: "Dan White is going to represent them.
There will be a voice in City Hall, you watch, I'll
    make it."

He did what he said he was going to do,
he ran, won the election.

SCHMIDT: Given these things that you mentioned about Dan White, was there anything in his character that you saw of him, prior to those tragedies of the 27th of November, that would have led you to believe that he would ever kill somebody cold-bloodedly?

NORMAN: Objection, irrelevant.

COURT: Overruled.

NORMAN: Let me state my grounds for the record.

COURT: Overruled.

NORMAN: Thank you, Judge. It's irrelevant and called for his opinion and speculation.

COURT: Overruled. *(To Falzon)* You may answer that.

FALZON: Yes, Your Honor.

I'm aware—I'm hesitating only because
there was something I saw in Dan's personality

that didn't become relevant to me
until I was assigned this case.

He had a tendency to run, occasionally,
from situations.
I saw this flaw, and I asked him about it,
and his response was that his ultimate goal
was to purchase a boat, just travel around the world,
get away from everybody,
and yet the Dan White that I was talking to
was trying to be involved with people,
constantly being a fireman,
being a policeman, being a supervisor.
He wanted to be helpful to people,
and yet he wanted to run away from them.
That did not make sense to me.

Today, this is the only flaw in Dan White's character
that I can cite up here, and testify about.

Otherwise, to me, Dan White was an exemplary
    individual,
a man that I was proud to know and be associated with.

SCHMIDT: Do you think he cracked? Do you think there was
    something wrong with him on November 27th?

NORMAN: Objection as calling for an opinion and speculation.

COURT: Sustained.

SCHMIDT: I have nothing further. *(Turns back)* Inspector, I have
    one last question. Did you ever see him act out of revenge
    the whole time you have known him?

NORMAN: Objection. That calls for speculation.

COURT: No, overruled, and this is as to his observations and con-
    tacts. Overruled.

FALZON:

            The only time Dan White could have acted out in
                revenge

is when he took the opposite procedure
in hurting himself,
by quitting the San Francisco Police Department.

SCHMIDT: Nothing further. Thank you, sir.

NORMAN: Inspector Falzon, you regard yourself as a close friend
to Mr. Daniel White, don't you?

FALZON: Yes, sir.

NORMAN: Do you regard yourself as a *very* close friend of Mr.
Daniel White?

FALZON: I would consider myself a close friend of yours, if that
can relate to you my closeness with Dan White.

(Pause. Norman uncomfortable.)

NORMAN: Of course, you haven't known me as long as you have
known Mr. Daniel White, have you, Inspector?

FALZON: Just about the same length of time, Counsel.

(Long pause.)

NORMAN: Inspector Falzon, while you've expressed some shock at
these tragedies, would you subscribe to the proposition that
there's a first time for everything?

FALZON: It's obvious in this case; yes, sir.

NORMAN: Thank you.

*(He sits. Falzon leaves the witness stand and takes his seat
beside him at the prosecutor's table.)*

The Prosecution rests.

*(Lights change. Screen: "The Prosecution Rests." Commotion
in court.)*

COURT: Order.

(Gavel. Lights. Freitas alone.)

FREITAS:

I was the D.A.
Obviously in some respects, the trial ruined me.
This trial . . .

*(Screen: Pictures of White as fire hero. Screen: "The Defense."
Subliminal music. Lights up. Four character witnesses dressed
as City Supervisor (suit), fire chief, police officer, fireman.)*

SHERRATT *(Fire chief)*: Dan White was an excellent firefighter. In
fact, he was commended for a rescue at Geneva Towers. The
award hasn't been given to him as yet, uh . . .
FREDIANI *(Fireman)*: Dan White was the valedictorian of the Fire
Department class. He was voted so by members of the class.

(Screen: Still of White as valedictorian.)

MILK'S FRIEND: When I was in the hospital, what galled me most
was the picture of Dan White as the All-American Boy.
SHERRATT: but a meritorious advisory board and fire commission
were going to present Mr. White with a Class C medal.

(Screen: Still of White as fire hero.)

FREDIANI: Everybody liked Dan.
SCHMIDT: Did you work with Dan as a policeman?
SULLIVAN *(Policeman)*: Yes, I did.
MILK'S FRIEND: Maybe as a gay man, I understand the tyranny of
the All-American Boy.

(Screen: Still of White as police officer.)

FREDIANI: He loved sports and I loved sports.

(Screen: Still of White as Golden Gloves boxer.)

SULLIVAN: Dan White as a police officer, was a very fair police officer on the street.

MILK'S FRIEND: Maybe because I am so often his victim.

GWENN: I followed the trial in the papers.

SCHMIDT: Having had the experience of being a police officer, is it unusual for persons that have been police officers to carry guns?

SULLIVAN: Uh, pardon me, Mr. Schmidt?

GWENN: I thought then something was wrong with this picture.

SCHMIDT: I say, it is uncommon that ex-police officers would carry guns?

GWENN: Something was wrong, we thought, when the Chief Inspector of Homicide became the chief character witness for the defense.

SULLIVAN: No, it is a common thing that former police officers will carry guns.

GWENN: Why didn't the Chief Inspector of Homicide ask Dan White how he got into City Hall with a loaded gun?

SCHMIDT: Without a permit?

SULLIVAN: Yes.

GWENN: White reloaded after shooting the mayor. If it was "reflex," police training, why didn't he reload again after shooting Harvey Milk?

SCHMIDT: Is there anything in his character that would have led you to believe he was capable of shooting two persons?

NORMAN: Objection.

COURT: Overruled.

SULLIVAN: No, nothing whatever.

GWENN:
>And what can explain the coup de grâce shots
>White fired into the backs of their heads as they lay
>   there
>helpless on the floor?

DOLSON *(Supervisor)*: Dan in my opinion was a person who *saved* lives.

GWENN: Where is the prosecution?

(Pause.)

FREITAS: I mean, I would have remained in politics. Except for this. I was voted out of office.

SCHMIDT *(To Dolson)*: Supervisor Dolson, you saw him on November 27th, 1978, did you not?

DOLSON: I did.

FREITAS: In hindsight, you know, I would have changed a lot of things.

SCHMIDT: What did you see?

FREITAS: But hindsight is always perfect vision.

(Screen: Still of White as City Supervisor outside City Hall.)

DOLSON:

What I saw made me want to cry . . .

Dan was always so neat.

Looked like a marine on parade;

and he made me feel ashamed of the way I usually looked,

and here he was, this kid, who was badly disheveled,

looking like he had been crying.

GWENN: What pressures were you under *indeed?*

DOLSON:

And he had his hands cuffed behind him,

which was something I never expected to see.

He looked crushed, looked like he was absolutely *devastated. (Sobs)*

GWENN:

As the *"victim"* sat in the courtroom

shielded by bulletproof glass,

we heard of policemen and firemen sporting
"Free Dan White" T-shirts
as they raised a hundred thousand dollars for Dan
    White's defense fund,
and the same message began appearing
in spray paint on walls around the city.
FREE DAN WHITE.

DOLSON:

I put my arm around him, told him that everything
    was going to be all right,
but how everything was going to be all right,
I don't know. *(He is deeply moved)*

(Mary Ann White sobs.)

GWENN: And the trial was still happening,
SCHMIDT *(Deeply moved)*: Thank you. I have nothing further.

(Dolson sobs.)

GWENN: but the tears at the Hall of Justice are all for Dan White.

(All exit. Lights change. Freitas alone in empty courtroom, nervous, fidgeting.)

FREITAS:

I was voted out of office.

(Screen: "Joseph Freitas, Jr., Former D.A.")

Well, I'm out of politics and I don't know whether
I'll get back into politics
because it certainly did set back my personal ah . . .
aspirations as a public figure dramatically.
I don't know . . .

You know, there was an attempt to not allow our
    office to prosecute the case
because I was close to Moscone myself.
And we fought against that.
I was confident— *(Laughs)*
I chose Tom Norman because he was the senior
    homicide prosecutor
for twenty years and he was quite successful at it.
I don't know . . .

There was a great division in the city then, you know.
The city was divided all during that period.
George was a liberal Democrat and Dick Hongisto.
I was considered a liberal Democrat
and George as you'll remember was elected
mayor over John Barbagelata who was the leader
of what was considered the right in town.
And it was a narrow victory.
So, after his election, Barbagelata persisted in
    attacking them
and keeping
I thought—
keeping the city divided.
It divided on emerging constituencies like
the gay constituency.
That's the one that was used to cause the most divisive
emotions more than any other.
So the divisiveness in the city was there.

I mean that was the whole point of this political fight
between Dan White
and Moscone and Milk:
The fight was over who controlled the city.

The right couldn't afford to lose Dan.
He was their swing vote on the Board of Supervisors.

He could block the Milk/Moscone agenda.
That was why Milk didn't want Dan White on the board.
So, it was political, the murders.

Maybe I should have,
again in hindsight, possibly Tom,
even though his attempts to do that may have been
    ruled inadmissable,
possibly Tom should have been a little stronger in
    that area.
But again, at the time . . . I mean,
even the press was shocked at the outcome . . .

But—
Well, I think that what the jury had already bought
was White's background—
Now that's what was really on trial.
Dan White sat there and waved his little American flag
and they acquitted him.
They convicted George and Harvey.
Now if this had been a poor black or a poor Chicano
or a poor white janitor who'd been fired,
or the husband of an alleged girlfriend of Moscone's
I don't think they would have bought the diminished
    capacity defense.

But whereas they have a guy who was a member of a
county Board of Supervisors who left the police
    department,
who had served in the Army, who was a fireman,
who played baseball—
I think that's what they were caught up in—
that kind of person *must* have been crazy to do this.
I would have interpreted it differently.
Not to be held to a higher standard, but uh . . .
that he had all the tools to be responsible.

One of the things people said was:
"Why didn't you talk more about George's
    background, his family life, etc.?"
Well . . .
One of the reasons is that Tom Norman did know that,
had he opened up that area,
they were prepared,
yeah—
they were prepared to smear George—
bring up the incident in Sacramento.
With the woman—
(And other things.)
It would be at best a wash,
so why get into it?
If you know they're going to bring out things
that aren't positive.
We wanted to let the city heal. We—
And after Jonestown . . .
Well—it would have been the
city on trial.

If the jury had stuck to the facts alone,
I mean, the confession alone was enough to convict
    him . . .
I mean, look at this kid that shot Reagan,
it was the same thing. All the way through that,
they said, my friends—
"Well, Christ, look at what the prosecutors went
    through on this one, Joe—"
It's tragic that this has to be the kind of experience
that will make you feel better.

And then about White being antigay
well . . .
White inside himself may have been antigay, but
that Milk was his target . . .

As I say—*Malice was there.*
Milk led the fight to keep White off the board,
which makes the murder all the more rational.
I know the gay community thinks the murder was
    antigay:
political in that sense. But
I think, they're wrong.

Ya know, some people—in the gay community—
ah—even said I threw the trial.
Before this, I was considered a great friend
to the gay community.
Why would I want to throw the trial,
this trial—
in an election year?

Oh, there were accusations you wouldn't believe . . .

At the trial, a woman . . . it may have been one of the
    jurors—
I can't remember . . .
Actually said—
"But what would Mary Ann White do without her
    husband?"
And I remember my outrage.
She never thought,
"What will Gina Moscone do without George?"
I must tell you that it's hard for me to talk about a lot
of these things,
all of this is just the—just
the tip of the iceberg . . .

We thought—Tommy and I—Tom Norman and I—
We thought it was an open-and-shut case
of first-degree murder.

(Lights.)

NORMAN: It wasn't just an automatic reaction when he fired those
    last two shots into George Moscone's *brains* was it, Doctor?
COURT: Let's move on, Mr. Norman. You are just arguing with the
    witnesses now.
NORMAN: Your Honor—
COURT: Let's move on.

*(Screen: "The Psychiatric Defense." Lights up. Psychiatrists,
conservative dress, in either separate witness stands or a
multiple stand unit.)*

SOLOMON: I think he was out of control and in an unreasonable
    stage. And I think if the gun had held, you know, maybe
    more bullets, maybe he would have shot more bullets. I
    don't know.
LUNDE: This wasn't just some mild case of the blues.
SOLOMON: I think that, you know, maybe Mr. Moscone would
    have been just as dead with one bullet. I don't know.
JONES: I think he was out of control.
DELMAN: Yes.
NORMAN: George Moscone was shot four times, Doctor. The gun
    had five cartridges in it. Does that change your opinion in
    any way?
SOLOMON: No. I think he just kept shooting for awhile.

(Norman throws his notes down.)

SCHMIDT: Now, there is another legal term we deal with in the
    courtroom, and that is variously called "malice" or "malice
    aforethought." And this must be present in order to convict
    for murder in the first degree.
JONES: Okay, let me preface this by saying I am not sure how mal-
    ice is defined. I'll give you what my understanding is.

In order to have malice, you would have to be able to do certain things: to be able to be intent to kill somebody unlawfully. You would have to be able to do something for a base and antisocial purpose. You would have to be aware of the duty imposed on you not to do that, not to unlawfully kill somebody or do something for a base, antisocial purpose, that involved a risk of death, and you would have to be able to act, despite having that awareness of that, that you are not supposed to do that, and so you would have to know that you are not supposed to do it, and then also act despite—keeping in mind that you are not supposed to do it.

Is that your answer—your question?

SCHMIDT: I think so.

(Pause.)

JONES *(Laughs)*:

> I felt that he had the capacity to do the first three:
> that he had the capacity to intend to kill,
> but that doesn't take much, you know,
> to try to kill somebody,
> it's not a highfalutin mental state.
>
> I think he had the capacity to do something for a base
> and antisocial purpose.
> I think he had the capacity to know that there was a
> duty
> imposed on him not to do that,
> but *I don't think he had the capacity to hold that notion*
> *in his mind while he was acting*;
> so that I think that the depression,
> plus the moment, the tremendous emotion of the
> moment,
> with the depression,
> reduced his capacity for conforming conduct.
> *(Pause)*

As ridiculous as this sounds, even to the point of
     instituting
to kill the mayor,
what he describes is more simply—
is striking out, not intending to kill,
well, obviously, if you have a gun in your hand,
and you are striking out,
you know you are going to cause at least great bodily
     harm,
if not death,
but as near as I can come to the state of mind at that
     time,
he was just, you know, striking out.
(Pause)
In fact, I asked him:
"Why didn't you hit them?"
And he was flabbergasted that I asked such a thing,
because it was contrary to his code of behavior,
you know, he was taken aback, kind of—
hit them seemed ridiculous to him—
because it would have been so unfair,
since he could have defeated them so easily
in a fistfight.

SCHMIDT: Thank you. *(He sits; to Norman)* You may examine.

NORMAN: Doctor Jones, when let off at City Hall the accused was
     let off at the Polk Street entrance and then walked a block
     and a half to Van Ness Avenue. Why wouldn't he just enter
     City Hall through the main entrance?

JONES: He got towards the top of the stairs, then looked up, saw the
     metal detector and thought: "Oh, my goodness, I got that gun."

(Pause.)

NORMAN: Doctor, why would he care whether there was a metal
     detector there, and that a gun would have been discovered
     upon his person?

JONES: Well, I would presume that would mean some degree of hassle. I mean, I presume that the metal detector would see if somebody is trying to bring a weapon in.

NORMAN: That is usually why they have it. *(Pause)* Did he realize at that time that he was unlawfully carrying a concealable firearm?

JONES: I presume so.

NORMAN: Dr. Jones, if it's a fact that Dan White shot George Moscone twice in the body, and that when George Moscone fell to the floor disabled, he shot twice more into the right side of George Moscone's head at a distance of between twelve and eighteen inches, he made a decision at that time, didn't he, to either discharge the gun into the head of George Moscone, or not discharge the gun into the head of George Moscone?

JONES: If decision means he behaved in that way, then, yes.

NORMAN: Well, didn't he have to make some kind of choice based upon some reasoning process?

JONES: Oh, no, not based on reasoning necessarily. I think—I don't think that I—you know, great emotional turmoil in context of major mood disorder—he was enraged and anxious and frustrated in addition to the underlying depression, I think that after Moscone says "How's your family?" or "What's your wife going to do?" at that point, I think that it's—it's over.

NORMAN: It's over for George Moscone.

SOLOMON: I think that if you look at the gun as a transitional object, you can see that transitional objects are clung to in—in situations of great—of anxiety and insecurity, as one sees with children—

NORMAN: Doctor, are you telling us that a person who has lived an otherwise law-abiding life and an otherwise moral life could not premeditate and deliberate as is contemplated by the definition of first-degree murder?!

SOLOMON: I'm not saying that absolutely. Obviously, it's more difficult for a person who lives a highly moral life. And this individual, Dan White, had, if you want—a hypertrophy complex. Hypertrophy meaning overdeveloped. Rigidly. Morally. Overdeveloped—

But I would say in general, yes.

I don't think you'd even kill Mr. Schmidt if you lost this case.

NORMAN: It's unlikely.

SOLOMON: You may be very angry, but I don't think you will do it because I think you are probably a very moral and law-abiding citizen, and I think if you did it, I would certainly recommend a psychiatric examination, because I think there would be a serious possibility that you had flipped. *(Pause)* It's most interesting to me how split off his feelings were at this time.

LUNDE: Dan White had classical symptoms that are described in diagnostic manuals for depression and, of course, he had characteristics of compulsive personality, which happens to be kind of a bad combination in those sorts of people.

NORMAN *(Frustrated)*: You are aware that he took a gun with him when he determined to see George Moscone, a loaded gun?

SOLOMON: Yes.

NORMAN: Why did he take that gun, in your opinion. Dr. Solomon?

SOLOMON: I might say that I think there are symbolic aspects to this.

COURT: Let's move on to another question.

NORMAN: Well, Your Honor . . .

COURT: Let's move on.

NORMAN *(Frustrated)*: All right. Dr. Delman, after he went in the building armed with a gun through a window and went up to see George Moscone, at the time he came in to see George Moscone, do you feel that he was angry with George Moscone?

DELMAN: Yes.

NORMAN: When George Moscone told him that he wasn't going to appoint him, do you think that that brought about and increased any more anger?

DELMAN: Yes.

NORMAN: All right. Now there was some point in there when he shot George Moscone, isn't that true?

DELMAN: Yes.

NORMAN: Do you know how many times he shot him?

DELMAN: I believe it's four.

NORMAN: Well, Doctor, do you put any significance upon the circumstances that he shot George Moscone twice in the head?

DELMAN: The question is, "Do I put any significance in it?"

NORMAN: Yes.

DELMAN: I really have no idea why that happened.

NORMAN: Well, Doctor, do you think he knew that if you shot a
man twice in the head that it was likely to surely kill him?

DELMAN: I'm sure that he knew that shooting a man in the head
would kill him, Mr. Norman.

NORMAN: Thank you! *(He sits)*

SCHMIDT: But, it is your conclusion, Doctor, that Dan White could
not premeditate or deliberate, within the meaning we have
discussed here, on November 27th, 1978?

DELMAN: That is correct.

(Norman slaps hand to head. Lights.)

BLINDER:

I teach forensic psychiatry.

I teach about the uses and abuses of psychiatry in the
judicial system.

The courts tend to place psychiatry in a position

where it doesn't belong. Where it becomes the sole
arbiter

between guilt and innocence.

There is also a tendency in the stresses of the
adversary system

to polarize a psychiatric statement so that a
psychiatrist finds himself trying to put labels on
normal stressful behavior,

and *everything* becomes a mental illness.

And I think that is an abuse.

(Refers to his notes)

Dan White found City Hall rife of corruption.

With the possible exceptions of Dianne Feinstein and
   Harvey Milk,
the supervisors seemed to make their judgments,
   their votes,
on the basis of what was good for them,
rather than what was good for the city.
And this was a very frustrating thing for Mr. White:
to want to do a good job for his constituents and find he
was continually defeated.

In addition to these stresses, there were
attacks by the press
and there were threats of literal attacks on supervisors.
He told me a number of supervisors like himself
carried a gun to scheduled meetings.
Never any relief from these tensions.

Whenever he felt things were not going right,
he would abandon his usual program of exercise and
   good nutrition
and start gorging himself on junk foods:
Twinkies, Coca-Cola.

Soon Mr. White was just sitting in front of the TV.
Ordinarily, he reads. (Mr. White has always been an
   identifiable Jack London adventurer.)

But now, getting very depressed about the fact he
   would not be reappointed,
he just sat there before the TV
binging on Twinkies

(Screen: "The Twinkie Defense.")

He couldn't sleep.
He was tossing and turning on the couch in the living
   room

so he wouldn't disturb his wife on the bed.

Virtually no sexual contact at this time.
He was dazed, confused, had crying spells,
became increasingly ill,
and wanted to be left alone.

He told his wife:
"Don't bother cooking any food for me.
I will just munch on these potato chips."

Mr. White stopped shaving
and refused to go out of the house
to help Denise rally support.

He started to receive information that he would not
   be reappointed
from unlikely sources.
This was very stressing to him.

Again, it got to be cupcakes, candy bars.
He watched the sun come up on Monday morning.

Finally, at nine o'clock Denise called.
He decides to go down to City Hall.
He shaves and puts on his suit.
He sees his gun—lying on the table.
Ammunition.
He simultaneously puts these in his pocket.
Denise picks him up.
He's feeling anxious about a variety of things.
He's sitting in the car hyperventilating,
blowing on his hands, repeating:
"Let him tell me to my face why he won't reappoint
   me.
Did he think I can't take it?

I am a man.
I can take it."

He goes down to City Hall, and I sense that time is
    short
so let me bridge this by saying that as I believe
it has been testified to,
he circumvents the mental [*sic*] detector,
goes to the side window,
gets an appointment with the mayor.
The mayor almost directly tells him,
"I am not going to reappoint you."

The mayor puts his arm around him saying:
"Let's have a drink.
What are you going to do now, Dan?
Can you get back into the Fire Department?
What about your family?
Can your wife get her job back?
What's going to happen to them now?"

(Pause. Lights up low on Mary Ann White.)

Somehow this inquiry directed to his family struck a
    nerve.
The mayor's voice started to fade out and Mr. White
    felt
"As if I were in a dream."
He started to leave and then inexplicably turned
    around
and like a reflex
drew his revolver.
He had no idea how many shots he fired.

The similar event occurred
in Supervisor Milk's office. [*sic*]

He remembers being shocked by the sound of the gun
going off for the second time like a cannon.
He tells me that he was aware that he engaged in a
    lethal act,
but tells me he gave no thought to his wrongfulness.
As he put it to me:
"I had no chance to even think about it."

He remembers running out of the building,
driving, I think, to church,
making arrangements to meet his wife,
and then going from the church
to the Police Department.

(Pause. Blinder exhausted.)

SCHMIDT: Doctor, you have mentioned the ingestion of sugar
and sweets and that sort of thing. There are certain theories
with regard to sugar and sweets and the ingestion thereof,
and I'd like to just touch on that briefly with the jury. Does
that have any significance, or could it possibly have any
significance?

BLINDER *(Turns to jury)*: First, there is a substantial body of evidence that in susceptible individuals, large quantities of
what we call junk food, high-sugar-content food with lots
of preservatives, can precipitate antisocial and even violent
behavior.

There have been studies, for example, where they have
taken so-called career criminals and taken them off all their
junk food and put them on meat and potatoes and their
criminal records immediately evaporate. *(Pause)* It's con-
tradictory and ironic, but the way it works is that for such a
person, the American Dream is a Nightmare. For somebody
like Dan White.

SCHMIDT: Thank you, Doctor.

(Lights fade on psychiatrists. Pause. Blazing white lights up on Mary Ann White. She is almost blinded. She comes forward.)

You are married to this man, is that correct?
MARY ANN: Yes.
SCHMIDT: When did you first meet him?
MARY ANN: I met him— *(Sobbing)*
SCHMIDT: If you want to take any time/ /just let us know.*
MARY ANN *(Pulling herself together)*: I met him in April 1976 . . .
SCHMIDT: And you were married/ /and you took a trip?
MARY ANN:

> Yes. Yes, we went to Ireland on our honeymoon
> because Danny just had this feeling that Ireland was
>   like a place
> that was just peaceful.

> He just really likes—loves—everything about Ireland
>   and so we— *(Sobbing)*

SCHMIDT: Excuse me.

MARY ANN: —so we went there/ /for about five wee—
SCHMIDT: During that period did you notice anything/ /unusual about his behavior?
MARY ANN:

> Yes, I mean, you know, when we went I thought—
>   went thinking
> it was going to be kind of romantic,
> and when we got there, it was all of a sudden,
> he went into almost like a two-week-long mood,
> like I had seen before, but I had never seen one, I guess,
> all the way through,

*Note: / / denotes overlapping dialogue; next speaker starts, first speaker continues.

because when we were going out, I might see him for
a day,

and being a fireman, he would work a day,

and then I wouldn't see him,

and when we got to Ireland . . .

I mean, I was just newly married and I thought:
"What did I do?"

SCHMIDT: After he was on the board, did you notice these
moods/ /become more frequent?

MARY ANN:

Yes, he had talked to me about how hard the job was
on him.

You know, from June he started to talk about how it
was.

Obviously you can sense when you are not sleeping
together,

and you are not really growing together,

and he would say,

"Well, I can't—I can't really think of anyone else
when I don't even like myself."

And I said, "It's just him.

He's not satisfied with what I'm doing

and I don't like myself/ /and so I can't . . . "

SCHMIDT: Did you see him on the morning of . . . November 27th?

MARY ANN: Yes/ /I did.

SCHMIDT: And at that time did he indicate what he was going to
do/ /that day?

MARY ANN:

It was just, he was going to stay *home.*

(With uncharacteristic force) He wasn't leaving the
house.

(Beat. Schmidt looks to jury.)

SCHMIDT: Later that morning, did you receive a call/ /to meet
him somewhere?

MARY ANN:

> Yes. I did. Yes, I went to St. Mary's Cathedral.
> I went
> and I saw him
> and he walked over toward me and I—
> I could see that he had been crying,
> and I, I just kind of looked at him
> and he just looked at me
> and he said,
> he said,
> "I shot the mayor and Harvey."

SCHMIDT: Thank you.

> *(Dan White sobs. Schmidt puts hand on White's shoulder.
> Mary Ann White stumbles off the stand to her husband.
> White shields his eyes. She looks as if she will embrace him.)*

> The defense is prepared to rest at this time.

> *(Mary Ann White sobs. Hyperrealistic sound of high heels
> echoing on marble. Mumbled Hail Marys.)*

COURT:

> Let me admonish you ladies and gentlemen of the
>   jury,
> not to discuss this case among yourselves nor with
>   anyone else,
> nor to allow anyone to speak to you about the case,
> nor are you to form or express an opinion until the
>   matter has been submitted to you.

> *(All exit. Screen: "The Defense Rests.")*

MILK'S FRIEND *(Enters alone)*:

> We got back from the airport the night of the 27th
> And my roommate said:

> There's going to be a candlelight march.
> By now, we thought it had to have reached City Hall.
> So we went directly there. From the airport to City Hall.
> And there were maybe seventy-five people there.
> And I remember thinking:
> My God is this all anybody . . . cared?
>
> Somebody said: No, the march hasn't gotten here yet.
>
> So we then walked over to Market Street,
> which was two or three blocks away.
> And looked down it.
> And Market Street runs in a straight line out to the
>   Castro area.
> And as we turned the corner,
> there were people as wide as this wide street
> As far as you could see.[§]

(Screens flooded with the lights of candles. Documentary footage of the march. We see what Milk's friend describes. Music: Barber Adagio. The entire company enters holding candles.)

YOUNG MOTHER: *(After a long while)*:
> Thousands and thousands of people,
> And that feeling of such loss.[§]

(Music continues.)

GWENN:
> It was one of the most eloquent expressions of a
> community's response to violence
> that I have ever seen . . . [§]

[§]Dialogue from *The Times of Harvey Milk*, a film by Robert Epstein and Richard Schmeichen.

A MOURNER *(Black armband)*:
>   I'd like to read from the transcript of Harvey Milk's
>   political will.
>   *(Reads)* This is Harvey Milk speaking on Friday,
>   November 18.
>   This tape is to be played only in the event of my
>   death
>   by assassination.

(Screen: Pictures of Milk.)

>   I've given long and considerable thought to this,
>   and not just since the election.
>   I've been thinking about this for some time prior to
>   the election
>   and certainly over the years.
>   I fully realize that a person who stands for what I
>   stand for—
>   a gay activist—
>   becomes a target for a person who is insecure,
>   terrified,
>   afraid or very disturbed themselves.

(White enters, stops.)

>   Knowing that I could be assassinated at any moment
>   or any time,
>   I feel it's important that some people should
>   understand
>   my thoughts.
>   So the following are my thoughts, my wishes, my
>   desires,
>   whatever.
>   I'd like to pass them on and played for the
>   appropriate people.
>   The first and most obvious concern is that

if I was to be shot and killed,
the mayor has the power,
George Moscone,

(Screen: Pictures of Moscone, the funeral, the mourners, the widow.)

of appointing my successor . . .
to the Board of Supervisors.
I cannot prevent some people
from feeling angry and frustrated and mad,
but I hope that they would not demonstrate violently.
If a bullet should enter my brain,
let that bullet destroy every closet door.

(Gavel. All mourners blow out candles. White sits. Blackout. Screen: "The People's Rebuttal." Screen: "Dr. Levy, Psychiatrist for the Prosecution." Lights up.)

LEVY: I interviewed the defendant several hours after the shootings of November 27th.

In my opinion, one can get a more accurate diagnosis the closer one examines the suspect after a crime has been committed.

At that time, it appeared to me that Dan White had no remorse for the death of George Moscone.

It appeared to me, he had no remorse for the death of Harvey Milk.

There was nothing in my interview which would suggest to me there was any mental disorder.

I had the feeling that there was some depression but it was not depression that I would consider as a diagnosis.

In fact, I found him to be less depressed than I would have expected him to be.

At that time I saw him, it seemed that he felt himself to be quite justified. *(Looks to notes)*

I felt he had the capacity to form malice.

I felt he had the capacity to premeditate. And . . .

I felt he had the capacity to deliberate,

to arrive at a course of conduct weighing
considerations.

NORMAN: Did you review the transcript of the proceeding
wherein the testimonies of Drs. Jones, Blinder, Solomon,
Delman and Lunde were given?

LEVY: Yes. *(Pause)* I found nothing in them that would cause me
to revise my opinion.

NORMAN: Thank you, Dr. Levy. *(Sits)*

SCHMIDT *(Stands)*: Dr. Levy, are you a full professor at the University of California?

LEVY: No. I am an associate clinical professor.

(Schmidt smiles, looks to jury.)

SCHMIDT: May I inquire of your age, sir?

LEVY: I am fifty-five.

SCHMIDT: Huh. *(Picking up papers)* Doctor, your report is dated
November 27, 1978, is it not?

LEVY: Yes.

SCHMIDT: And yet the report was not written on November 27,
1978?

LEVY: No. It would have been within several days/ / of that time.

SCHMIDT: And then it was dated November 27, 1978?

LEVY: Yes.

SCHMIDT: Well, regardless of the backdating, or whatever, when
did you come to your forensic conclusions?

LEVY: I'd say the conclusions would have been on November
27th.

SCHMIDT: And that was after a two-hour talk with Dan White?

LEVY: Yes.

SCHMIDT: Doctor, would it be fair to say that you made some snap
decisions?

LEVY: I don't believe/ /I did.

SCHMIDT: Did you consult with any other doctors?

LEVY: No.

SCHMIDT: Did you review any of the witnesses' statements?

LEVY: No.

SCHMIDT: Did you consult any of the material that was available to you, save and except for the tape of Dan White on the same date?

LEVY: No. That was all that was made available to me/ /at that time.

SCHMIDT: Now I don't mean to be facetious, but this is a fairly important case, is that fair?

LEVY: I would certainly think so,/ /yes.

SCHMIDT: But you didn't talk further with Mr. White?

LEVY: No. I was not requested to.

SCHMIDT: And you didn't request to talk to him further?

LEVY: No. I was not going to do a complete assessment.

SCHMIDT: Well, in fact, you didn't do a complete assessment, is that fair?

LEVY: I was not asked to do a complete assessment.

COURT: Doctor, you are fading away.

LEVY: *I was not asked to do a complete assessment.*

SCHMIDT: Thank you.

(Blackout. Commotion in court.)

She wants to tell the story so it's not responsive to the questions.

(Lights up. Screen: "Supervisor Carol Ruth Silver, Witness for the Prosecution.")

SILVER *(Very agitated, speaking fast, heated)*: He asked in what other case did a dispute between Dan White and Harvey Milk arise! And it was the Polk Street closing was another occasion when Harvey requested that Polk Street, which is a heavily gay area in San Francisco, I am sure everybody knows, and on Halloween had traditionally had a huge number of people in costumes and so forth down there and has/ /traditionally been recommended for closure by the Police Department and—

SCHMIDT: I am going to object to this, Your Honor.

SILVER: It was recommended—

COURT: Just ask the next question.

SILVER: I am sorry.

NORMAN: Did Mr. Milk and Mr. White take positions that were opposite to each other?

SILVER: Yes.

NORMAN: Was there anything that became, well, rather loud and perhaps hostile in connection or consisting between the two?

SILVER: Not loud but very hostile. You have to first understand that this street closure was recommended by the police chief and had been done customarily in the years past/ /and is, was—came up as an uncontested issue practically.

SCHMIDT: Your Honor, I again—

COURT: Please, just make your objection.

SCHMIDT: I'd like to.

COURT: Without going through contortions.

SCHMIDT: There is an objection.

COURT: All right. Sustained.

NORMAN: Miss Silver, did you know, or did you ever see Mr. White to appear to be depressed or to be withdrawn?

SILVER: No.

NORMAN: Thank you. *(Sits)*

(Silver flabbergasted, upset.)

COURT: All right. Any questions, Mr. Schmidt?

SCHMIDT: Is it *Miss* Silver?

SILVER: Yes.

(Schmidt looks to jury, smiles. Lights up on Moscone's friend.)

SCHMIDT: Miss Silver, you never had lunch with Dan White, did you?

SILVER: Did I ever have lunch?

MOSCONE'S FRIEND: George was socially brilliant in that he could find the injustice.

SCHMIDT: I mean the two of you?

SILVER: I don't recall having done so/ /but I—

MOSCONE'S FRIEND: His mind went immediately to what can we do?

SCHMIDT: Did you socialize frequently?

MOSCONE'S FRIEND: What can we practically do?

SILVER: No, when his son was born/ /I went to a party at his house and that kind of thing.

SCHMIDT: Did Mr. Norman contact you last week, or did you contact him?

MOSCONE'S FRIEND: Rather like the image of Robert Kennedy in Mississippi in 1964.

SILVER: On Friday morning I called his office to—

MOSCONE'S FRIEND: Y'know, he'd never seen that kind of despair before

SILVER: because I was reading the newspaper—

SCHMIDT: Yes.

MOSCONE'S FRIEND: but when he saw it/ /he said,

SILVER: And it appeared to me that—

COURT: Don't tell us!

MOSCONE'S FRIEND: "This is *intolerable.*"

SILVER: I am sorry.

MOSCONE'S FRIEND: And then he did something about it.

(Beat.)

COURT: The jurors are told not to read the newspaper, and I am hoping that they haven't/ /read the newspapers.

SILVER: I apologize.

COURT: Okay.

SCHMIDT: Miss Silver—

COURT: I am sorry, I didn't want to cut her off—

SILVER: No, I understand.

COURT: from any other answer.

SCHMIDT: I think she did complete the answer, Judge. In any event, you contacted Mr. Norman, did you not?

SILVER: Yes, I did.

SCHMIDT: And at that time, you offered to Mr. Norman to round up people who could say that Dan White never looked depressed at City Hall, is that fair?

SILVER: That's right. Well, I offered to testify to that effect and I suggested that there were other people/ /who could similarly testify to that fact.

SCHMIDT: In fact, you expressed it though you haven't sat here and listened to the testimony in this courtroom?

SILVER: No, I have never been here before Friday when I was subpoenaed/ /and spent some time in the jury room.

SCHMIDT: But to use your words, after having read what was in the paper, you said that the defense sounded like *(As if he were spitting on his mother's grave)* "bullshit" to you?

SILVER: That's correct.

(Subliminal music.)

DENMAN: I thought I would be a chief witness for the prosecution.

SCHMIDT: Would that suggest then that perhaps you have a bias in this case?

DENMAN: What was left unsaid was what the trial should have been about.

SILVER: I certainly have a bias.

SCHMIDT: You are a political enemy of Dan White's, is that fair?

SILVER: No, that's not true.

DENMAN: Before, y'know, there was a lot of talk about assassinating the mayor among thuggish elements of the/ /Police Officers Association.

SCHMIDT: Did you have any training in psychology or psychiatry?

DENMAN: And those were the cops Dan White was closest to.

SILVER: No more than some of the kind of C.E.B. courses lawyer's psychology for lawyers/ /kind of training.

DENMAN: I think he knew a lot of guys would think he did the right thing and yeah they would make him a hero.

SCHMIDT: I mean, would you be able to diagnose, say, *manic depression depressed type*, or could you distinguish that from *unipolar depression*?

SILVER: No.

(Pause.)

DENMAN: I was Dan White's jailer for seventy-two hours after the assassinations.

SCHMIDT: Did you ever talk to him about his dietary habits or anything like that?

DENMAN: There were no tears.

SILVER: I remember a conversation about nutrition or something like that, but I can't remember/ /the substance of it.

SCHMIDT: I don't have anything further.

DENMAN: There was no shame.

COURT: Any redirect, Mr. Norman?

NORMAN: Yes.

DENMAN: You got the feeling that he knew exactly what he was doing and there was no remorse.

(Pause.)

NORMAN: Miss Silver, you were asked if you had a bias in this case. You knew Harvey Milk very well and you liked him, didn't you?

SILVER: I did; and also George Moscone.

NORMAN: Miss Silver, speaking of a bias, had you ever heard the defendant say anything about getting people of whom Harvey Milk numbered himself?

(Lights up on Milk's friend.)

SILVER: In the Polk Street debate—

MILK'S FRIEND:

> The night Harvey was elected,
> I went to bed early
> because it was more happiness than I had been
>   taught
> to deal with.

SILVER:

> Dan White got up and gave—
> a long diatribe—

MILK'S FRIEND:

> Next morning we put up signs saying "Thank You."

SILVER:

> Just a—a very unexpected and very uncharacteristic of
>   Dan,
> long hostile speech about how gays and their lifestyles
> had to be contained and we can't/ /
> *encourage* this kind of thing and—

SCHMIDT: I am going to object to this, Your Honor.

COURT: Sustained, okay.

MILK'S FRIEND:

> During that, Harvey came over and told me
> that he had made a political will
> because he expected he'd be killed.
> And then in the same breath, he said (I'll never
>   forget it):
> "It works, it works . . . "

NORMAN: All right . . . that's all.

MILK'S FRIEND: The system works/ / . . .

NORMAN: Thank you.

(Pause.)

DENMAN: When White was being booked, it all seemed fraternal.
One officer gave Dan a pat on the behind when he was
booked, sort of a "Hey, catch you later, Dan" pat.

COURT: Any recross?

DENMAN: Some of the officers and deputies were standing around with half-smirks on their faces. Some were actually laughing.

SCHMIDT: Just a couple.

DENMAN:

> The joke they kept telling was,
> "Dan White's mother says to him when he comes home,
> 'No, dummy, I said milk and baloney, not Moscone!'"

(Pause.)

SCHMIDT: Miss Silver, you are a part of the gay community also, are you?

SILVER: Myself?

SCHMIDT: Yes.

SILVER: You mean, am I gay?

SCHMIDT: Yes.

SILVER: No, I'm not.

SCHMIDT: I have nothing further.

MOSCONE'S FRIEND: George would have said, "This is intolerable," and he'd have done something about it.

COURT: All right . . . You may leave as soon as the bailiff takes the microphone off.

(Silver sits for a while, shaken.)

COURT: Next witness, please.

DENMAN:

> I don't know . . .
> All I can say is, if Dan White was as depressed
> as the defense psychiatrists said he was before he
>   went to City Hall,
>   then shooting these people sure seemed to clear up
>   his mind . . .

(Silver exits towards door. Lu with TV lights.)

LU *(On camera)*: Miss Silver, Supervisor Silver, would you like to elaborate on Mr. White's antigay feelings or hostility to Harvey Milk or George Moscone?

SILVER: No comment, right now.

(Silver distraught, pushes through crowd, rushes past.)

LU *(On camera)*: Did you feel you were baited, did you have your say?

SILVER: *(Blows up)*: I said I have no comment at this time!!! *(Exits)*

COURT: Mr. Norman? Next witness?

NORMAN: Nothing further. Those are all the witnesses we have to present.

COURT: The People rest?

NORMAN: Yes.

COURT: Does the Defense have any witnesses?

SCHMIDT *(Surprised)*: Well, we can discuss it, Your Honor. I am not sure there is anything to rebut.

(Lights. Commotion in court. Screen: "The People Rest."
Lights up on Schmidt at a lectern, a parish priest at a pulpit. Screen: "Summations.")

> *(In a sweat, going for the home stretch)*
> I'm nervous. I'm very nervous.
> I sure hope I say all the right things.
> I can't marshal words the way Mr. Norman can—
> But—I believe strongly in things.
>
> Lord God! I don't say to you to forgive Dan White.
> I don't say to you to just
> let Dan White walk out of here a free man.
> He is guilty.
> But the degree of responsibility is the issue here.

The state of mind is the issue here.
It's not who was killed; it's why.
It's not who killed them; but why.
The state of mind is the issue here.

Lord God! The pressures.
Nobody can say that the things that happened to him
days or weeks preceding
wouldn't make a reasonable and ordinary man
at least mad,
angry in some way.

Surely—surely, that had to have arisen, not to kill,
not to kill, just to be mad, to act irrationally,
because if you kill, when you are angry, or under the
     heat of passion,
if you kill, then the law will punish you,
and you will be punished by God—
God will punish you,
but the law will also punish you.

Heat of passion fogs judgment, makes one act
     irrationally,
in the very least,
and my God,
that is what happened at the very least.

Forget about the mental illness,
forget about all the rest of the factors that came into
     play
at the same time:
Surely he acted irrationally, impulsively—out of some
     passion.

Now . . . you will recall at the close of the
     prosecution's case,

it was suggested to you this was a calm, cool,
     deliberating,
terrible terrible person
that had committed two crimes like these,
and these are terrible crimes,
and that he was emotionally stable at that time
and there wasn't anything wrong with him.

He didn't have any diminished capacity.
Then we played these tapes he made directly after
he turned himself in at Northern Station.

My God,
that was not a person that was calm and collected and
     cool
and able to weigh things out.
It just wasn't.

The tape just totally fogged me up the first time I
     heard it.
It was a man that was, as Frank Falzon said, broken.
Shattered.
This was not the Dan White that everybody had
     known.

Something happened to him and he snapped.
That's the word I used in my opening statement.
Something snapped here.

The pot had boiled over here,
and people that boil over in that fashion,
they tell the truth.

Have the tape played again, if you can't remember
     what was said.
He said in no uncertain terms,

"My God,
why did I do these things?
What made me do this?
How on earth could I have done this?
I didn't intend to do this.
I didn't intend to hurt anybody.
My God,
what happened to me?
Why?"

Play the tape.
If everybody says that tape is truthful, play the tape.
I'd agree it's truthful.

With regard to the reloading and some of these little
discrepancies that appeared to come up.
I am not even sure of the discrepancies, but if there
    were
discrepancies,
listen to it in context.
(Picks up transcript, reads)
"Where did you reload?"
"I reloaded in my office, I think."
"And then did you leave the mayor's office?"
"Yes, then I left the mayor's office."
That doesn't mean anything to me at all.
It doesn't mean anything to me at all.
And I don't care where the reloading took place!

But listen to the tape.
It says in no uncertain terms,
"I didn't intend to hurt anybody.
I didn't intend to do this.
Why do we do things?"
I don't know.

It was a man desperately trying to grab at
    something . . .

"What happened to me?
How could I have done this?"

If the District Attorney concedes
that what is on that tape is truthful,
and I believe that's the insinuation we have here,
then, by golly,
there is voluntary manslaughter,
nothing more and nothing less.

Now, I don't know what more I can say.
He's got to be punished
and he will be punished.
He's going to have to live with this for the rest of his
    life.
His child will live with it
and his family will live with it,
and God will punish him,
and the law will punish him,
and they will punish him severely.

But please, please.
Just justice.
That's all.
Just justice here.
(He appears to break for a moment)
Now I am going to sit down and very soon,
and that's it for me.

And this is the type of case where, I suppose,
I don't think Mr. Norman is going to do it,
but you can make up a picture of a dead man,
or two of them for that matter,

and you can wave them around and say
somebody is going to pay for this
and somebody *is* going to pay for this.

Dan White is going to pay for this.
But it's not an emotional type thing.
I get emotional about it, but
you can't because you have to be objective about the
    facts . . .

I get one argument.
I have made it.
And if I could get up and argue again,
God,
we'd go on all night.

I just hope that—
I just hope that you'll come to the same conclusion
that I have come to.
And thank you for listening to me.

(Schmidt holds the lectern, then sits.)

NORMAN:

Ladies and gentlemen of the jury, having the burden
    of proof,
I am given an opportunity a second time to address
    you.

I listened very carefully to the summation just given
    you.
It appears to me, members of the jury,
to be a very facile explanation and rationalization
as to premeditation and deliberation.
The evidence that has been laid before you
screams for murder in the first degree.

What counsel for the defense has done is suggest to
    you
to *excuse* this kind of conduct and call it something
    that it isn't,
to call it voluntary manslaughter.

Members of the jury, you are the triers of fact here.
You have been asked to hear this tape recording
    again.
The tape recording has been aptly described
as something very moving. We all feel a sense of
    sympathy,
a sense of empathy for our fellow man, but you are
    not to let
sympathy influence you in your judgment.

To reduce the charge of murder to something less—
to reduce it to voluntary manslaughter—
means you are saying that this was not murder.
That this was an intentional killing of a human being
upon a quarrel, or heat of passion.
But ladies and gentlemen,
that quarrel must have been so extreme
at the time
that the defendant could not—
was incapable of forming
those qualities of thought which are
malice, premeditation and deliberation.
But the evidence in this case doesn't suggest that at
    all.
Not at all.

If the defendant had picked up a vase or something
that happened to be in the mayor's office
and hit the mayor over the head and killed him
you know,

you know that argument for voluntary manslaughter
might be one which you could say the evidence admits
a reasonable doubt. But—

Ladies and gentlemen:
The facts are:
It was *he*—Dan White—who brought the gun to City
    Hall.
The gun was not there.
It was *he* who brought the extra cartridges for the gun;
they were not found there.

He went to City Hall and when he got there
he went to the Polk Street door.

There was a metal detector there.
He knew he was carrying a gun.
He knew that he had extra cartridges for it.

Instead of going through the metal detector,
he *decided* to go around the corner.
He was capable at that time of expressing anger.
He was capable of, according to the doctor—
well, parenthetically, members of the jury,
I don't know how they can look in your head and tell
    you
what you are able to do. But—
They even said that he was capable of knowing at that
    time
that if you pointed a gun at somebody and you fired
    that gun
that you would surely kill a person.

He went around the corner,
and climbed through a window into City Hall.

He went up to the mayor's office.
He appeared, according to witnesses,
to act calmly in his approach, in his speech.

He chatted with Cyr Copertini;
he was capable of carrying on a conversation
to the extent that he was able to ask her how she was,
after having asked to see the mayor.
(Looks to audience)
He stepped into the mayor's office.
After some conversation,
he shot the mayor twice in the body.
Then he shot the mayor in the head twice
while the mayor was disabled on the floor.
The evidence suggests that in order to shoot the
     mayor
twice in the head
he had to *lean down* to do it.
(He demonstrates, looks to jury)
Deliberation is premeditation.
It has malice.
I feel stultified to even bring this up.
This is the *definition* of murder.

He reloaded the gun.
Wherever he reloaded the gun,
it was *he* who reloaded it!

He did see Supervisor Milk,
whom he knew was acting against his appointment
and he was capable of expressing anger in that
     regard.

He entered the supervisors' area
(a block from the mayor's office across City Hall)

and was told, "Dianne wants to see you."
He said, "That is going to have to wait a moment,
I have something to do first."

Then he walked to Harvey Milk's office,
put his head in the door and said,
"Can I see you a moment, Harv?"
The reply was, "Yes."

He went across the hall and put three bullets
into Harvey Milk's body,
one of which hit Harvey directly in the back.
When he fell to the floor disabled,
two more were delivered to the back of his head.

Now what do you call that but premeditation and
    deliberation?
What do you call that realistically
but a cold-blooded killing?
Two *cold-blooded executions.*
It occurs to me that if you don't call them that,
then you are ignoring the objective evidence
and the objective facts here.

Members of the jury, there are circumstances here
which no doubt bring about anger,
maybe even rage, I don't know,
but the manner in which that anger was felt
and was handled
is *socially something that cannot be approved.*

Ladies and gentlemen,
the quality of your service is reflected in your verdict.

(Norman sits. Joanna Lu, at door, stops Schmidt. TV lights.)

LU *(On camera)*: Mr. Schmidt, do you—

SCHMIDT: Yes.

LU *(On camera)*: Do you feel society would feel justice is served if
     the jury returns two manslaughter verdicts?

SCHMIDT *(Wry smile)*: Society doesn't have anything to do with it.
     Only those twelve people in the jury box.

COURT:

>   Ladies and gentlemen of the jury,
>   Now that you have heard the evidence,
>   we come to that part of the trial where you are
>   instructed
>   on the applicable law.
>
>   In the crime of murder of the first degree
>   the necessary concurrent mental states are:
>   Malice aforethought, premeditation and deliberation.
>
>   In the crime of murder of the second degree,
>   the necessary concurrent mental state is:
>   Malice aforethought.
>
>   In the crime of voluntary manslaughter,
>   the necessary mental state is:
>   An intent to kill.
>
>   Involuntary manslaughter is an unlawful killing
>   without malice aforethought
>   and without intent to kill.
>
>   The law does not undertake to limit or define the
>   kinds of passion
>   which may cause a person to act rashly.
>   Such passions as desperation, humiliation,
>   resentment,

anger, fear, or rage,
or any other high-wrought emotion . . .
can be sufficient to reduce the killings to manslaughter
so long as they are sufficient to obscure the reason
and render the average man likely to act rashly.
There is no malice aforethought
if the killing occurred upon a sudden quarrel
or heat of passion.

There is no malice aforethought
if the evidence shows that due to diminished capacity
caused by illness, mental defect, or intoxication,
the defendant did not have the capacity
to form the mental state constituting malice
    aforethought,
even though the killing was intentional,
voluntary, premeditated and unprovoked.

(A siren begins. Screen: Images of the riot at City Hall—broken glass, cop cars burning, riot police, angry faces. Audio: Explosions.)

GWENN *(On video)*: In order to understand the riots, I think you have to understand that the Dan White verdict did not occur in a vacuum—

COURT: Mr. Foreman, has the jury reached verdicts/ /in this case?

GWENN: that there were and are other factors which contribute to a legitimate rage that was demonstrated dramatically at our symbol of Who's Responsible, City Hall.

(Screen: Images of City Hall being stormed. Line of police in riot gear in front.)

FOREMAN: Yes, it has, Your Honor.

GWENN: The verdict came down and the people rioted.

COURT: Please read the verdicts.

GWENN: The people stormed City Hall, burned police cars.

(Screen: Image of City Hall. Line of police cars in flames.)

FOREMAN *(Reading)*: The jury finds the defendant Daniel James
   White guilty of violating Section 192.1 of the penal code.

GWENN:
   Then the police came into our neighborhood.
   And the police rioted.

FOREMAN: Voluntary manslaughter, for the slaying of Mayor
   George Moscone.

*(Mary Ann White gasps. Dan White puts head in hands. Ex-
plosion. Riot police enter.)*

GWENN:
   The police came into the Castro and assaulted gays.
   They stormed the Elephant Walk Bar.
   One kid had an epileptic seizure and was almost
      killed for it.
   A cop drove a motorcycle up against a phone booth
   where a lesbian woman was on the phone,
   blocked her exit
   and began beating her up.

COURT: Is this a unanimous verdict of the jury?

FOREMAN: Yes, it is, Judge.

GWENN *(Off video)*: I want to talk about when people are pushed
   to the wall.

COURT: Will each juror say "yea"/ /or "nay"?

(Violence on stage.)

YOUNG MOTHER: What about the children?

MOSCONE'S FRIEND:
   I know who George offended.
   I know who Harvey offended.

JURORS *(On tape)*: Yea, yea, yea/ /yea, yea, yea.

MOSCONE'S FRIEND: I understand the offense.

YOUNG MOTHER: What do I tell my kids?

GWENN: Were the ones who are responsible seeing these things?

YOUNG MOTHER: That in this country you serve more time for robbing a bank than for killing two people?

JURORS *(On tape)*: Yea, yea, yea/ /yea, yea, yea.

GWENN: Hearing these things?

MILK'S FRIEND: I understand the offense.

GWENN: Do they understand about people being pushed to the wall?

YOUNG MOTHER: Accountability?

(Yea's end.)

MILK'S FRIEND:

> Assassination.
> I've grown up with it.
> I forget it hasn't always been this way.

YOUNG MOTHER:

> What do I say?
> That two lives are worth seven years and eight
>   months/ /in jail?

MILK'S FRIEND:

> I remember coming home from school in sixth
>   grade—
> JFK was killed—
> six years later, Martin Luther King.
> It's a frame of reference.

(Explosion.)

COURT: Will the foreman please read the verdict for the second count?

DENMAN: It's a divided city.

MOSCONE'S FRIEND: The resentment of change is similar. I can understand that. It's my hometown. *(Irish accent)* They're changin' it, y'know?

DENMAN:

> The people are getting caught up in the change
> and didn't know.

MOSCONE'S FRIEND: You grew up in old Irish Catholic/ /San Francisco . . .

DENMAN:

> Then didn't know why it was—
> like Armageddon.

MOSCONE'S FRIEND: and Bill Malone ran the town and "these guys" are disruptin' everything.

FOREMAN: The jury finds the defendant Daniel James White guilty of Section 192.1 of the penal code, voluntary manslaughter, in the slaying of Supervisor Harvey Milk.

(Dan White gasps. Mary Ann White sobs. Norman, flushed, head in hands. Explosions. Violence ends. Riot police control the crowd. TV lights.)

BRITT *(On camera)*: No—I'm optimistic about San Francisco.

COURT: Is this a unanimous decision by the jury?

FOREMAN: Yes, Your Honor.

BRITT: I'm Harry Britt. I was Harvey Milk's successor.

CARLSON: If he'd just killed the mayor, he'd be in jail today.

YOUNG MOTHER: To this jury, Dan White was their son.

MILK'S FRIEND: Harvey Milk lit up my universe.

YOUNG MOTHER: What are we teaching our sons?

(White raises his hands to his eyes, cries. Mary Ann White, several jurors sob.)

BRITT:

> Now, this is an example I don't use often because
> people will misunderstand it.
> But when a prophet is killed . . .

It's up to those who are left
to build the community or the church.

MOSCONE'S FRIEND:
Dan White believed in the death penalty;
he should have gotten the death penalty.

YOUNG MOTHER:
How do you explain/ /the difference?

BRITT:
But I have hope and as Harvey said,
"You can't live without hope."

MOSCONE'S FRIEND: I mean, that son of a bitch/ /killed somebody
I loved.

MILK'S FRIEND: It was an effective/ /assassination.

MOSCONE'S FRIEND: I loved the guy.

(Pause.)

MILK'S FRIEND: They always are.

GWENN *(Quiet)*: Do they know about Stonewall?

BRITT: Our revenge is never to forget.

(The foreman walks to the defense table, gives Schmidt a handshake. Norman turns away.)

LU *(On camera)*: Dan White was examined by the psychiatrist at the state prison. They decided against therapy. Dan White had no apparent signs of mental disorder . . . Dan White's parole date was January 6, 1984. When Dan White left Soledad Prison on January 6, 1984, it was five years, one month, and eight days since he turned himself in at Northern Station after the assassinations of Mayor George Moscone and Supervisor Harvey Milk. Mayor Dianne Feinstein, the current mayor of San Francisco, has tried to keep Dan White out of San Francisco during his parole for fear he will be killed.

(The cop enters. Sister Boom Boom enters.)

BOOM BOOM: Dan White! It's 1984 and Big Sister is watching you.

LU *(On camera)*: Dan White reportedly plans to move to Ireland after his release.

MOSCONE'S FRIEND:

What do you do with your feelings of revenge?

With your need for retribution?

BRITT: We will never forget.

(Screen: Riot images freeze. A shaft of light from church window.)

BOOM BOOM: I would like to close with a reading from the Book of Dan. *(Opens book)* Take of this and eat, for this is my defense. *(Raises a Twinkie. Eats it. Exits)*

LU *(On camera)*: Dan White was found dead of carbon monoxide poisoning on October 21, 1985 at his wife's home in San Francisco, California.

(Lights change. Dan White faces the court.)

COURT: Mr. White, you are sentenced to seven years and eight months, the maximum sentence for these two counts of voluntary manslaughter. The Court feels that these sentences for the taking of life are completely inappropriate but that was the decision of the legislature.

Again, let me repeat for the record:

Seven years and eight months is the maximum

sentence

for voluntary manslaughter, and this is the law.

(Gavel. Long pause. White turns to the audience/jury.)

WHITE:

I was always just a lonely vote on the board.

I was just trying to do a good job for the city.

(Long pause. Audio: Hyperrealistic sounds of high heels on marble. Mumbled Hail Marys. Rustle of an embrace. Sister Boom Boom enters. Taunts police. Police raise riot shields. Blackout. Screen: "Execution of Justice." Gavel echoes.)

END OF PLAY

GREENSBORO

(A REQUIEM)

Overleaf: Jon DeVries, Michael Countryman, Philip Seymour Hoffman and Deborah Hedwall in McCarter Theatre's world premiere production. Photo by T. Charles Erickson.

This play is dedicated to Arthur Mann
and John Hope Franklin who marched together
from Selma to Montgomery with Dr. King

Special thanks to Sally Bermanzohn for permission to use material from her doctoral dissertation "Survivors of the Greensboro Massacre."

I gratefully acknowledge the following people for their contribution to this play:

Lewis Pitts
Dr. Martha A. Nathan
Kathryn Watterson
Rev. Nelson Johnson
Sally Alvarez
Dr. Paul Bermanzohn
Willena Cannon
Ned Canty
Jean Chapman
Bobby Daye
Oskar Eustis
Prof. John Hope Franklin
Doris Gordon
Loretta Greco
Kate Greene
Joyce Johnson
Eva Mae Jones

Gail Korotkin
Michael Lupu
Nancy Malkiel
Carolyn McAllaster
Brian Mitchell
Eugene R. Palmore
Imani Parker
Shirley Richardson
Dale Sampson
Karine Schaefer
John Spencer
Skipp Sudduth
Flint Taylor
Maria Tucci
Signe Waller
Floris C. Weston

Greensboro (A Requiem) received its world premiere on February 6, 1996 at the McCarter Theatre. The production was designed by John Boesche, with sets by Robert Brill, costumes by Catherine Homa-Rocchio, lights by Pat Collins and original music by Baikida Carroll. Mark Wing-Davey directed the following cast:

INTERROGATION OFFICER
DR. PAUL BERMANZOHN, a survivor
LEWIS PITTS, lawyer for the plaintiffs 1
SKINHEAD   Michael Countryman

EDWARD DAWSON   Jeffrey De Munn

ROLAND WAYNE WOOD
DAVID DUKE
LAWYER FOR GOLDBERG 2
JUDGE 3
VIRGIL GRIFFIN   Jon DeVries

SALLY BERMANZOHN, a survivor 4   Lisa Eichhorn

SIGNE WALLER, widow of Dr. Jim Waller 5
DR. MARTY NATHAN, widow of 6
   Dr. Michael Nathan
JANE, a survivor 7   Deborah Hedwall

DAVID MATTHEWS, a Klansman
ANONYMOUS KLANSMAN
/ FBI AGENT GOLDBERG   8
CHAPMAN, lawyer for the defense 9
MINISTER   Philip Seymour Hoffman

REVEREND NELSON JOHNSON,
    a survivor
BIG GEORGE, a survivor   Robert Jason Jackson

INTERROGATION OFFICER
DEMONSTRATOR
AMIR, a survivor
MINISTER   Stanley Wayne Mathis

INTERVIEWER   Angie Phillips

RONNIE, a survivor
FLORIS CAUCE WESTON, widow of
    Cesar Cauce
DORIS GORDON, a survivor
JOYCE JOHNSON, wife of Reverend
    Nelson Johnson   Myra Lucretia Taylor

ROSE, a survivor   Carol Woods

A bare stage. Projection surfaces.

  The play can be performed by an ensemble of eleven.

  This is a documentary.

  The time is the present and the remembered past.

Some names have been changed at the interviewees' request.

A slash mark (/) in the script indicates that the next speaker's line begins at that point, overlapping the current line.

  In some cases, multiple overlaps are indicated with asterisks. For instance, in the following segment, the line "How do we fight these dogs?" overlaps the previous speech beginning at the word "tarred"; and the line "Do we stay home behind closed doors and tremble?" overlaps beginning at the word "ridden":

  voice 2: They have shot and lynched thousands of black people /* tarred and feathered black and white union organizers /** ridden in the night shooting into people's homes.

  voice 3: *How do we fight these dogs?

  voice 4: **Do we stay home behind closed doors and tremble?

RONNIE, a survivor, African-American

JOYCE JOHNSON, wife of Reverend Nelson Johnson, African-American

FLORIS CAUCE WESTON, widow of Cesar Cauce, African-American

DORIS GORDON, a survivor, African-American

ROSE, a survivor, African-American

SIGNE WALLER, widow of Dr. Jim Waller

DR. MARTY NATHAN, widow of Dr. Michael Nathan

JANE, a survivor

INTERVIEWER

SALLY BERMANZOHN, a survivor

REVEREND NELSON JOHNSON, a survivor, African-American

BIG GEORGE, a survivor, African-American

EDWARD DAWSON, Klansman

LEWIS PITTS, lawyer for the plaintiffs

SKINHEAD

INTERROGATION OFFICER

DR. PAUL BERMANZOHN, a survivor

KLANSMAN

DAVID MATTHEWS, Klansman

FBI AGENT GOLDBERG

CHAPMAN, lawyer for the defense

MINISTER

VIRGIL GRIFFIN, Klansman
DAVID DUKE
ROLAND WAYNE WOOD, Klansman
JUDGE
LAWYER FOR GOLDBERG
AMIR, a survivor, African-American
INTERROGATION OFFICER, African-American
MINISTER
MORDECHAI LEVEY, Voice-Over

ACT ONE

On screen: "The play consists entirely of verbatim interview material, courtroom transcripts, public record and personal testimony. All of the play's characters are real people."

In blackness, the company (without actors playing Dawson, Griffin and Matthews) sings "It's So Hard to Get Along," a song of infinite sorrow. Rose, a black woman in her fifties, leads.

COMPANY *(Singing a cappella)*:
      It's so hard to get along,
      My Lord, it's so hard to get along.
      It's so hard to get along,
      Oh, just can't hardly get along.
      Just can't hardly get along.
      Hm-mmm.

(Spoken)
I'm gonna say that one more time for those of you
    who didn't understand it.
It's so hard to get along,
My Lord, it's so hard to get along.
It's so hard to get along,
Oh, just can't hardly get along.
I just can't, just can't hardly get along.
Hm-mmm.

Master hear me, while I'm weeping and body-bound
So many trials and tribulations
But I'll make it home somehow.
My Lord, I got to pray to get along,
My Lord, I got to pray to get along.
Oh yeah, pray to get along,
Oh, Lord, just can't hardly get along.
I just can't, just can't hardly get along.
Hm-mmm.

Listen. I got enemies camped all around me,
Tryin' to make it down here on my own.
Every tear that I shed way down here
It ain't nothin' but my train fare home.
My Lord, we got to cry to get along,
My Lord, we got to cry to get along.
Whoa, we got to cry to get along,
Oh, just can't hardly get along.
I just can't, just can't hardly get along.
Hm-mmm.

Hard to get along,
My Lord, it's so hard to get along.
Whoa, it's so hard to get along,
Oh, just can't hardly get along.

I just can't, just can't hardly get along.
Hm-mmm.

So hard to get along,
My Lord, it's so hard to get along,
Oh, just can't hardly get along.
I just can't, just can't hardly get along.
Hm-mmm.

(Lights up slowly. Nelson Johnson stands, head down. He looks up.)

NELSON: Something happened in Greensboro, North Carolina I think you should know about.

(On screen: "November 3, 1979, Greensboro, North Carolina." "Eighty-Eight Seconds."
In blackness, very quietly, we hear the song "We Shall Not Be Moved." Image on screen: Demonstrators at an anti-Klan rally surround an effigy of a Klansman.
The cast is in a line: Only their faces are lit as images of the demonstration and massacre are projected on screens. Nelson is not in the line.)

November 3rd, 1979. A group of people, many of us members of the Communist Workers' Party, were organizing black and white workers in the local textile mills. This was a time when the Ku Klux Klan was on the rise again in North Carolina. We organized a demonstration and rally against the Klan for the morning of November 3rd.

ALL: DEATH TO THE KLAN!

NELSON: The march was to start at 11:00 A.M. at Morningside Homes, an almost entirely black working-class neighborhood where most of the people worked in the nearby textile mills.

ALL: DEATH TO THE KLAN!

(Nelson joins them.

The following sequence is an aural re-creation of the actual march and massacre. The pace is very quick and many of the lines are overlapped. The massacre is not acted out.)

VOICE 1 *(As Sally)*: For a hundred years the Klan has beaten / murdered and raped.

VOICE 2 *(As Floris)*: They have shot and lynched thousands of black people, /* tarred and feathered black and white union organizers, /** ridden in the night shooting into people's homes.

VOICE 3 *(As Paul)*: *How do we fight these dogs?

VOICE 4 *(As Signe)*: **Do we stay home behind closed doors and tremble?

VOICE 5: Do we say ridiculous things like . . . /*

VOICE 6: "This is a quarrel between two hate groups?"

VOICE 7 *(As Rose)*: *Do we make public statements to the press saying we deplore violence / then do nothing?

NELSON: THE KLAN MUST NOT BE ALLOWED TO GROW!

VOICE 8: They have to be exposed for what they are—servants / of the ruling bourgeoisie.

VOICE 9: They should be physically beaten and chased out of town.

VOICE 1: *This is the only language they understand.*

VOICE 2: Armed self-defense is the only defense.

ALL: DEATH TO THE KLAN!!

VOICE 4: We call on the people to join with us to SMASH THE KLAN!

(They all begin to chant "Death to the Klan!")

VOICE 3: Come to the W.V.O. anti-Klan conference! SMASH THE KLAN!

(The chanting continues.

Images flash on the screen: A line of cars, rebel plates on cars, a rebel flag, an arm with a Nazi tattoo, a Klan insignia, men in pickup trucks, an effigy of a Klansman, Communist Workers' Party signs, "Death to the Klan" posters.)

VOICE 2: Here comes / the Klan!
DAWSON: You asked for the Klan, you communist sons of bitches, /*
you got the Klan./**
*VOICE 10: Come on, come on. Get out.

(Signal shot. A woman [Voice 2] screams.)

**VOICE 5: Move it out, move it out. /*
VOICE 10: Come on, come on out.

("Death to the Klan" chant begins to fade out.
On screen: A man with a shotgun, cigarette dangling out of his mouth. Other Klansmen with long guns, shotguns. People fleeing.
We hear children crying. Screams. Gunshots.)

MATTHEWS: Show me a nigger with some guts and I'll show /
you a Klansman with a gun!/**
VOICE 1: They've got guns! /
DAWSON: They've / got Roy.
*VOICE 7: Hit the ground!
**VIRGIL GRIFFIN: Move it, move it!

("Death to the Klan" chant has finished by now.
Sound: Series of gunshots. Image: Cesar Cauce shot. Paul Bermanzohn shot. Mike Nathan shot.
Sound: Screams. Chaos. Image: Jim Waller shot. Bill Sampson shot.
Sound: Cracking of wood on Sandy Smith's head.
Sound: Three single shots, then irregular set of three.)

VOICE 2: Take care of the children, / I can't move.

VIRGIL GRIFFIN: Let's get the hell out of here, come on / Jerry before we get killed.

MATTHEWS: I got three of 'em, I got three of 'em.

(Sound: Car wheels screeching. Image: Finally, a still of Sandy Smith, slumped against a wall, bullet between her eyes. Newsmen, cameramen running. Long pause.)

NELSON: Oh God, my God.

(Brief pause.)

VOICE 10: Nelson! Nelson!

VOICE 2 *(Overlapping)*: Where the heck are the /* damn cops! /**

*VOICE 1: Where are the cops?

**VOICE 4: We don't want / the cops, we want justice.

VOICE 3: They had it planned, / they had it planned.

VOICE 2: Help us, help us, he's dead, / help us.

VOICE 10: We need an ambulance / soon right here.

VOICE 4: Put your hand over the hole in his head.

VOICE 8 *(Reporter)*: You kiss my ass. / You started this shit, you put your hand on the hole in his head.

VOICE 1: It's the Klan. I'm not gonna hush, it's my husband, / mother fuckin' Klan came in here.

VOICE 4 *(Signe)*: Long live the Communist Workers' Party, long live /*

(Sound: Sirens.)

the working class. In spite of you goddamn cops there's gonna be a /** socialist revolution.

*VOICE 7: Mommy, Mommy! The police are back.

**VOICE 1: The cops did this.

VOICE 2 *(Floris)*: Officer, I think my husband / is alive. I'm concerned no one is helping.

VOICE 1: The Klan and the state got together and planned this, that's why there were . . . no cops here, / do you hear me.

VOICE 10: The state protects the Klan /* and this makes it clear. Goddamn bourgeoisie did this! /**

*VOICE 4: They came through, they opened fire, they opened fire on us, and we fired back to protect ourselves.

**NELSON: We declare war! / WAR! WAR! *(He continues chanting "WAR!")*

VOICE 7: And the police did this directly or indirectly; they set it up.

NELSON: WAR! *(He stops the chant)*

(Silence.)

ROSE *(Very softly)*:
        It's so hard to get along, my Lord
        It's so hard to get along, my Lord
        It's so . . .

CHORUS *(Joining her)*: Hummmm

(Nelson comes forward. Mourners exit, still humming.)

NELSON: In eighty-eight seconds, the Klan shot thirteen people. They killed five of us. No Klansman was shot.

(Blackout. On screen: "Greensboro, North Carolina. The Present. Reverend Nelson Johnson and Interviewer."
"Extremist Informant.")

INTERVIEWER: So how come I never heard about this? Why don't I know about the massacre?

NELSON: Well, the hostages were taken in Iran the day after the Greensboro event.

INTERVIEWER: Oh . . .

NELSON: So, it got pretty much pushed off the front page.

INTERVIEWER: Right . . .

NELSON: Now, see this dive here? This is where the Klan and Nazis had breakfast on the morning of November 3, here at this dive right off the interstate. Then they all got together at a Klansman's house, a friend of Eddie Dawson. Eddie Dawson is a key figure here.

(Lights up on Eddie Dawson.)

INTERVIEWER: Oh yes, I know. So, tell me about him.

NELSON: Well, where do I start—uh—he was a member of the Klan's Inner Circle since 1969—

INTERVIEWER: The Inner Circle?

NELSON: The Klan's murder squad.

(A beat. She looks at him. He nods.)

NELSON: The FBI approached him after they found out he'd had a falling out with the Klan . . .

INTERVIEWER: Oh really.

NELSON: . . . and asked him to become an informant. He informed on the Klan for over eight years *(A beat)* The FBI even labeled him an "extremist informant."

INTERVIEWER: *Extremist* informant . . .

NELSON: Absolutely. He had an incredible record of violence—convicted twice for cross-burnings and violent night riding, that kind've thing. *(A beat)* Then in the late seventies he was terminated by the FBI.

INTERVIEWER: After the COINTELPRO investigation?

NELSON: Right.

INTERVIEWER: But how did he end up working for the Greensboro police?

NELSON: Well, okay, when we started organizing against the Klan in '79, the police felt they needed someone to monitor the Klan from the inside, so they logically went to Dawson.

INTERVIEWER: I see . . .

NELSON: So you have to understand, Dawson recruited, organized, and *led* the Klan, fully armed, to Morningside Homes while he was working for the Greensboro Police.

INTERVIEWER: Wait . . . he organized it . . .

*(On screen: "Greensboro, North Carolina. Eddie Dawson."
"An Escape Goat.")*

DAWSON:

It was a frame-up job.
I couldn't control this thing.

Coupla half-wits got themselves into a jam
now they're lookin' for an escape goat.

And the cops . . .
They discard ya, that's for sure.
This happened on a Friday.
I didn't hear anything. Nothin' over the weekend.
Nobody called. Tuesday, nothin'.
In fact, they never called.
Police, FBI
let me go down the drain
like a rotten piece'a meat.

*(On screen: "Go to Lunch."
Nelson and the Interviewer at a Y-intersection. He shows
her some pictures.)*

NELSON: A few minutes before the attack, the Klan and Nazis drove here to this Y-intersection. They stopped and waited for the last vehicle to join the caravan.

INTERVIEWER: Why?

NELSON: It was the arsenal car. A blue Ford Fairlane. *(Shows her the picture, then another picture)* Nine cars, thirty-five Klansmen and Nazis.

INTERVIEWER: How do you have these pictures?

NELSON: Rooster Cooper took them. They were shown at the trial.

INTERVIEWER: "Rooster"—?

NELSON *(Laughs)*: Yeah. Rooster's a good ol' boy. Rooster Cooper was Dawson's supervisor in Intelligence.

INTERVIEWER: Cooper—

NELSON: He was shadowing the Klan caravan that whole morning and transmitted his information back to police headquarters. He photographed the Klan arriving at Dawson's friend's house with their weapons. *(Shows picture)* He photographed the arsenal car joining the caravan here.

INTERVIEWER: Where was Cooper when he took this picture?

NELSON: Just over that ridge.

INTERVIEWER: Why didn't he stop—

NELSON: He said in court that he saw no reason to stop the caravan.

INTERVIEWER *(After a beat)*: How far away are we from Morningside—from Carver and Everitt streets?

NELSON: Just a few miles.

INTERVIEWER: Really.

NELSON: Eddie Dawson was right here trying to rush these Klansmen to Morningside Homes by eleven o'clock.

INTERVIEWER: Why?

NELSON: Because, at 10:57, "someone" at police headquarters gave the police officers the order to *leave* the Morningside area—

INTERVIEWER: Leave the area?

NELSON: *Leave the area . . .* and go to lunch.

> *(The Interviewer shakes her head. Lights reveal Eddie Dawson. The Interviewer turns to him.*
> *On screen: "You Get Reminiscing on It.")*

DAWSON *(Filling out a form)*: Oh, I should know what it is.

INTERVIEWER: Huh?

DAWSON: I should know the date.

INTERVIEWER: Oh, I bet you do. I know, it's—I wondered how it would hit you if we came to see you on this date.

DAWSON: I beg your pardon?

INTERVIEWER: I wondered how it'd hit you coming to talk about this on the day, November 3rd. Fifteen years later.

DAWSON: No, no, I'm more or less over that part; you know, the being shaken up about it. I just, the other night, I was—you know, you get reminiscing on it—and you look at your watch, it's eleven o'clock at night, and you say: "Well, five, four people had, you know, twenty-four hours to live." I wonder if they, you know, felt anything.

INTERVIEWER: Yeah.

DAWSON: The Grim Reaper—guy that rides around with a sickle—he was on their back. *(Laughs)*

INTERVIEWER: Yeah. Yeah, he sure was.

(She plays back the tape: "guy that rides . . . ")

DAWSON: So . . . Why do you want to know?

INTERVIEWER: About you?

(He nods.)

I'm writing about the Greensboro event . . . maybe a play . . .

DAWSON: Yeah? I like plays.

INTERVIEWER: Good.

DAWSON: So. It was a terrible ordeal. You know, regardless what they were, what you are, Ku Klux Klan, Nazi, communist. To get killed like that, it's terrible. It was. And it bothered, it has to, if you're a human being.

INTERVIEWER: Did you . . . um . . .

DAWSON: Some people it didn't.

INTERVIEWER: Some people it didn't?

DAWSON: Like Matthews, the one that killed—he only killed four out of five—he said, "I'm not a criminal." And they just don't have no feeling, I guess. So. He was a little wacky. He was in the Klan for a long time, Matthews.

INTERVIEWER: Yeah. Yeah. Yeah.

DAWSON: So.

INTERVIEWER: What happened to him?

DAWSON: Matthews?

INTERVIEWER: Yes.

DAWSON: Nothing. He lives here. Up the road.

(Lights up on a small interrogation room. Matthews is hunched over a tape recorder. Two interrogating officers—one white, one black, both dressed in suits—stand near Matthews. The white officer asks the questions.

On screen: "November 3, 1979. 9 P.M. Greensboro Police Headquarters. Interrogation of David Matthews."

"I Thought I Hit the Niggers.")

MATTHEWS: They said we were scum, that we were hiding under a rock, that we were chicken shit to come out and meet them head-on. Fine and dandy. We decided to come.

At first we was talkin' about it and we took some guns. We heard that the communists and the niggers was going to shoot us on the side, so we took some shotguns. We were cautious. So the niggers started shooting, and there was some spectators around and some communists. So just like anybody with any common sense, anybody starts to shoot at you, you better defend yourself. They were trying to protect theirselves and finally got stopped. Niggers and communists, you could hardly tell who was the niggers and who was communist.

We didn't take guns there just to kill people. There were some innocent people shot, I reckon, as I'm told anyway. But I was shooting at the niggers.

WHITE OFFICER: I've been told that when you got back in the van, you said, "I got three of them." Did you make that statement?

MATTHEWS: At that time, I thought I did. Yes.

WHITE OFFICER: At that time? What was that statement, David?

MATTHEWS: The people was dropping. I was shooting at them niggers that had riot guns.

WHITE OFFICER: What was that statement?

MATTHEWS: I thought I hit the niggers.

WHITE OFFICER: Okay . . .

(Lights up on Dawson and Interviewer. On screen: "Bucket of Blood.")

DAWSON *(Getting coffee, adding cream, sugar)*: Yeah, sure. The police paid me. My police contact agent was Cooper and Lieutenant Talbert, of the Intelligence.

INTERVIEWER: Rooster Cooper?

DAWSON: Yeah. You know how he got that name?

INTERVIEWER: No.

DAWSON *(Laughs)*: He was a "cocksman."

(No response.)

Yeah, I can play with you, play games with you. So.

I'll tell ya how, about October the twenty-sixth, or whatever, in that neighborhood though, I was gettin' real nervous from this whole thing. I just, you know, like I said before, puttin' these people together.

INTERVIEWER: Yeah, yeah, yeah. You put them together.

DAWSON: It don't take a college graduate to know you put these two groups together and you got trouble. So I'm in Lieutenant Talbert's office, and Cooper's in there, and he says to Talbert: "I think the best thing to do,"—he's not talkin' about November the 3rd now, he's talkin' about his own case, somethin' in his case—

"I'll get an injunction on that. That'll be my best bet." I said: "That's it!" when he walked out. "We'll get an injunction against the damn march. That's what we'll do." Talbert says: "Well who's gonna get the injunction?" I said: "Me!" So I called Bogaty, FBI, always callin' Bogaty, even after I left the bureau. He told me to go see the city attorney. He says: "Ed, get down there, and act like a gentleman. Don't go in there hollerin' at him, and screamin'. He'll listen to ya."

INTERVIEWER: Did you go?

DAWSON: Yeah I did—I went down there. And I told him what I wanted, an injunction against the parade, because of blah blah, trouble with the Ku Klux Klan was comin' up. "And I feel it's best that . . . " you know, like that. Now, I wasn't finished but he stood up, and he says: "I'll tell you what. I can't get no injunction." He said: "I advise you to go down and talk to the police department about what you just told me." So I lose my damn cool. I said: "Okay, you don't have to get up and throw me out of the damn door. I know where it's at. I tell you what though, the next damn time I'll bring you a bucket of blood."

(On screen: "July 8, 1979."
"China Grove."

On screen, we see a segment from the movie Birth of a Nation—*night riders in sheets, burning crosses, saving a white maiden accompanied by loud old-timey Confederate music on piano. The Klan, armed, is inside a clapboard house watching the film. Dressed in their robes, they are jovial and loud, hooting and cheering the movie. Lights up on Nelson.)*

NELSON: November 3rd was really the Klan's response to an incident just a few months before in a small town, mostly black, called China Grove. The Klan was planning on holding a recruitment drive in China Grove, showing the movie the *Clansman*, better known as *Birth of a Nation.*

We helped organize a demonstration with the people of the town against the Klan and this recruitment. That time the cops were there, as well as the press.

(A group of demonstrators lines the stage. A Confederate flag burns.

On screen: Coming up a hill, holding sticks and placards, a huge angry mob of black and white people is calling out: "Death to the Klan."

A Grand Dragon steps out onto the porch, his sheets flying. He has a shotgun and angrily yells back. His Klan brothers join him, also armed. A TV cameraman records the following.)

PAUL LUCKY *(Black demonstrator, holding the burning Confederate flag)*: We just want the Klan to go—go home. If they live here, go home, if they live there, go there. But we will not have it. We will not tolerate it. If we have to die here, we'll die here. But there will not be any Klan. Today, tomorrow— NEVER! DEATH TO THE KLAN! DEATH TO THE KLAN!
(He throws down the flag)
DEMONSTRATORS *(Joining in)*: DEATH TO THE KLAN! DEATH TO THE KLAN!

(The Grand Dragon picks up the still-smoldering remains of the burnt Confederate flag.)

GRAND DRAGON: But I *will* have revenge for this.
KLANSMAN 1: Oh, it'll be revenged.

(Lights up on Nelson.)

NELSON: November 3rd was the Klan's revenge.

(On screen: "Ronnie and Rose, Survivors."
"Unkept Fellows."
Lights up on two black women. Ronnie, very thin, high-strung, and Rose, a big, older woman with a carved walking stick.)

ROSE: I never ever, in my heart of hearts, expected any Klansmen or Nazis to come to Greensboro . . . Then the caravan of

Klansmen came through, driving by, giving us the finger, shouting stuff. I said: "Who are those people?" People around me said: "Those are the Klans." They were all unkept fellows.

Then the shooting began. I heard a gunshot. All of a sudden, it was unreal.

(Lights up on Interviewer and Dawson.)

INTERVIEWER: After China Grove, didn't you speak at a Klan rally in Lincolnton and encourage them to seek revenge in Greensboro?

DAWSON: Now I know where you're going. Look—I was very cagey. I always am; and I never never tell anybody to bring guns or anything like that. I said: "If you bring a gun, you can be sure the police will be there. They will be all over the place. And if they see a bulge on you, they are gonna take you, and you will be arrested. For carryin' a concealed weapon. Now it's up to you. I am not your daddy, I cannot tell you what to do. You go from there." And that's what I said at the Klan rally at Lincolnton. But the interpretation is: "Ed said to bring your guns! Bring all the guns you can." Blah blah blah. *(Laughs)*

INTERVIEWER: Yes, well . . . but you knew they would bring guns, didn't you?

(Lights up on Ronnie and Rose.)

ROSE: I didn't know it was a gunshot, I thought it was a back fire. Someone else in the crowd remarked that it was a gunshot. I just stood there, dumbfounded. I tripped backwards over my friend. She was eight months pregnant, and had gotten sprayed with bird shot. She had fallen against the car door, and it had cut her head. The firing was beginning, and all I could think of was to get behind something.

RONNIE: Sandy saved my life . . . I was disoriented and didn't know which way to go. Sandy had just been severely bashed in the head, yet she could think better than I could in that situation. She was herding children out of the street, trying to save the children, and saw me standing there disoriented, and she grabbed my arm, and said: "Go!" and pointed a way to cover. As I ran for cover, I was shot, but not seriously. Now, Sandy must have gone back to get more kids because when I turned around to take Sandy's hand . . . I saw her kinda slumped up against a wall . . . she was dead. Shot between the eyes.

(Images flash as lights come up on Paul and Sally Bermanzohn. Sally looks at a photo album.
On screen: "Paul and Sally Bermanzohn, Survivors."
"Made Ancient.")

PAUL: I remember trying to run back and help Cesar out . . .

SALLY: Here's Cesar . . .

PAUL: And Cesar, being an old friend of mine . . .

SALLY: You can see him on the videotape, with just a stick in his hand—just guarding . . .

PAUL: I really couldn't understand exactly what was going on . . .

SALLY: . . . just letting the rest of us run back, getting away from the gunfire . . .

PAUL: He was shot . . .

SALLY: I ran up to Cesar. I didn't see Paul.

PAUL: Suddenly I was hit with a tremendous force in my head and arm and I couldn't get up.

SALLY: I tried to pick Cesar up. He was so big; he musta weighed twice what I weighed.

PAUL: When the gunfire stopped, I heard voices, some people say or yell: "Jim's dead. Sandy's dead." And I remember thinking—I'm a doctor—somebody with some medical expertise needs to go over and take a look at this, someone could think they are dead and not give them proper treatment.

SALLY: When I tried to pick him up . . .

PAUL: I tried to get up.

SALLY: . . . this gush of air came out of his lung. I thought at first: "Oh, good! He's breathing!" But then it just kept on going, and going, and going.

PAUL: I really tried as hard as I could to get up but I guess you know by this time I, well, I must have been paralyzed.

SALLY: It was just the air coming out of his lungs, because he had been shot, right in the chest.

PAUL: But the thing that stopped me from getting up was, I just felt like I was a thousand-year-old man. All of a sudden, I had been made ancient, you know . . .

(Lights change. On screen: "Personally Invited.")

DAWSON: Oh, when this first happened, the chief of police got on television, I thought: Oh God, another lie. Another one, another one. They went on and on. Lies. "We showed up late cuz we didn't know where the start of the march was." Balon-ey. That's a buncha crap. Cooper of the Police Intelligence told me, as I was leaving the police station two days before, Cooper says: "Now you know that the beginning of the march has been changed to Morningside Homes?"

And I went outside then, but Morningside Homes meant nothing to me, and Covert Street . . .

INTERVIEWER: Carver and Everitt.

DAWSON: Everitt. Carver and Everitt meant nothing. I went outside of the police station, and I saw these signs: "Death to the Klan." So I walked over there, and I saw Paul Bermanzohn with some literature on his arm, there, you know. I'm gonna talk to him; I said: "What the hell is this 'Death to the Klan' crap?" And Nelson Johnson came over, and got talkin'. He says: "Ya never heard of the Ku Klux Klan?" I said: "Hell yeah! What, you gonna kill them?" You know, tryin' to get him to say somethin'.

INTERVIEWER: What'd they say?

DAWSON: So he said: "No."

INTERVIEWER: Uh-huh.

DAWSON: He says, "I'll tell ya what. Why don't you come to the rally Saturday?" So I'm the only one that was personally invited out of the Ku Klux Klan. I said: "Okay, I'll try to see if I've got time to come." Nelson says: "Try to be there." I says: "Oh, I'll be there." *(He laughs)*

(Nelson enters with Interviewer. On screen: "Your Life Ain't Worth a Nickel, Nigger.")

NELSON *(At Morningside)*: So here we are at Morningside. I was way over there when I was attacked. *(He points)* I was lucky it was somebody with a knife instead of somebody with a gun. By the time I got free, it was all over. I just started running, just running looking for Sandy—

INTERVIEWER: Sandy Smith?

NELSON: My wife's and my best friend. Sandy *(He shakes his head)*

SALLY *(Continuing from previous scene)*: I was three months pregnant with my daughter on November 3rd. She is named after Sandy Smith.

NELSON: Sandy was somthin'—an amazing woman. She came from South Carolina. An only child. Her parents didn't want her to stay up here. I was the one who told Sandy's mother. "It's all right. I'll take good care of her." I assured her.

SALLY: Sandy Smith was head of her student council at Bennett College . . . chair of a union organizing committee up at the mills . . .

NELSON: I found Sandy sitting up against that wall. *(He indicates with his head)* Bullet between her eyes. Then I saw Jim Waller . . . lying on the ground just about here. I was holding Jim when he died. His wife, Signe, came up to us. She just started screaming. I got up and started to say some stuff to the press about who was responsible for this attack, about the police and the Klan working together. The police—who had just gotten there—arrested me. At the hospital, the doctors sewed up my arm. Then the police took me to the station. I was interrogated by the FBI and Greensboro police. The agent said that my name was on the lips of every Klansman in the state, that my life was over, that I needed to talk to them.

I refused to speak. They threatened to rip my bandages off. The FBI agent whispered in my ear: "Your life ain't worth a nickel, nigger." Finally they took me to a jail cell. I stayed up all night, trying to figure out what had happened. I didn't know who was dead, except Jim and Sandy. I didn't know who was alive.

(They exit.)

SALLY: Oh, now I'm looking at Bill Sampson—God, what a gorgeous guy. He was a southerner, a divinity student who graduated magna cum laude from Harvard. He went back down South to join the civil rights movement. People always used to ask him: "Now tell us, Bill, what went wrong?" He'd say: "No, no. Coming down to Greensboro is what went right."
   (A beat. She turns a page in the album)
   Then there's Jim Waller. When he quit being a doctor full-time, he got himself hired as a worker at Haw River Mills—a textile plant that made corduroy—he led a strike—till management figured out he was the same person as somebody named Dr. James Waller who had given some workers a doctor's note for being sick. Jim and Signe had been married eighteen months, and . . . *(She is unable to speak)*

(Lights up on Signe Waller. On screen: "Jim Waller's Widow, Signe Waller."
   "That Less Than Human Thing.")

SIGNE: They said we widows weren't human. We had no feelings of grief. The press said look at that woman. She can stand over her dead husband's body and scream about the party. What they didn't hear me scream was: "I can't go on living without Jim." I really felt like I couldn't go on living. For at least a year it was a matter of total indifference to me whether I lived or died. However people treat you, they give you an identity. I had to deal with this monster image.

I was the one left holding the red banner. I was the lightning rod. It's funny because when I was a teenager, my nickname in summer camp was Lightning Rod. So I was put out there. I did it voluntarily. I was happy doing it. I wanted to take most of the flak that way for being the up-front communist.

What I'm afraid of now is the same prejudices are operating, just attaching to different people. I live in Milwaukee now. This guy Dahmer—you know about him. He raped, mutilated, killed his young male victims. He lured people to his apartment, took photographs of them both before and after, put their hearts, their skulls in his refrigerator, put their heads in acid, ate their hearts, their body parts, it's unbelievable, unbelievable. Anyway, I heard that one of his victims, somehow managed to get away. He was naked. Dahmer ran out after him. The boy had found a police officer, and Dahmer said to the cop: "Oh he's just upset." So the police officer gave him *back to Dahmer!* He gave him to his killer. The cop's attitude was: "Oh, he's just some faggot."

I mean, once there are categories of people who do not qualify as having full human stature—whether they are gays or communist or black people or whoever they are—I mean, once you can separate humanity that way, then you have already created an entire framework in which you can practice all kinds of oppression on people. And you can get away with it. As soon as you have that less than human thing operating, boy, you can do anything to people. And I can understand that, having been a communist.

(On screen: "No. He Didn't Do a Thing.")

INTERVIEWER: Okay. Now so, you got there, you're at Morning-side, you turned the corner, and you were going down, you see: Okay, this is the place for the march. There are no po-lice there. Then what happened?

DAWSON: Bermanzohn was standing there; they had an eiffel [sic] of the Ku Klux Klan; there was people screamin' and hol-lerin' and carryin' on. And this is one thing that I regret in my life, of course. There's nothing I can do to change it though, nothing. Paul was standin' there. And as we ap-proached, Buck was drivin', I had the window down, and we were the lead truck. And our eyes met at the same time. And Paul went to wave, just when I was still movin', you know, real slow. I said: "You communist son of a bitch you; you asked for the Ku Klux Klan, well here we are." So. Then we kept goin'. We got through okay—nobody knew yet, you know. There were three of them, three of the cars got through. And then they got in front of the fourth car, more or less. Blocked them. So then, of course, they got down, and they was all beatin' the crap out of one another. In the meantime, Rooster Cooper is two blocks up.

INTERVIEWER: Watching the whole thing.

DAWSON: Yeah.

INTERVIEWER: Did he radio for help?

(A look from Dawson.)

No, he didn't do a thing.

(Lights up on Nelson. On screen: "Alotta Hate in Those Eyes.")

NELSON: The bad blood between me and the Greensboro police is old, very old. Goes all the way back to my student activist days, late sixties at North Carolina A&T . . . I'll never forget this one cop—Gibson—who gave me the permit for November 3rd . . . There I was at the Greensboro Police Station, he was handing me the permit—which was also a guarantee of police protection, by the way—he looked me in the eye—there was alotta hate in those eyes—and he said: "So you gonna be armed?" I said: "Do you always ask people wanting a parade permit if they're gonna be armed?" "Well are you?" he said. "It's not illegal to carry unconcealed weapons," I said. "No, but the permit states for you to be unarmed." "Yeah," I said, "we'll be unarmed. Why? Are you expecting trouble?" "Nope." The man said no. Just like that. Nope. When we were shot down on November 3rd, that scene flashed through my mind. I *knew* at that moment I *knew* we were set up.

(Lights up on Interviewer and Dawson. On screen: "At People.")

INTERVIEWER: What about the people who were killed, in terms of their relationship and rank. Who were they—is it just random?

DAWSON: No, they were the leaders. *(Scornfully)* You know that.

INTERVIEWER: No, I don't know enough about it. *(Long pause)* So the people that were killed were the high-up people.

DAWSON: Yeah, they were. And that's been a good question: I mean, the question why did they pick out this, this and this to kill? You're right. I think I know where you're goin'. I've been through this before. *(Laughs)* It's a good question. But it was just one of them things. The Klan ain't that intelligent, to plan something like that. They can't plan burning a cross, really. Now, I'm not tellin' you something I didn't say on the damn witness stand. I said: "They don't have sense enough to come out of the damn rain." I said: "They got a gun, half of them don't know if they've got the right bullets in it! They're liable to turn around and watch the bullet come out!" I said, "That's what you got here." So, the intelligence is limited. Very limited.

INTERVIEWER: But didn't Matthews have that telescope? I mean, he knew what he was going.

DAWSON: Matthews?

INTERVIEWER: Yeah, wasn't it him? Who had that—

DAWSON: Well one of them had a telescope, yeah. But, well that mighta got—the black, Smith, could have got her. You know she wouldna never got hit if she'da kept her damn dumb face in the doorway. Like, the street ran here, and she was up here, in the apartment, the houses, the development more or less. And she came out the alley there, and they just—bingo! That's how she got it.

INTERVIEWER: How'd you feel when suddenly everyone was getting—there were people being shot at?

DAWSON: Well, we didn't find out—Buck and I left there, and we went over to a barroom. And I had a Coke, and he had a—

INTERVIEWER: Didn't you ever hear the noise? You didn't hear it? You didn't hear anything?

(No answer.)

You left while it was going on?

DAWSON: Yeah.

INTERVIEWER: Did you hear any noise?

DAWSON: Yeah.

INTERVIEWER: Oh, right. So you knew something had happened.

DAWSON: Yeah, we heard the shots; you couldn't help it. It sounded like blasting. I said "Let's get the hell out of here" to Buck. "Long Gone John."

INTERVIEWER: So you took off as soon as they started to shoot at people.

DAWSON: Well, I don't know. You use the word "at people." I didn't see nobody point a gun at anybody.

(Lights up on Sally Bermanzohn. On screen: "And That's When Mike Was Shot.")

SALLY: And finally there's Mike.

I was standing with Mike when the Klan and Nazi caravan drove up. We were talking about the first-aid car, that was his station wagon. He—Mike was a doctor. He was a pediatrician in Durham, in the middle of a poor black neighborhood.

And so, he was gonna drive his station wagon right behind our march; and there were first-aid supplies, in case somebody . . . fell, or twisted an ankle, or got tired, or . . . little things like that. We always had a first-aid car.

And then this line of cars just drove very slowly, right in front of us, and I didn't know who they were. And then I saw the Confederate license plate tags; and then I heard somebody yell out of the car: "You nigger; you kike; you nigger lover." *(Pause)*

And then—actually, it was a teenage girl yelling—and then there was a shot. And I saw this guy at the front of the caravan, with his body snaked out of the front window of the pickup truck, and a pistol that he had just shot in the air; and I remember the smoke of the gun just kinda hanging in the air there. And people started to run, and scream, and run back. And I was right there between two cars, and I just ducked down between two cars. And then I saw Mike, running back along the buildings. And I thought: Should I run back with him? Maybe it's safer to run back that way, away from this signal shot, this first shot. And I thought, well, I'll stay right here. I think I'm okay right here. And then suddenly there was a barrage of shots, and I thought it was from where that signal shot, that first shot was.

But it wasn't—it was from the back of the caravan. It was from the direction that people were running towards. So Mike, thinking he was running away from that first shot, was actually running towards the guys who had the long rifles, and who knew who they wanted to shoot—were aiming carefully at people. And apparently, Jim Waller was fighting with a Klansman. And Mike went up to help him out.

And that's when Mike was shot. In the head.

(Lights up on Lewis and Marty in his office. On screen: "Lewis Pitts, the Lawyer for the Plaintiffs for the Civil Trial. Dr. Marty Nathan, Widow of Dr. Michael Nathan."
"The Paradigm.")

LEWIS *(South Carolina accent)*: There were three trials over six years. The first trial was a murder trial in state court and an example of good old-fashioned southern justice.

MARTY: The prosecutor, who was ostensibly our lawyer, said to us, his clients: "Most people in Greensboro believe you got what you deserved." They then proceeded to impanel a jury hostile to us, picked with his approval.

LEWIS: See, North Carolina is an anti-union state, and Klan presence is strong. Most of those folks let on the jury weren't against the Klan. In fact, apparently during jury selection, one of them even said the Klan was like "the NAACP for white folks." And communism! *(Shakes his head)*

MARTY: I remember one man saying, again during jury selection: "Well, we fought against the communists in World War II . . . " *(Laughs)* I remember the D.A. kinda smiled and shook his head, and the man said: "Uh, i'n't that right?" The D.A. said: "Well, no sir. That's incorrect." The man was *dumbfounded*. But he was still let on the jury.

LEWIS: Well . . . Marty and Floris were held in contempt for refusing to participate.

MARTY: When the first trial opened, we already knew that we were not going to get any kind of justice—it was just gonna be aimed at us and not at the Klan and Nazis who had killed us—Floris Cauce and I stood up in that courtroom that first day and said: "This trial is a farce. This trial is a sham. The police killed our husbands. They let the Klan come in and kill our husbands." Our mouths were taped. We were hauled out of court and thrown into jail for contempt of court for thirty days.

LEWIS: When the Klan and Nazis were acquitted by this all-white jury, progressive people were outraged. "Hey, we saw this on videotape," they said, "what happened?"

MARTY: This was when Lewis and his team came in.

LEWIS: Our side organized and tried to call for a federal investigation.

MARTY: This time we fully cooperated—

LEWIS: But it was what I like to call "the fox guarding the henhouse." The indictment used a very narrow statute of the civil rights law. They made it so you had to prove racial animus—a racial motivation for the murders—so the defense used anti-communism again—"outside agitators and communists came down here and caused trouble, your honor . . . "

MARTY: You know—historically how racial violence has *always* been dodged in the South.

LEWIS: Again, an all-white jury acquitted the Klan and Nazis.

MARTY: The third trial, the civil trial in 1985, was our last chance.

LEWIS: Our strategy was simple.

MARTY: We tried to tell the whole story—about the pre-planning, about the police and Klan collusion, about the federal involvement.

LEWIS: You know, what happened on November 3rd is part of a long line of civil rights abuses with the Klan and local police working together.

MARTY: Greensboro fits the paradigm perfectly.

LEWIS: Take the Freedom Riders in the sixties, same thing. The Klan'd go to the local police and say: "Hey, these integrationists are comin' down here. We want to go in and bash some heads," and the police'd look at their watches and say: "Okay—we'll give you twenty minutes." So, the buses full of Freedom Riders would arrive on schedule—the Klan was there to greet them and where were the cops? Well—the cops had "gone to lunch."

MARTY *(Echoes)*: "Gone to lunch."

(Lights out. In the black, we hear the voice of Wood: "Roland Wayne Wood." On screen: "1985, Winston Salem. The Civil Trial."

"5 Skulls."

Lights up. Roland Wayne Wood swears in using a Heil Hit-
ler salute. Wood wears a cheap suit, five skulls on his lapel.
Lewis Pitts examines him. He is angry. It shows.)

LEWIS: Mr. Wood, are you the same Roland Wayne Wood who is a
defendant in this case?

WOOD: Yes, I am.

LEWIS: And, Mr. Wood, when you were sworn in, did you put your
hand out in a Hitler and Nazi salute—

WOOD: No, sir, I did not.

LEWIS: —instead of swearing with your hand up?

WOOD: Open fingers.

LEWIS: Open fingers. What does that mean, Mr. Wood?

WOOD: The Father, the Son, the Holy Ghost and myself through
salvation is one.

LEWIS: May I approach the witness for a moment, Your Honor?
Thank you. *(Into Wood's face)* Mr. Wood, is that five skulls
you have on your lapel there, sir?

WOOD: Yes, sir, it is.

LEWIS: Do these five skulls stand for the five people that were
killed on the streets of Greensboro, North Carolina, on November 3rd, 1979, Mr. Wood?

WOOD: No sir, it does not. It stands for the five attacks being committed against me by communists when I tried to express my
freedom of speeches.

LEWIS: And it just happened to be five skulls, is that right?

WOOD: Yes, sir.

LEWIS: And you are proud that you're a racist, aren't you?

WOOD: Yes, sir. I believe in the sovereign rights of the sovereign
people of the sovereign states of the Confederacy that has
never surrendered. Lee, the traitor, surrendered, but not my
Confederate government. I believe that my country is occupied. And I will fight as my forefathers fought to give me a
free Christian republic.

LEWIS: You left the Klan sometime after 1976, didn't you?

WOOD: Yes, sir.

LEWIS: And you started to talk with another defendant in this
case, a Nazi leader, state party leader, by the name of Harold
Covington, am I right? *(He waves a deposition)*
WOOD: Yes, sir.
LEWIS: Did he say in your presence that *(Reads)* "The Jews were
the root of all evil"?
WOOD: I don't recall those exact words, no sir. Maybe Judaism.
LEWIS: Well, do you remember singing a little old song of his that
went like this—page 65: *(Reads)*

> "Shooting all the kikes, rat-a-tat-tat, rat-a-tat-tat
> Mow the kike, mow the kike, mow the kikes down
> Oh, what fun it is to have the Nazis back in town."

Do you remember that?
WOOD: That's not the words. It's—

(Starts to sing to the tune of "Jingle Bells.")

LEWIS: You're not going to put music to that, are you?
WOOD: Sir I could give you the exact words, I don't remember
them words. The song that I remember him singing, now,
not me, and it come out of a book from George Lincoln
Rockwell. It wa—

> *(Sings)*
> "Riding through the town
> In a Mercedes Benz . . . town in a Mercedes Benz . . .
> Having lots of fun."

Something like that. I'm trying to think of the words myself,
and I can't now . . .

> *(Sings)*
> "Riding through the town
> In a Mercedes Benz

Having lots of fun
Shooting Jews down.

Rat-a-tat-tat-tat
Rat-a-tat-tat-tat
Shoot the kikes down
Oh, what fun it is to have
The Nazis back in town."

Something on that line there, but it's a lot different than what you went through.

(It is a surreal moment. The courtroom is stunned. Lights up on Paul and Sally Bermanzohn, Ronnie, Rose, Jane—a white woman in her fifties and Big George—a black man in his late fifties. On screen: "Paul and Sally Bermanzohn, Ronnie, Rose, Big George and Jane, Survivors."
"This Race Mess.")

PAUL: For me, fighting the Nazis wasn't an abstraction. My parents are both Holocaust survivors. My mother survived, probably because, well *(Laughs)* she was so small—someone helped her climb out through a very small window of the death train on its way to Treblinka through a very small window while the train was moving, fast. She knew it was her only chance.

SALLY: She never wanted Paul to do anything that would draw attention to himself.

PAUL: Yeah. If you're a Jew, "Oyb du bist ein Yid," you have to be "ein gruer mensch . . . "

SALLY *(Translates)*: A gray person.

PAUL: . . . blend in, be invisible.

SALLY: She couldn't understand . . .

PAUL *(Imitating his mother)*: "How could you be a doctor," she'd say. *(He smiles)* Her dream—*(Imitates again)* "And give up everything, work in a factory? In a mill? For what? Is this why we escaped from Germany? So you could maybe get yourself killed here?" But of course what happened to them was *exactly* why I was doing what I was doing.

SALLY: Yes . . .

PAUL: Since the time I was a very little kid, I heard Holocaust stories from my mother about Jews being rounded up and people being killed in front of her eyes. And one of the more gruesome and memorable things was my mother seeing Nazi dogs, literally dogs, German shepherds, dragging bodies through the streets. And she was about seventeen when the war started, and her parents were taken. It's just about the same age as my older daughter, which is really a kind of sobering and frightening thought. But she remembers these dogs dragging bodies through the street, and running after them to see if the bodies they were dragging were her parents.

BIG GEORGE: I grew up in South Carolina in the 1930s. I remember the Klan going into people's houses, dragging them out, beating them, hanging them. Naturally, being a kid, I asked myself: "Is this the way it's gotta be?" What I said to myself is: "It won't happen to me. If you do, you're going to have to kill me first."

PAUL: I remember I was lying in the hospital—I didn't know whether I would live or die—I'd had six hours of surgery on my brain—and my mother, tiny as she is . . . well . . . she could terrify me. I lay there more frightened of facing her than I'd been facing the Klan-Nazi guns and she came into the hospital room, looked at me a long time, then she hugged me. She said: *(Choked up)* "Son, I'm proud of you."

(Sally laughs.)

RONNIE: I remember thinking when I was very little: "Maybe if I could save a white person's life, maybe then we would be accepted." It sounds silly now, but I remember thinking:

"Maybe we are not doing enough. Maybe if I did a great thing, like they were hit by a car, and I pulled them out of danger, then this would be the opening." In my young way of thinking, I was just trying to figure this race mess out. My mother was a domestic worker all her life. She would say to me, "When you grow up and get a job, you're going to have to learn how to get along with these white folks. You can't be high and mighty with them, or voice your opinion . . . You just forget about all that trying to change white folks, you can't do anything with white people, that's just the way they are. You can't do anything about it. Well . . .

BIG GEORGE: The grownups kept it hid from you. Something happened to such and such a one, he was dragged out in the middle of the night, and beat up or shot, and if you asked questions, they would say: "You don't need to know about that." If you asked them about a cross-burning, they wouldn't explain it to you, they just didn't want you to know.

SALLY: I know the moment I became a radical: April 4, 1968. When Martin Luther King was killed. I was in a parking lot at Duke . . . *(Looks to Paul)*

RONNIE: I never really been a great follower of Dr. King. I appreciated what he was doing, but I never could get into all this passive resistance—somebody wants to kill you, you fall down on your knees and start praying for that bastard? Me and Dr. King, our philosophy is so different. I was more into what Malcolm was saying. So I would read a lot of Malcolm to tune into him.

ROSE: Well, what really made me want to do something about the system was when they took Miss Cary, my friend who's an old lady, to the hospital. She was real sick, and they rushed her to the hospital. But everyone at Duke Hospital was so busy, and they just overlooked her because she had no insurance. But then Paul told them at the emergency room that someone should see her, raising his voice, and looking mad. He made them give her health care.

When Miss Cary came home, she told me: "Paul really

stood up for me. I wouldn't trade nothing for that college boy." Miss Cary talked about that for years and years and years!

And this did something to me. And everything that Paul got into, I would get into. Workers' Viewpoint and everything.

BIG GEORGE: I liked the people in WVO. Many were highly educated. I wondered, why would they jeopardize their careers to work in the mills? I remember Black Beard . . .

JANE: Jim Waller.

BIG GEORGE: Yeah, that's what we called him. He was a doctor. He'd say that he didn't want to just nurse the wound, but to cure the disease. He'd say: "People keep coming into your medical office with broken legs, so you set their legs. And then one day you notice right outside your office is a big pothole, and people keep falling into that pothole and breaking their legs. So our job is not to keep setting the broken legs! Our job, as doctors, is to fill in the pothole!"

ROSE: As long as it was Workers' Viewpoint, it was like safe; it was respectable. But when this whole debate came on about going communist, I felt like we wasn't doing the right thing.

BIG GEORGE: We was still just working for the people.

ROSE: But once you said you were a communist, you just isolated yourself from everybody. It was so hard to convince people you stood for the same things you did when you were Workers' Viewpoint. A lot of people said: "Couldn't you just not say that word?"

BIG GEORGE: Uh-huh . . .

ROSE: We changed our name to Communist Workers Party just two weeks before the massacre. *(She shakes her head)* People never understand the word "communist." I think it would've still been going on—if it had a different name.

RONNIE: I thoroughly enjoyed the study of Marxism. I went to a school when they had all these federal programs in the late sixties. We came across something called communism. We said: "What is communism?" There were some congressmen coming down from D.C. because they were the ones funding the program. Our instructor said: "When they come, ask them what communism is." When the congressmen came in the room, someone said: "What is communism?" I remember it got quiet, and they never gave us an answer. They tried to laugh it off, you know how politicians can do. We never did know what communism was. When the movement started studying Marxism, and I heard the word communism again, I said: "Well, Lord, I'm gonna find out what communism is." After I started studying, I said: "No wonder they didn't want us to know what it was!"

BIG GEORGE: The anti-Klan campaign was right on time, just right on time. I just loved it. I just loved it. It was right on time. Should have been a long time ago. Seemed like to me we couldn't do enough.

JANE: We were really on a roll then. We had been doing a lot of work, and had a big presence in the county. People either hated us or thought we were great. We were certainly known, we were always on the front page of the local newspaper. We had led the first strike there ever, and the first civil rights march there since Reconstruction. Every black church knew us and we knew every black minister in the county.

BIG GEORGE: We were trying to educate people on the Klan. A lot of people today don't know what the Klan's all about. They think it's just a few little poor white guys with sheets on.

ROSE: During the anti-Klan campaign, I think we were a little cocky locally.

BIG GEORGE: They don't realize the support it gets in the government.

JANE: People knew we were tough. I remember driving around with Big George in the middle of the night putting up posters on the doors of every known Klansman in the county!

When November 3rd came, it never crossed my mind ... There were always campaigns. I never thought twice about it. I remember going to Greensboro with no thoughts—it was just another demonstration.

(Lights up on Amir, a young black man. On screen: "Amir, a Survivor.")

AMIR: The first demonstration I went to was Greensboro and it was my last experience of protesting. When the Klan came, it was like the whole world had fell.

And afterwards, I went into a shell myself. I was scared. I still had this rebel feeling, I wanted to go out there and say: "You can't do this to people." I still want to do the things I did before, but there's a lot of fear, knowing that someone out there doesn't want you to have your rights or to be happy. I was eight years old that day.

(Lights up on Jane.)

JANE: When I was about eight, I remember my mother told me she wanted to show me something. I can see the picture in my mind of her taking me to this hall closet in our house and pulling out this Klan robe. My father was in the Klan. I remember being shocked. I don't remember having the sensibility to be offended . . . I just was shocked. There was a point where I realized what he was doing was very racist, but he was very loving, and would bring people home off the street, hitchhikers—everybody, black or white. He was one of those curious Southern paradoxes, because he was a kind person one-on-one to either black people or white people. He would give you the shirt off his back. He drove my mother crazy. But in group process, he projected his unhappiness on black people, the logical people you did that to in the 1940s or 1950s, as a Southern man—a Southern white man.

My mother was one of these typical Southern religious women, very quiet. I remember thinking that if she ever had an independent thought in her life, I never knew what it was. She never talked about bigoted stuff; she just sort of nodded a lot.

(Lights change.)

SALLY: No, I don't consider myself a Marxist anymore.

PAUL: I no longer have any central political beliefs.

SALLY: I think a lot about what I want our kids to come away with.
I hope they'll work for social change. And I hope they won't
be as radical as their parents were.

PAUL: It was not just the impact of November 3rd . . .

SALLY: I just, you know, I'm not a revolutionary.

PAUL: . . . not getting shot . . .

SALLY: I'm not.

PAUL: . . . not any particular event.

SALLY: Even though I know why I was. But I'm not.

PAUL: It has been a whole chain of events.

SALLY: I very much appreciate The Powers That Be, and I want to
be part of making changes—I'm still a activist—at the same
time knowing that some changes that I'd like to see probably will not happen in my lifetime. And I feel bad about that.

PAUL: I guess I feel like I'm just a vaguely progressive guy.

SALLY: I know that too great militancy . . . hurts. Can hurt. That's
sort of a painful realization, and I don't want my children to
get hurt.

(Lights up on Ronnie.)

RONNIE: My earliest memory is a black man and a white woman
going together. They both consented. White men came and
locked them in a barn and set it on fire. They threw stones at
the woman and somehow she ran away. The sheriff came
out and said it was "people's business." He didn't stop it. He
just left. The man burned to death. You could hear the man
in the barn holler for awhile and that screaming went on in
my nightmares for a *long* time.

*(Lights up on Nelson and Dawson. On screen: "November 1,
1979. Greensboro.")*

NELSON *(To TV camera)*: The police hate us, we know it; they are not neutral. They are out to do everything they can to disrupt us. And we are here to say that we are going ahead with the march, permit or no permit. And I want to add that we just picked up the permit a few minutes ago after running around the building two or three times this morning. The people in Greensboro are intent on smashing and driving out the scum Ku Klux Klan and their secret supporters. The march will be more powerful than ever. We fully expect the police to continue their slimy tactics. They will do anything to disrupt this march and disguise themselves. They might harass us or send provocateurs into our ranks to try to disrupt the march.

What we want to do is say the Klan's nothing but a bunch of cowards. They're not going to come here. If they come here, right, it'll be because the police aided them in coming here, you know, and attacking us.

DAWSON *(Posing as a reporter)*: Do they have Klansmen in Greensboro here?

NELSON: Oh yeah. They have Klansmen everywhere.

(Lights up on Paul.)

PAUL: You know, the biggest mistake the post-war generation made, I think, was teaching their kids the Nazis were monsters, like they were a different species from us. The Nazis weren't "monsters." They were people. —That's the problem . . .

(Lights change.)

NELSON *(To Dawson)*: Why don't you come to the rally Saturday?

DAWSON: Okay, I'll try to see if I've got time to come.

NELSON: Try to be there.

DAWSON: Oh, I'll be there.

(Lights fade out.)

ACT TWO

Lights up. The mourners' circle at graveside. All the survivors (the whole cast except Dawson, Griffin and Matthews—a multiracial group) circle the grave. Marty, Sally and Amir each place flowers on the grave during the song. Ronnie places a packet of peppermint candy. This is a ritual they know well.

ROSE *(Sings)*:
> Now Michael was a soldier.

RONNIE AND AMIR:
> Oh yeah.

ROSE:
> He put his head on the battle line.
> Then one day he couldn't take it no more.
> So I took his place in line.

RONNIE:
> Now Sandy was a soldier.
> She joined Cesar on the battle line.

Then one day they couldn't take it no more.
So we took their place in line.

ALL:

We are soldiers in the army.
We got to fight
Though some fall at our side.
We got to hold up
The blood-stained banner.
We got to hold it up
Until we die.

RONNIE:

Now Bill was a soldier.
He joined Jim on the battle line.
Then one day they couldn't take it no more.
So we took their place in line.

ALL:

We are soldiers in the army.
We got to fight
Though some fall at our side.
We got to hold up
The blood-stained banner.
We got to hold it up
Until we die.

(On screen: "A Klansman. White Aryan Resistance (W.A.R.) Conference."
"Invisibility."
A middle-aged man in a white shirt and a white cap with black insignia stands at a church podium with a microphone. Behind him are the Confederate flag, the National Socialist flag, and a silver Viking broadsword mounted into a stone block. He's been talking and is agitated.)

KLANSMAN: We can't use the same techniques we've been using for the last forty years. Look at Louis Farrakhan—black leader, separatist—Nation of Islam. He should be a model to the Klan. And when Louis Farrakhan speaks, he doesn't speak in a small church like this. He gets a sports amphitheater that seats 50,000 people. A half million black men went to Washington. That just shows you what white people are up against. We're going to have to get started here.

We are the White Knights of the Ku Klux Klan. We are not supremacists. Okay . . . We are separatists. We're not supreme anymore. We've been degenerated. The last thirty years the white race has gone downhill so fast it's unbelievable.

We of the White Knights of the Ku Klux Klan are not going to sugarcoat our ideology. We are pro-white. We like the "r" word. We are revolutionaries. Look—the masses respect power. Look at the IRS. They grumble and groan but come April what is it? April 14, they come right out with their 1040 forms. The masses respect who's in power. And I don't think it shows power when you have half a dozen Klansmen walkin' down the street in sheets with a hundred cops around in fronta five hundred jeerin', screaming white protesters. When Joe Six-Pack sees that, he's got nothin' but contempt for the Klan. But we can win over Joe Six-Pack with our ideology. Why? Because Joe Six-Pack agrees with us.

Let's talk about tactics. Let's talk about invisibility. It's time for the Klan to go Invisible. Put on a coat and tie like David Duke can get forty percent of the vote in Louisiana. David Duke hasn't changed his ideology one bit but he's changed his tactics. We have to get started here. Now let's talk about courage and let's talk about fear. Most of the Knights have lost their jobs. We live near the ghetto. We live near these blacks. You have to deal with fear every day. But when you get fulla anger and rage, you'll overcome that fear. We'll ally with you—National Socialist, Identity Christian, Aryan Nation, militia—what have you. We'll work with you. We make the best fighters. Why? The White Knights have been hurt by the system, knocked down by the system, kicked by the system. We make the best fighters because we got nothing more to lose.

(On screen: "David Duke, Former Grand Dragon of the Ku Klux Klan, Former President of the National Association for the Advancement of White People, (NAAWP) Former Representative of the State of Louisiana, Currently Head of the Office of the Conservative Network, New Orleans."
"I Have a Dream."
He's on the phone. He speaks beautifully, quietly, rationally—articulate and charming. He looks like an Ivy Leaguer.)

DUKE:

Yes . . . I ran for Governor, got forty percent,
ran for Senator, got forty-five percent of the votes.
I think my ideas show the Republican Party the way.
The average working man in this country is
    conservative
of philosophy, of values; in terms of unions,
they might have a liberal point of view . . .
that's the only place they have a liberal *(Laughs)*
    point of view.
Taxes, welfare, affirmative action, all the issues—
the hard hats in this country are natural troops
of the Republican Party.
I haven't been in the Klan for years. And I'm not
    associated with the National Association for the
    Advancement of White People,
the NAAWP, that organization anymore,
but I wouldn't be ashamed of that fact.
I think if there's an NAACP then NAAWP is perfectly
    appropriate.
I am proud of my heritage.
We . . . we . . . the cultural, religious, racial . . .
    heritage
of the country is being split apart now.
And uh even if we have not always been of one race
    or one
faith

uh . . . the Europeans, Christian, value system . . .
Western European value system has been the bedrock
   of the country.
And if that erodes, I think that the foundations of our
   country
will erode.
Pretty straight talk. I hope you don't mind.
No one's undergone the kind of smear campaign I
   did . . .
They'll accuse anybody of being a fascist or a racist or
   a Nazi
if you talk about these kinda things.
I left the Klan because I got sick of fighting that
   stereotype.
I wanted to uh discuss the issues confronting my
   heritage
without being accused of violence or hate.
I started NAAWP when I got sick of being labeled
with that moniker.
This thing is not about hating others but loving your
   own.
I think the people of the world are turning
   conservative and I think the European-Americans
and European-Europeans for that matter
are starting to realize like every culture and every
   heritage they have a right to preserve what's theirs
   and their way of life.
We're people that look at conservatism in more of a
   historical way, much like Patrick Buchanan has
   adopted.
I think Patrick Buchanan got some of his ideas for
   political activism from what he saw in my election.
He feels he has to disassociate himself from anything
   I might say
and he did in the presidential primaries and that's his
   right.

If it helps him politically, I don't have any problem
    with it.
Segregation comes about through people's choices.
Schools have become resegregated as you know.
I think not only should we not fight that trend
but we should facilitate it.
I mean there's a real cultural clash that takes place
    with integration.
black kids even listen to different kind of music than
    white kids do.
They dress differently.
They have different languages, different lifestyles,
    different uh values.
I was just in D.C. a while back, Department of Labor
    cafeteria
Eight hundred maybe a thousand people in the
    cafeteria
Eight hundred whites, maybe two hundred blacks
Two hundred blacks sitting all together eating lunch
Eight hundred whites sitting together eating lunch
that's one of the more liberal departments right in
    our federal government! So you know—give people
    a choice!
So, no, I don't think segregation has to be legislated.
See—that's quite different from what happened in
    1954.
Segregation by law.
You give people freedom of choice in the matter,
it will take place naturally
and the racial harmony will be much greater.
One reason why you have phenomena like the
    skinheads
and a lot of the white kids that that uh
are very radical on this issue
is because of forced integration.
Because they've endured it,

they've endured uh
violence and uh put downs and uh racial slurs
and by the time they get out of their public
    educational process they come out with not so
    much racial self-respect and awareness, but they
    come out with uh sometimes a burning racial
    hatred toward minorities.
And that's what integration's produced.
It hasn't produced love and harmony,
it's produced more racial antagonism than ever.

*(Slowly a slide of a map from a newspaper published by
Duke fades up. The map sections off America into racial
zones. For instance, Long Island is New Israel; Florida, New
Africa, etc.)*

No, no, that map was really a joke.
This was not a serious thing
about how to solve the problem in America.
Y'know every piece in every magazine is not
    endorsed by the editors. That's one of the
    typical political tricks used against me.
Anything can be distorted and taken out of context.
I never advocated any forced removals, repatriation
    of blacks to Africa
or forcible partitioning of America.
The most I've ever said on that is what I just told you
those who want separation, blacks that want
    separation,
give it to 'em!
Those that want it, let 'em have it!
I'll pay the way for Al Sharpton, Jesse Jackson . . .
    (Laughs)
I have a dream for America—
that America will someday be again a nation
that respects and reveres

its magnificent, European, Western heritage
at the same time tolerates or is tolerant of diversity.
A nation based on excellence in all areas of life
rather than mediocrity
a nation that believes in equal opportunity
based solely on ability and talent and industriousness.
A nation that each generation *removes*
a little more of its underclass . . .
a country based on merit, a true meritocracy . . .

INTERVIEWER *(On speaker phone)*: Mr. Duke, you sound almost like a progressive. What separates your dream from the dream of, say, Martin Luther King?

DUKE:

Martin Luther King's dream was a fraud.
The "I Have a Dream" speech was a fraud . . .
That's pretty tough, okay?
Because I don't think it was ever the intention
of the civil rights movement from the early days
to have equal rights; it was always special rights
affirmative action went right with it
The "I Have a Dream" speech was written by a
    Marxist
which you probably know already.
King didn't write that speech, it was a communist.
I'm sorry I can't remember his name, but it's common
    knowledge . . .
The media in this country—so many of 'em—Marxists
that's how our schools learned about the antebellum
    South
and reconstruction . . .
But ostensibly, that idea of Martin Luther King of
    equal rights
I can agree with.
And one more thing I can agree with—and this'll
    shock you—
he said in his "I Have a Dream" speech he said:

"Someday we could have a world where we have
     white children
hand in hand with black kids, and red kids, and
     yellow kids."
He says that "I have a dream that that will someday
     be possible."
And let me tell you something.
I can share in a way in that dream of Martin Luther
     King uh and if the present trend continues
with immigration and differential birth rates
and the rising numbers of the underclass
if those things continue
that dream will be impossible
because there won't be any more white kids
for the black and red and yellow kids to hold hands
     with.
That's a different way to look at the dream.
I guess this is why I'm called a racist.
I'll be honest. I want to preserve my heritage.
I love the traditions of Shakespeare and Milton and
     Nietzsche and Hegel and uh the great music
say Mozart *(He pronounces it "Mo-zart")* or Handel
     or Beethoven or for that matter
some of the modern writers we still have today
which are European in outlook
and uh I love our traditions and our value system
and I think genocide is the worst crime.
I can't think of a worse crime
than the purposeful eradication from this earth of a
     people.
I am a very strong naturalist—I believe in the
     environment
and the preservation of all kind of life on earth
human life or animal life—
or for that matter flora.
But for me there is no greater crime.

Genocide really means the destruction of the genes.
And if we are destroyed whether it be by gas chamber
which is probably not on the horizon
or whether it simply be by the fact we don't have any
    kids—
you understand?
It would be a great tragedy.
The real minority on the planet right now is
    Caucasian mankind.
Europeans built this country
are responsible for the Declaration of Independence
and I believe that if we lose that base,
then we will lose America.
Now a lot of people
think that
and will say that
behind closed doors.
I just speak out.

(On screen: "A Skinhead."
"W.A.R."
Lights come up on a young man, very thin, almost
waiflike. He is hunched over, vulnerable.)

YOUNG MAN: It starts early. They start to drain your white pride in
school.

We are the master race—intellectually, creativity—we are
the master race. —How did we come enslaved by the Jews? I
think the answer is easy—it's in our culture, it's in our heritage, it's in our blood from day one to be honest, honorable,
hard-working people. It's in their blood from day one to
learn how to deceit the Gentiles.

You know a Jew is not a white man. Y'ever heard the ex-
pression "blood in the face"? Well, lemme ask you, can a
Jew blush? Listen, he's just a nigger in disguise.

And now what do we have? A whole bunch of reverse discrimination. We have the anti-hate law which might as well be called the anti-white law cuz I never heard it used against any of those mud races.

There are a lot of angry white people out here now. We have to prepare for war, and we know that. The time has come—it's going to be too late. That means food storage, target practice, ammunition . . . There's going to be a lot of bloodshed. Personally, I can't think of a better way to go than to die for my people. *(He raises his arm in a Heil Hitler salute)* White Power!

(On screen: "The Inner Circle.")

DAWSON: And why, people ask me, why'd ya join the Klan. I joined the Klan for experiments. I was always curious about their activities. And how that came about. Right down here in the restaurant, I was sitting there, and this fellow sitting next to me just started to talk. About enigration, and stuff like that, and then they feel what your answers are. And he says: "You'd make a good Klan member." So he says: "Why don't you fill this application out?" and hands me an application.

INTERVIEWER: For the Klan?

DAWSON: For the Klan.

INTERVIEWER: A written application.

DAWSON: Right. He was the Exalted Cyclops. *(Laughs)* He was the president.

INTERVIEWER: That's his name? Exalted Cyclops.

DAWSON: Exalted Cyclops. That's the wise man. Okay? So, that's what he was. I found out later. But Buck and I got together right away. You know, he was from Wisconsin, and they used to call us the Yankees. I'm from Jersey. Never by name; it was always the Yankees. So. I ended up Titan. *(He stresses the second syllable)*

INTERVIEWER: Titan? How do you spell that?

DAWSON: Titan? I don't know. I'm a sixth-grade dropout.

INTERVIEWER: T-I-T-A-N.

DAWSON: T-I-T-I-A-N. I think. Yeah. See—in each state, there's a Grand Dragon. He's in charge of the state. And each city has maybe three or four meeting halls. They're called Klavern Halls, and they're meeting halls. And I was in charge of them all in this Greensboro area here.

And my biggest downfall was, I guess, I got in with the Echelon immediately, the higher-ups. The Grand Dragon, George Foster, with people like that. And I was with the Echelon. I was curious.

INTERVIEWER: Curious.

DAWSON: Curious . . . Because of the blacks. I don't uphold blacks. I just can't help it; that's the way I am.

INTERVIEWER: You don't uphold—you mean you hate 'em. You don't like 'em.

DAWSON: You're using the word hate. That's a strong word.

INTERVIEWER: Is it accurate?

DAWSON: "You don't bother me, I don't bother you." I'm not doin' it to deliberately go out of my way to harm a black, or anything like that. No. I think I'd go off the deep end quicker for a black to do something small to me.

To actually boil down, when I first went to Klan meetings, you know, I guess I was like a lot of people. You expect to see a black hanging in the corner there. Or one hanging over there, or something like that.

INTERVIEWER: Hanging?

DAWSON: That's exaggeratin' now. But, you know, the meetings, like I said, are just meetings. That's all. It's like they're Moose meetings. And what they did at the rally and the next rally and so on. But after the meetings are over, you meet in the car, the back of a car, and that's called the Inner Circle. And that's where the—out of the meeting hall, there might be two, three hundred people in the Klan Klavern Hall, but there's only about six, eight or ten that's in the Inner Circle, and the rest of the people don't even know what happened.

INTERVIEWER: So that's when it gets interesting right? When you're in the Inner Circle.

DAWSON: You're the only one who knows about it—the grand jury, nobody would tell 'em what the Inner Circle was. That was kept quiet. Stop bitin' your nails. You nervous?

INTERVIEWER: Yeah, well, it's a nervous-making day, you know?

DAWSON: Well, you can bite 'em if you wish. *(Laughs)*

INTERVIEWER: You're right, I was biting my nails . . . In the early seventies, you had a falling out with the Klan, didn't you?

DAWSON: I'll have a falling out with you before the day is out.

(Lights up on Marty Nathan. On screen: "Marty Nathan." "This Abyss.")

MARTY: Mike went to China Grove, and I stayed home with Leah, who was only three months old. He came back, and everyone was saying how exciting it was, and how it was a working-class victory, and how the community was all with it. And after everybody left, Mike said: "I was scared to death. We almost got ourselves killed." My response to that was: "What's wrong with you, Mike? Why don't you have more spirit?" That was a rift between us.

Just a week before November 3, I was sitting in Shoney's—this restaurant we all went to—with Mike, and we had just gotten a copy of that letter to the Klan that had been made into a leaflet. Mike looked at it and said: "This is crazy. This is really off the wall." I got angry at him. Why didn't I listen to him? Because deep inside of me, it didn't make any sense to me either.

That morning—November 3, we got into a fight, and he said something about not wanting to go. I got mad at him. We had to take separate cars anyway, which we did. But then it was all right. We picked some folks up and we were just waiting at the other starting point when Jim came over and told me to send a first-aid car for any accidents on the march and I asked Mike to go over to Morningside. That was the last I ever saw of him.

Al came over and said some people had been shot. Joyce

Johnson and I went over to Morningside. And that's where I
saw . . .

(Long pause) You know what sticks in my mind? I didn't
actually hear it, it's from the videotapes, it's Signe's screams
after she saw Jim . . . That sticks in my mind—this unbelief—
this abyss.

*(Lights up on Interviewer and Dawson. On screen: "You're
Not in It for the Money.")*

DAWSON: Yeah. I had a falling out with the United Klans, yeah.
INTERVIEWER: You were arrested in a shoot-out in Middletown
between the Klan and some black people, weren't you, and
the Klan didn't stand by you?
DAWSON: Yeah. We all got fined a thousand and a year suspended
for five years. Now, they always said if it was Klan activity,
the Klan would stand in back of you. So I got rather upset.
And they had an Imperial meeting there, and I called them a
buncha damn thieves at the meeting, because they wouldn't
pay: "You're just a buncha damn thieves, that's all you are."
I called 'em a buncha scum. Pay outta my own pocket . . .
   Then the FBI, after I made that statement, the FBI had
informants to inform on the informants. So they brought me
downtown here, and you know, well, they came over the
house, and they want to talk to you.
   And he says: "You see that pack of papers there?" "Yeah."
"That's your background, and your buddy James Buck. If
we go through this paper real real good, we'll have enough
to put your unh unh where it belongs." I says: "Well, I can't
stop ya. If that's your thing, you go do it." So.
INTERVIEWER: Was that from Klan activities?
DAWSON: Ah, you don't know. It was a stack of papers. They could
have been all blank. You don't know. You're never sure.
They said: "Now look! What's the difference? You're goin' to
these meetings, and you're goin' to the rallies; you'll go, and
you'll get paid to go!" And finally I got thinking about it, and

I said: "You get me off that probation for Middletown, and
I'll work for you for a year." So what they did, they give ya
twenty-five dollars for going to a local meetin', fifty dollars
out of town, eight cents a mile travelin', eight dollars a hundred to Charlotte and eight dollars back. So that was your
pay, ya know. What they paid you. No big deal.

INTERVIEWER: No big deal, right.

DAWSON: No. You're not in it for the money you know. People say,
was ya in it for the money? You're not, 'cause there's no
money there. Now, don't forget, we're goin back in time too,
you know.

INTERVIEWER: Oh, I know.

DAWSON: So it's not bad.

INTERVIEWER: So what were the guidelines? Did they just say they
wanted information? During the eight years you informed
for the FBI, didn't they tell you what you could or couldn't
do?

DAWSON: Absolutely not. They give you no guidelines to go on.
None whatsoever. You're on your own.

(On screen: "Lewis Pitts."
"It Ain't Our Jurisdiction."
Lewis Pitts in his office.)

LEWIS: You have to wonder if November the 3rd would evena
happened without the federal involvement . . . or federal
negligence. You know Dawson was an agent provocateur inside the Klan for the FBI—but another federal agency was
involved, too. Bureau of Alcohol, Tobacco and Firearms.
ATF had infiltrated the Nazis. There was a guy named
Butkovich—federal agent for the Bureau of Alcohol, Tobacco and Firearms. He was working undercover inside the
American Nazi Party, also—it was *his idea* to get the Klan
and Nazis together—to form something called the United
Racist Front. This is a law enforcement officer! *(Opens his
briefcase, looking for the documents and pictures)*

Like Dawson—incredible record of violent acts. He loved to wear his Nazi uniform. He was picked to come down here cuz he busted the most heads at a Jewish Defense Organization meeting in Ohio . . . *(Finds them. Throws down the pictures. Long pause)*

ATF sent him to Greensboro to investigate whether the Nazis were in possession of automatic weapons. We now know Butkovich was actually teaching the Nazis how to make explosives and automatic weapons. But when all they brought to Greensboro on November 3rd were long guns and semi-automatics, the Feds saw they didn't have a bust so they just . . . walked away. During the trial one ATF officer said to me: "Hey, we do bombs and guns, not civil rights. That ain't our jurisdiction!" . . . or some such shit . . . *(Shakes his head)*

(Lights up on Dawson and Interviewer. On screen: "A Pebble on the Hood.")

INTERVIEWER: Why did they call you an "extremist informant"? The FBI labeled you an "extremist informant." What does that mean?

DAWSON: I think they knew that I just didn't worry about nothin'. James Buck and I were feared around here. We had a reputation. They needed anything done—cross-burning, intimidation—they called James Buck and Eddie Dawson to do the dirty work. My truck, I had it set up that you pushed a button and the back lights went out. If anything had to be done, they'd call the extremist. You didn't scare me. I put up a good front. Don't think for one minute I wasn't scared a lot of times— you're damn right I was. But I wouldn't show it. You know, they got this advertisement: "Never leave 'em see you sweat."

INTERVIEWER: What were you scared of that you weren't showing?

DAWSON: What was I scared of? Well, I was scared of the police department, I was scared of the FBI. I was never scared of the Klan—

INTERVIEWER: You weren't. Uh-huh.

DAWSON: Because I knew them. And I knew that they ran scared. Even when—the shooting. After that. I knew too much on the police department; I knew too much about the FBI. And I was worried about them sending me away—I mean, forever.

INTERVIEWER: You mean, killing you.

DAWSON: I got to a point where I used to put a pebble on the hood of my truck at night, and in the morning, I'd look at that first—to make sure they didn't lift the hood up, ya know. You're damn right.

INTERVIEWER: You thought the cops, or the FBI, might kill you, is that what you're saying?

DAWSON: Yeah. They get rid of you and think nothing of it. Hell yeah. You see, what didn't help much any: Len Bogaty— FBI—turned against me. So Bogaty makes this statement to me, that after the trials are over, after things settle down, he'll give me more information on what happened. Okay? So maybe two months after the trials are over, and everything is settled down, I was over his house—now I got this on tape. I says, "Hey, we're alone here. What happened during that mess, you know? What's the bottom line on this?" He says: "Whaddaya mean?" I says: "Well you said you were gonna tell me something, you know, after the trial was over." He says: "I never said that." *(Laughs)* I said: "You lyin' son of a bitch you," you know, to myself. I got you on damn tape!

And on November 2nd, the day before it happened, Len Bogaty—FBI—had made a statement to me: "You did everything you could; stay the hell away from the thing now. Don't go near it." Why? *(Laughs)* Why did he tell me that? That comes to my mind, you know. That he knows somethin' that they'll never tell.

(Blackout. From the darkness, we hear Levey Voice-Over.)

LEVEY *(Voice-Over; speaking over a crackling phone line)*: Lewis Pitts? My name is Mordechai Levey, Jewish Defense Organization. I want to tell you that we got information prior to the massacre that the Nazis were going to go to Greensboro with the Klan on November 3rd, to "kill some people . . . "

LEWIS: Uh-huh . . .

LEVEY: And I informed the FBI in North Carolina on November 2nd—asked for a Jewish agent—got a guy named Goldberg—told him exactly this information . . .

(Lights up. Deposition room. Lewis conducts a deposition on Goldberg. Present are: a lawyer for the FBI, Nelson, Marty, a court reporter and a tape operator.

On screen: "Deposition of FBI Agent Goldberg. Greensboro, 1985."

"Not That I Recall.")

LEWIS: Agent Goldberg, did you receive a call on November the 2nd, that related to the upcoming November 3rd anti-Klan demonstration?

GOLDBERG: Not that I recall.

(A beat. Lewis is stunned.)

LEWIS: You don't recall receiving a call from Mordechai Levey?

GOLDBERG: No, sir.

LEWIS: Do you know that Mr. Levey has asserted that he did and we have further documentation?

GOLDBERG: I saw the affidavit, yes.

LEWIS: You received no phone call at any time prior to November the 3rd that purported to provide information about an expected confrontation in North Carolina between Klan, Nazis and other demonstrators?

GOLDBERG: Not that I recall, no sir.

LEWIS *(Annoyed)*: Well, explain to me what you mean by "Not that I recall," can't you say yes or no to that?

GOLDBERG *(Looking at the lawyer)*: No, I think I can say not that I recall.

(Lawyer nods. Lights change. Half an hour later. Lewis sits.)

LEWIS: Mr. Goldberg! . . .

GOLDBERG: All right. I received a phone call which caused me to call telephonically the Greensboro resident agency and ask if there was anything going to take place that weekend. What *caused* me to make the phone call, I don't know.

(Lewis groans, gets up.)

LEWIS *(Exasperated)*: So you don't—what was—I think I can guess that answer, but let me ask the question. Why did you make the call when you learned that there was going to be some demonstration and why didn't you do anything with regard to that information?

(Goldberg looks to his lawyer, who shakes his head.)

GOLDBERG: If I—if I knew how to answer it I would, I wish I knew what you were getting at, sir. I wish I would know why she's laughing also.

(Marty ducks her head down.)

LEWIS: I can probably answer that, but I won't.

(Lights shift again, indicating another half hour has passed.)

LEWIS: Did the anonymous call that you received make reference that you'd been contacted because you were Jewish?

GOLDBERG: I don't believe it did. If anybody had investigated me they would have known that I was not.

LEWIS: But that call prompted you to call the FBI office in Greensboro—because you heard from the Jewish Defense Organization that some Nazis were going to Greensboro to "kill some people"—

GOLDBERG: No, you're trying to put words in my mouth. I don't know why I called Greensboro. If I knew I would tell you! How can I be more emphatic?

LEWIS: So then within roughly a week after November 3rd—

(Goldberg suddenly doubles over in pain.)

GOLDBERG: Aaah! Let me just stand—I got a cramp! *(He grabs his leg)* Aah! Aah! Aah! Aah! Aah! Aah!

(He hobbles in pain, doubled over and holding his leg, which is in spasm. Lewis is amazed, shakes his head. He looks at Marty.)

LEWIS: Unbelievable . . .

*(Lights up on Floris Cauce Weston; she sits in a chair. On screen: "Floris Cauce Weston, Widow of Cesar Cauce."
"I'm Quiet.")*

FLORIS: I guess I haven't dealt with a lot of the anger. I'm the only one of the survivors, I think, who stopped doing any social justice work, any political work at all. I feel guilty I didn't spend full-time on my own case. I'm really grateful to Marty and Dale and Signe, the other widows, that they followed through with that process, due process. It was very important, but I couldn't stay through to the end. The widows and Nelson helped the lawyers uncover the full extent of the conspiracy, the role of the government and the police. See—there were police people who really knew a lot. The murders have the character of an accident, but someone let it happen.

I became firmly convinced it was preventable. But I didn't know where to place my anger. See, I could always understand the Klan's point of view. They have always identified who they hate. They have always admitted they're violent people. I suppose I'm most angry at the police. In my eyes, they were on trial more than the Klan. And I'm angry at us for letting it happen. Even though we didn't mean to. But we were fighting armed men with ideas, with *words*.

I don't know . . . I guess, Greensboro was a place where I lost my purpose in life. I still don't go to demonstrations. I don't think they work. I don't know if they ever did. I think what really gets done gets done someplace else. If social change is going to be accomplished, it's going to be done in somebody's office, I don't know. I was twenty-four years old when this happened. I thought I was doing the right thing. I went straight out of college into a social movement . . . I didn't have the skills necessary to interpret this. Cesar . . . I don't know. Talking helps. I try to put a piece of the puzzle together every day. And I'm quiet. I guess that's what they wanted. It's fifteen years later, and I'm still quiet.

(Blackout. Lights up on Nelson Johnson on the witness stand.
On screen: "1985/The Civil Trial. Cross-Examination of Nelson Johnson."
"Words Have Meaning."
Chapman, lawyer for the defense, examines Nelson. Lewis looks tense, worried. His head is down.)

CHAPMAN: The CWP membership application we found in your briefcase says:

(Nelson looks up, checks his anger.)

"What is your outlook on the need for armed struggle and violent revolution in the United States," is that correct?
NELSON: Yes, it is. *(He takes a sip of water)*
CHAPMAN: And why does the application ask that?
NELSON *(Speaking very slowly, very quietly, looking to Lewis)*: We want to know how people think, what are their views for social change. I think that's a very important discussion.

(Lewis nods.)

CHAPMAN *(To the jury)*: But my question is, isn't that really why you wanted the information ... because the people you wanted were people who believed in armed struggle and violent revolution, isn't that a fact?

NELSON *(Very measured)*: Are you asking me whether we wanted people in the party who wanted violent overthrow of the United States government?

CHAPMAN: Yes.

NELSON *(Angry)*: *No*. That is not correct.

(Lewis is about to rise.)

JUDGE: Now members of the jury, I want you to be very careful about this. I told you earlier, and I repeat it, this is not a case in which the Communist Party is on trial, or the Ku Klux Klan or the FBI or the BATF, they're all individuals. We're not trying people for their political views. In America, you have a right to have whatever views you want to have.

(Chapman signals for a video tape to roll. Slides show Nelson screaming for war and resisting his arrest after the murders. We hear a voice-over: "We declare war! War! War!")

CHAPMAN: Mr. Johnson, when the officer placed you under arrest, you did not willingly go, did you?

NELSON: I believe I resisted, because I believe I was improperly arrested.

CHAPMAN: Yes, sir. *(Looks to the jury)* And you were kicking and holding on to the chain there at the corner, weren't you?

NELSON: And I was being stomped as I was bleeding from a knife wound inflicted on me by a Klansman.

CHAPMAN: And you had said "We declare war against them, war," didn't you?

NELSON *(Controlled anger)*: Yes, sir. And it expressed the intensity of my feeling about what I believed had happened, sir.

CHAPMAN: Thank you. *(He looks to the jury, shaking his head)*

(Hours pass. On screen: "Death to the Klan" posters.)

NELSON: No, it's *not* my view that people who have the name Nazi and Klan don't have the right to exist. What that document is talking about is that I think we need to try to reduce and minimize racism and racist violence . . .

CHAPMAN: I see. You think that views which you perceive to be racist should not even exist?

(Nelson looks to Lewis.)

NELSON: It would be very good if racist views didn't exist, yes.

CHAPMAN: And to that extent, the First Amendment should not protect those ideas?

NELSON: I didn't say that. But again, I don't think that makes them wholesome views that we necessarily want.

CHAPMAN: Well, what you're saying now is that you would like to oppose those ideas whereas a minute ago, I thought you said you didn't think those ideas should even exist?

NELSON: Well, the reason to oppose them is to minimize them, and I would hope that at some point there isn't racism in this society. I really would hope that.

CHAPMAN: Mr. Johnson, all your materials say: "Smash the Klan," "Death to the Klan." Words have meaning. You wanted violence at China Grove and you wanted violence on November the 3rd Mr. Johnson, didn't you?

NELSON *(Loses his cool)*: No, that is not true!

(Blackout. On screen: "Sally Bermanzohn."
"We Made Mistakes.")

SALLY: Yes, we made mistakes. We did make mistakes. I think we made a big mistake by calling our rally, by saying "Death to the Klan." But I want to talk about why we said that, what we meant by it. The Klan has a history that goes back more than a hundred years, back to the end of the Civil War. And during the early part of this century, the lynchings that they know, the lynchings that have been publicly recorded, the murders of black men, women and children, as well as any white person who tried to help blacks get their rights, there were an average of one lynching per day. People murdered, and nothing ever happened to them. The Klan had this aura that they could do this, they could terrorize people, scare people, kill people, and nothing would ever happen to them. They were night riders, they were covered, they were in sheets, and nobody knew exactly who they were, and they could do just anything they wanted.

And during the civil rights movement the Klan backed off. But then, in the seventies, in the mid-seventies as the movement died down, the Klan started stirring again. And in 1979, it was on a real resurgence. There were all kinds of Klan public meetings, and open recruitment drives by the Klan. And it was in this context that we had done our own anti-Klan campaign. And our slogan, "Death to the Klan," we didn't—it meant not to hurt any individual, not to hurt any Klansman, but to say to the Klan: "We are not afraid of you. We are not. We are black, and white, and we are united and we will not be scared into fearing you. You will not prevent us from building unions, and from people working together on all the issues that concern them." And so, the rally was supposed to be militant, it was supposed to be bold; and it was supposed to just try to break that aura of invincibility that the Klan had.

But the Klan used our words as an excuse to open fire and kill us. And clearly, in retrospect, our slogan was a big mistake. But I think it's really important to see that we made mistakes. We made mistakes. We did not commit crimes. The Klan and Nazis committed crimes. They murdered five people. And did they ever pay for their mistakes? They never served a day in jail. Not one day. No one ever served time for what they did to us. They committed crimes, and this society let them walk free.

And I feel that letting the Klan get away with what they did to us, as well as what they've done to hundreds of thousands of other people in this country in their bloody history is part of the reason that we have a big problem on our hands today. Because they think they can get away with it. And people turn a blind eye in this country. It's like they see other countries as having big problems with terrorists. The Klan is a terrorist organization. That has been their sole purpose for over a hundred years in this country. That's what they do: they terrorize people. And yet there's been a reluctance to face that fact, or to come down on them, or to make them pay for their crime! Even when we know, even when we have it on TV who did the shooting!

When I heard about the Oklahoma bombing, I was horrified, along with the rest of the country, and the daycare center was particularly painful. My kids went to a daycare center like that one, and I taught in public daycare for several years, and it just—well, it was terrible.

When the news came out, that it was American right-wingers who had done this attack, I was frankly not surprised. I was not surprised, because we had experienced that kind of hatred, we had experienced that kind of terror.

(Blackout. On screen: "1985, The Civil Trial. Virgil Griffin."
"I Didn't Do Anything."
Lights up. Virgil Griffin is on the stand.)

LEWIS: And you are the Grand Dragon of the Invisible Empire of the Knights of the Ku Klux Klan?
GRIFFIN: Yes, sir, I am. *(He touches the American flag behind him)*
LEWIS: Aren't you a convicted felon, Mr. Griffin?
GRIFFIN: Yes, sir, I am.
LEWIS: Do you deny advocating violence at your rallies, sir?
GRIFFIN: No, sir, I do not.

LEWIS: Can you see this, Mr. Griffin?

(Lewis holds up the Klan poster encouraging members to go to Greensboro. There is a picture of a black man being lynched, the caption calls for old-fashioned American justice, "Race-mixers, Jews, communists, niggers, beware, the crosshairs are on your neck," etc.)

GRIFFIN: I recognize it.

LEWIS: All right sir, don't you talk at your rallies about having a hundred dead people in the street, using a word other than "black" in those speeches?

GRIFFIN: In my phrases I use "a hundred dead niggers in the street."

LEWIS: You have said that?

GRIFFIN: I have said if a white woman was raped and killed, they should find a hundred dead niggers in the street the next day. Yes, sir.

LEWIS: And didn't you make a statement to the effect that all of the communists in the United States should be executed?

GRIFFIN: I think I said they should be charged for treason against the United States *(He touches the flag again)*, put in front of a firing squad and shot. I believe that's the words I said.

LEWIS *(To the jury)*: Sir, did you see any *guns* at the house that morning before you departed on November 3rd for the rally in Greensboro?

GRIFFIN: I believe I saw two shotguns, and a rifle, two long guns or three long guns, I'm not sure, a pistol, and the pistol I had at the house.

LEWIS *(Nodding)*: All right and didn't Roland Wayne Wood ask you if he ought to take his tear gas grenade with him?

GRIFFIN: Yes, sir, he did.

LEWIS: And Eddie Dawson reiterated that if fights and an arrest situation occurred "We'd all go to jail together" and he had arrangements for bond?

GRIFFIN: Yes, sir.

LEWIS: And you still deny there were plans for violence on November 3rd in Greensboro?

GRIFFIN: Like I said before we just wanted to stand on the sidewalk and fly the American flag and the Christian Confederate flag and watch the communists march. I didn't *do* anything.

(Lewis looks wildly to the jury.)

LEWIS *(Outraged)*: Mr. Griffin, didn't you co-lead with Edward Dawson the armed caravan that went to Carver and Everitt Streets which resulted in the deaths of five people?

GRIFFIN: Yes, sir.

(Lights up on Doris Gordon, a survivor. On screen: "Doris Gordon, a Survivor."
"But What Can You Do?")

DORIS: I'm a child of the movement. It started for me as a child, going with my mom and them, following in their footsteps, and just coming on through the struggle. I remember six, seven years old, me and my sisters looking in at those A&T students—standing outside Woolworth's, looking through the windows. The first sit-ins. We were scared to go in but we knew something exciting was going on.

That's why the young generation now is so messed up, they had no kind of strong guidance like that. If we hadn't had that, I guess we would be crazy into drugs. The kids of today, they didn't have the kind of guidance we had. They didn't have things to do that was meaningful.

Like my little cousin, laying over there in the hospital with a bullet in him. That's crazy. The rage inside, but what can you do? You can't fight these city officials, these politicians, there ain't nothing you can do. 'Cause they're going to win. But when you stuck together there was some victories that you could see, that people can still see today. But ain't nobody doing anything.

What my friends died for, should be going on full force to-day. They really believed in what they were doing, and they put all their heart and soul in it. I know somewhere, they know what's going on. And one day they gonna walk back and touch all them souls and they going to get on back out there, and let us know we was wrong for stopping . . . They're somewhere out there, whether they're a bumble bee or a bird, they are waiting on us to wake up. It's wrong what happened, the way it went down . . . If I could see the Controller today, I would have two, three words with Him, because it didn't go down the way it should . . .

Why did everybody drop everything? Because I want to know. Where's the movement now? I want to know who said: this is over with—and there go all my friends—*gone*.

(Lights up on Nelson and Interviewer. On screen: "I Was Not on the Road to Damascus.")

INTERVIEWER: You know I realized there's a whole chapter that I missed and that's when you went from post-November 3rd and went into the ministry, what that thought process was.

NELSON: Let me tell you what it's not, because many people have tried to present me as some kind of Paul, the biblical figure Paul?, who was possessed by evil thoughts, who had some gifts but who was hit by a bolt of light and knocked off of his horse on the Damascus Road? And the Lord spoke to him and that was his moment of conversion? Are you kind of fa-miliar with that biblical story?

(Interviewer nods; she halfway knows it. Nelson laughs.)

Okay. Now, the problem with that, when it comes to me, is that it first establishes my prior life as hurtful and hateful and mean; and I'm not even sure that's accurate with Paul, but it's there in the record. The reason I drifted away from the church was mainly because I thought that the church needed to be doing more of what I was doing, okay? *(Laughs)* And it wasn't, and I met people who had, you know, sources of analysis, things that they studied, got me into Marxism, that was very helpful, and to this very day, there's much value in that study. I think I've learned to critique it better, in terms of my own understanding, things that I think are very valid, and things that perhaps are not. But in the early eighties, I really was so rejected around here, that— I think I shared with you—once I went to a job, and the guy went to call the police; I sat in the courtroom, everyone got up and moved to the other side of the court. I listened to radio talk shows when people said they wished I had been shot, and all this kind of stuff. And my children had to listen to it. I started to reflect, think, actually talk to a lot of people, and I really was taken back to the faith of my youth.

INTERVIEWER: Tell me about that.

NELSON: Well, where I grew up, my grandfather founded a church; my father was a deacon in it, my mother played piano, and I believed it. But I didn't think other people did. That was why I moved away from it. And actually, the mistake that I made was to draw too close a relationship between the institution of the church and a concept of the Divine. And I would advise anyone: never get those two mixed up.

INTERVIEWER: Right.

NELSON: But one connection to my political past, I think, is I think that the people who say they are atheists and express that, and show a lot of love and good work, are probably closer to whatever the Divine is. I saw that with some . . . *(Laughs)* it's not an empty thought.

INTERVIEWER *(Laughs)*: Yes, I understand.

NELSON: They have kind of decided not to drag along behind a lot of symbols and empty talk and it's almost a confession, that: "Here I am, and that's all I am. I do the best that I can." I want to appreciate that. In point of fact, everyone would be much better off to acknowledge that all of us are pretty much in the same place, close to it. I try to teach that, and I honestly believe that something like that is what I have intended to be most of my life.

Therefore I don't accept that I was on the road to Damascus, and the Spirit hit me, and I got up and I was headed right. I think mine is a more of a deepening process than it is a fundamental shift of direction. And therefore I'm not given to negating my past.

(Lights up on Dawson. On screen: "Some Kinda Jerk.")

DAWSON: How do I feel about that now? I feel like I was some kinda jerk. *(Laughs)* You know.

During the trials—you know, you sit in court and every day, you know, off and on for six years, with them people, and I just . . . I shouldn'ta waited, but I did, until after the trial was over—then I joined the church. Told my wife, I says, I started to realize that's not a good life!

(On screen: "Faith Community Church. Nelson Johnson, Minister."
"The Arc of the Moral Universe Is Long."
Music starts. Rose sings "Behind Every Cloud.")

ROSE *(Sings)*:

> Behind every dark cloud there's a silver lining,
> and behind each rainstorm there's a bright new dawning.

> If trouble greets you, good friends deceive you
> Oh, don't worry, it will pass over,
> Pass over, in the morning.

CHOIR:

> Weeping may endure for a night,
> but joy, joy, joy, joy

joy, joy will come
Hmmmmm . . .

(Chorus continues to hum very quietly under Nelson's speech.)

NELSON: It is a great honor for all of us to have all of you here, from all over the country, to worship together this November morning

(The congregation responds.)

—to remember, to mourn, to heal together.

(The humming and music end.)

Frederick Douglass said that if there is no struggle, there is no progress. And if you examine the scripture a little bit, it says that if there *is* no persecution, no standing up, no struggling for righteousness, then there *is* no progress towards the Kingdom of God. Compassion and love of God and love of people destroys suffering, by suffering with and on behalf of those who suffer.

It's a close identity to people, and the identity is *so* deep, that the Person who was going and teaching says: "When you do it to them, you're doing it to me. If you hate the poor, then you hate me, because you'll always find me shoulder to shoulder with them. If you kill them, then you're gonna kill me first, because I'm standing at the front of the line." He said some words like these: "Blessed are the poor, blessed are the weak, blessed are those who hunger, blessed are those who mourn." If you examine it closely, with the finest magnifying glass, you will not find him saying: "Blessed are the rich and the famous."

Jesus also said: "I want you to understand that even though you're going to suffer, it's not going to be in vain. I want you to know that when you stand up for righteousness, when you stand up, you take part in creating a whole new reality." I want you to see it and feel it: a reality in which everybody's somebody. A reality in which there is no *need* for racism, because we're *all* somebody equal to each other. A reality in which there *are* no Nazis, there *are* no Klan, there *is* no shooting, because *somebody* suffered for righteousness' sake. Jesus said that if you stand up for righteousness, you will be persecuted.

And then there's an interesting thing in the scripture. It says that when you do that, don't hang your head down. And this is almost unbelievable: it says don't hang your head down when people talk about ya, and call you ugly names, and drag your name through the mud and say all kinds of evil things about you. It says: "Stand up and jump for *joy* because you know you're onto the right thing." I read these words. And I tried to believe them. There is something to be said for believing in the future and forgiveness. But you see, my faith has not always been deep enough to keep on believing in the absence of evidence.

You see, if I can make this a little more concrete, sometimes when your closest friends are killed, and you see their names drug through the mud, treated as nothing, you start to ask the question: what did it all mean? When you look in the faces of people that you have come to know and love, and see the pain in those faces because a spouse has been snatched from life together, and the very persons themselves have been placed in a jail, you start to ask yourself: what does it *all* mean? You start to ask: what does it mean when you see yourself accused of trying to get your own children killed in order to get some publicity, so that your own narrow ends might be served? What does it mean when folk that you love can't get a job, pushed outside of the workforce? What does it mean when you find yourself beaten in the back of a judge's chamber, with your head bleeding, and taken to jail? What does it mean when there's so much suffering and persecution?

I want to conclude this message by saying that dying is not the worst thing in the world, but perhaps living for nothing, and then dying. We're all gonna die—why don't we stand for something while we're living? And if we look at suffering, if we suffer for righteousness' sake, there's a beautiful thing on the other side of suffering. King said that the arc of the moral universe is long, but it bends toward justice. Somebody said that truth, crushed to the earth, will rise again; Greensboro yet will have to bear witness to the truth of its own history, because the truth of the *love* of those, by whatever names they were called, has been crushed to the ground but I believe it will rise again.

(Music begins, playing under Nelson's speech.)

Suffering doesn't last always. There is a psalm which says that you might suffer for a long time, that you might carry pain for a long time, that you might hurt for a long time, that you might be confused for a long time, they said that trouble might endure for a night, but thanks be to God, the joy still comes in the morning. On the other side of suffering, there is joy. On the other side of pain, there is *joy*. On the other side of hardship, there is *joy*! And this is the pretty part: it says that if you just keep on walking, if you don't give up, if you just stay on the course, if you come back year after year and keep on fussin' anyhow, that the glory of God will be revealed; all of us will see it together, and we will be brothers and sisters in a new community on the other side. On the other side of sorrow.

(Rose and chorus sing chorus of "Joy." Lights up on Eddie Dawson and Interviewer.
    On screen: "Hate Literature.")

DAWSON: Yeah, you get to reminiscing. *(Laughs)* Yeah use that word. I miss the excitement. In the Klan you never knew what was gonna happen. Once, at this restaurant, I had literature, it's about that big, that wide. It's a free boat trip back to Africa. And this waitress up there, I says: "You look bad." She says: "I need a vacation. I can't afford it." So, can't mind my own damn business, I walked her into this conversation, about goin' on vacation. I says: "You oughta go on vacation." She says: "I can't afford one!" White girl now, she's white.

INTERVIEWER: Oh!

DAWSON: Yeah, no, white! And I hand her this letter, I said: "Here. Free trip." So she reads it: "Oh, *you*." Well, the next thing I know, I'm eatin' my eggs, and I hear this black guy hollerin': "You think you're a real smart ass, bringin' this hate literature in." He says: "You bring this hate literature around, I got a .357 Magnum home. I'll go home and get that. I'll blow a damn hole in you big enough to walk through!" I says: "You do what you have to do." You know, I can't back up—these people are lookin' at me. You could hear a pin drop in the place. I says: "You do what you have to do. But you take my word: don't miss. I'll make you eat the damn gun." And he got up, big—I mean big guy—and I thought: "Oh gosh, he's gonna kill me right here." *(Laughs)* But he just stood in back of me, and he said: "I'm leavin', before I do somethin' I'll regret." I said: "Don't leave on my account—you stay as long as you want." So he left.

Okay, not knowin', I was down at federal building, about three weeks later, FBI agent was in there. He says: "Why don't you have him arrested? That nigger, he threatened your life." I said: "Sure he threatened my life. I brought hate literature in that place too." Imagine standin' in front of a judge. He's got the hate literature, and I got what he said he's gonna do to me. What would the outcome be? I'd spend maybe two weeks in court, and the judge'd tell me: "Don't bring this hate literature in. You can't run around callin' people niggers, and Polacks, and tellin' nigger jokes. You're not allowed to do that no more. That's against the law." So, creates a problem. That educated me—I threw all that stuff away. Yeah.

INTERVIEWER: When did that happen, that incident?

DAWSON: About a year ago.

INTERVIEWER *(Stands, starts packing up)*: Uh-huh.

DAWSON: So did you get what you needed?

INTERVIEWER: Absolutely.

(Nelson's office in the Shiloh Baptist Church.
On screen: "Reverend Nelson and Joyce Johnson, His Wife."
"First Step."
Nelson Johnson sits with his wife, Joyce.)

NELSON: You know, in the end, I hope what we believed in represents what's best in the people of this country.

(Lights up dim on two ministers, one white, one black, flanked by the survivors.
On screen: "Morningside Homes Greensboro Ministers."
"Dedication of the Ground.")

WHITE MINISTER: This is hallowed ground. This is a dedication of the ground.

NELSON: I have difficulty with the idea that "racism has gotten worse." Now society is working on problems that are deeper, problems that have always been there but were ignored. Many people are fatalistic, seeing it as an impossible struggle. But I don't see it that way.

BLACK MINISTER: We dedicate this earth to the five who died at the hands of the Klan and Nazis on November 3rd, 1979.

NELSON: I've never told this to anyone before—but this year I met with the Klan.

(Joyce nods.)

JOYCE: He did.

NELSON: I needed to do it. It was a faith venture, I guess. I asked to meet with them. And they actually showed up—in their pickup trucks—

JOYCE: I stayed at home. I prayed and prayed.

WHITE MINISTER: This is a memorial to Sandy Smith, Dr. Michael Nathan . . .

NELSON: I went to the Grand Dragon's house. I was scared, but I said look, we have something in common now—we have the Lord. And they said: "Well, you niggers just taking all our jobs" and I said: "no." Black people are not taking your jobs. We don't have any jobs either—they've gone outta the country—we're outta work, too. Black people are *not* your *enemy*. That's what the system wants you to think.

BLACK MINISTER: . . . Cesar Cauce, Bill Sampson and Dr. Jim Waller.

NELSON: The point is you can turn your energy away from hating to do good for your families, good for your people—we got to go forward now—together, as one people—and I actually got them to kneel down and pray with me.

(Joyce shakes her head in wonder.)

WHITE MINISTER: In your names we dedicate this ground—in your honor we erect this memorial, so our city—

BLACK MINISTER: all the people of our city—

WHITE MINISTER: will never forget.

NELSON: And when I got outta there, and got home, I wrote a letter to the white clergy here. I told them: I made the first step. Now it's up to you—up to all of us—we got to turn these people, your people, *around*.

(On screen: "First Step."
As lights fade to black, new slide lingers and then fades: "In 1985, for the first time in American legal history, local police and the Ku Klux Klan were found jointly liable in a wrongful death. The city of Greensboro paid the judgment for the police. No Klan or Nazi member has paid the judgment."
Fade out.)

END OF PLAY

EMILY MANN is in her seventh season as Artistic Director of Princeton, New Jersey's McCarter Theatre—recipient of the 1994 Tony Award for Outstanding Regional Theatre. Ms. Mann wrote and directed *Having Our Say: The Delany Sisters' First 100 Years*, for which she received Tony, Outer Critics and Drama Desk award nominations, and was awarded the prestigious Hull-Warriner Award, presented by The Dramatists Guild. *Having Our Say* had its world premiere at the McCarter, followed by a successful Broadway run and a national tour. Ms. Mann made her Broadway debut as playwright and director of *Execution of Justice*, which received the Helen Hayes Award, the Bay Area Theatre Critics Circle Award, the HBO/USA Playwrights Award, a Burns Mantle Yearbook Best Plays Citation, a Playwriting Award from the Women's Committee of The Dramatists Guild for dramatizing issues of conscience and a Drama Desk nomination. Her play *Still Life* premiered at Chicago's Goodman Theatre and opened Off-Broadway at the American Place Theatre under her direction in 1981, winning six Obie Awards, including Distinguished Playwriting, Distinguished Directing and Outstanding Production of the Season. *Still Life* has been presented at major theatres throughout the United States, Europe (Fringe First Award for Best Play at the Edinburgh Festival) and at the Market Theatre in South Africa. Her other works include *Annulla, An Autobiography*, the rhythm and blues musical *Betsey Brown* (co-written with Ntozake Shange and Baikida Carroll) and, her most recent,

Greensboro (A Requiem). Her numerous awards for artistic excellence include a Guggenheim, a Playwrights Fellowship and Artistic Associate Grant from the National Endowment for the Arts, a McKnight Fellowship and a Rosamund Gilder Award for Outstanding Creative Achievement in the Theatre. In recognition of her achievements illuminating the possibilities for social, cultural and political change, Ms. Mann was awarded the Lee Reynolds Award from the League of Professional Theatre Women/NY.